TOXIC

Cold-blooded
Australian murders

Lindy Cameron has written several true crime books over the years and is also a writer of crime, historical and science fiction. She's the author of the archaeological mystery *Golden Relic*; the Kit O'Malley PI trilogy; the action thriller *Redback*; and the science fiction novella *Feedback*.

Her published short stories include 'Hauntings Inc.' in the anthology *Who Sleuthed It?*; and, with co-author Kerry Greenwood, 'A Wild Colonial' in *Sherlock Holmes: the Australian Casebook,* and 'The Saltwater Battle' in *War of the Worlds: Battleground Australia.*

Lindy is currently working on a crime novel and a series of historical novellas featuring time-travelling archaeologists.

She is a founding member and national co-convenor of Sisters in Crime Australia, and the Publisher of Clan Destine Press (visit www.clandestinepress.com.au).

Fin J Ross is a journalist, creative writing teacher and writer of fact and fiction, who also runs a boarding cattery in East Gippsland and breeds British Shorthair cats.

Fin's first historical novel, *Billings Better Bookstore and Brasserie*, set in Melbourne in the 19th century, is the story of young Fidelia Knight, whose thirst for knowledge changes the lives of everyone she meets.

Her first novel, *AKA Fudgepuddle*, is the journal/memoir of the oh-so-true adventures of a demanding cat called Megsy.

Fin has won nine category prizes (over six years) in the annual Scarlet Stiletto Awards for crime and mystery short stories. The competition has been run by Sisters in Crime Australia since 1994.

In her spare time Fin compiles cryptic crosswords for fun, and is the co-compiler, with Willsin Rowe, of *Nifty Fifty: 50 Cryptic Crosswords with an Aussie Flavour.*

TOXIC

Cold-blooded
Australian murders

Lindy Cameron
& Fin J Ross

◢ LAKE PRESS

 LAKE PRESS

Lake Press Pty Ltd
5 Burwood Road
Hawthorn VIC 3122 Australia
www.lakepress.com.au

Some of these stories have been
previously published.
This edition first published 2021
Printed and bound in Australia at McPherson's
Printing Group, Maryborough, Victoria 5 4 3 2 1
LP21 016

 A catalogue record for this
book is available from the
National Library of Australia

CONTENTS

INTRODUCTION

Toxic masculinity – it's a thing.

It's a personality type. A misguided sense of what makes a real man. An archaic belief in male superiority. A deluded concept of what men deserve.

It's insidious. It's damaging. It's a defect.

Before anyone starts with the infantile 'not all men' – no-one has ever said the term applies to all men.

And no-one has ever said the word 'toxic' cannot apply to women. It does. It's just much less rampant. And it's never called toxic femininity – just a toxic personality.

And while the toxic traits that manifest in women may well end in murder – and this is a book about murderers – generally speaking, there's often little physical violence on the way there. All sorts of other behaviour, such as manipulation, subterfuge and lying, yes – but rarely physical violence. Until the murder.

We've all known men and women with toxic personalities, usually in a work environment; their progress through life depends entirely on the control and abuse of those less powerful than them. It's never a level playing field; if it were, they'd be unmasked and dealt with, before things got nasty. They're always bullies, sometimes passive aggressive, usually less competent and, oddly, often cowards.

They rarely commit murder. Not at work, anyway. Well, not in Australia at least.

But in domestic situations – where love and hate are part of the mix – the toxic personality, in an effort to grasp and maintain control, too often slides into something more dangerous.

'I am entitled to more … I am entitled to her … I am entitled to his money … I am entitled to be in control of them' are merely selfish notions, in men or women, until we get to: 'My life is more important than theirs'.

Which brings us back – while still not ignoring women who kill – to toxic masculinity.

1

In the social sciences, *toxic masculinity* refers to traditional cultural masculine 'norms' that say boys and men are tough, strong, aggressive, and have a right to anger; that they're born to be providers and therefore must be protective and dominant. These old-fashioned ideas are now regarded as potentially harmful to women, to children, to men themselves, and therefore to society as a whole.

Toxic masculinity is described by Dr Terry A Kupers in the February 2005 edition of the *Journal of Clinical Psychology* as 'a constellation of socially regressive male traits that tend to foster misogyny, homophobia, greed, cruel domination, and wanton violence'.

When we remove the presence of aggression and domination, the need for power and control, from what is considered 'masculine', clearly there's nothing wrong with masculinity.

The problem is that *toxic* masculinity is too often also drenched in a sense of entitlement and narcissism that informs power plays of all kinds – in business, politics, even sport – in the wider world. But it also fuels so much violence – psychological and physical – in the domestic arena.

This male entitlement plays a significant role in domestic abuse. These men consider abusive behaviour not only acceptable, but justified – both a right and a privilege. And when they treat someone they claim to love as less than equal, and deserving of punishment and harm, it's because they feel – they *believe* – they are entitled to do so.

As this entitlement is often specific to an intimate relationship, it's hidden from those outside the home. Domestic abusers do not abuse their bosses, their colleagues or their friends, which means these people rarely know what goes on in that man's home. This is because these men understand that power at work, or in public, has to be negotiated, but believe power at home is their right.

And domestic abuse does not have to involve physical violence; nor does it have to be induced by stress or triggered by drugs or alcohol – the old 'I couldn't help myself' routine.

'Coercive control' is an ongoing and unrelenting abuse that pervades a victim's daily life, and covers a wide variety of abusive social, financial and psychological behaviours.

The man (usually it's a man) works at overriding their partner's independence to extinguish their sense of self, to make the person they 'love' totally subordinate to, and dependent on, them. To do this, they isolate the woman (most often) from friends and family, and micromanage their daily life while also working to humiliate, monitor and gaslight them. Basically, they create a domestic life that involves confusion, contradiction and extreme threat.

It's so insidious that the victim finds they're trapped inside a world they don't recall entering, because the oppression happened slowly, little by little. Amnesty International has classified coercive control as torture. The abusers may use extreme sexual or physical violence as well, or no violence at all. Survivors often say the complete mental dislocation from themselves and their lives is the hardest thing to recover from.

There are increasing calls to make coercive control a criminal offence across Australia, as it is in some other parts of the world, such as the UK. Advocates in favour of criminalisation argue that it will help change the legal response, so domestic violence can be regarded as a pattern of abuse, rather than an isolated incident, especially as coercive control is the most common risk factor leading to intimate partner homicide.

It is, however, by no means the only risk. Because another version of the toxic entitled man is the one who wants or had that control but feels unable to grasp it, or fears it's being taken from them. In a sense it's the entitlement without the strength of personality to maintain it. Or a wannabe alpha male who's just an ordinary bloke.

This perceived loss of power and control – in the toxic macho man or ordinary male – too often has deadly consequences. The humiliated fury of the man whose wife threatens to leave, or walks out and takes the kids, fires a need to beat the manly chest and reassert their version of dominance.

On average, one woman a week dies at the hands of a current or former partner in Australia because a dangerous mindset is born out of this insecurity, shame and thwarted entitlement; or the already-dangerous man who is habitually aggressive and controlling. And sadly, while our society is angry and despairing of the way things 'seem to be', we're not surprised anymore when yet another man kills someone – nearly every other day.

Oh, but not all/only men ...

Women are supposed to be the fairer sex, the nurturing gender, the caring members of society. And women who kill most often do so to protect themselves or their children *from* an abusive partner.

But the women who commit murder for greed, perversion or power are definitely out there. Though fewer in number, they are, like any wilful murderer, usually tainted with a toxic temperament, a lack of empathy, and an innate ability to lie. They also tend to antagonise, manipulate and treat those around them with callous indifference.

Because of the whole gentler, more-caring myth surrounding women, the rest of us are always surprised when a woman kills for pleasure or profit. Even so, some women can be truly scary. And the women murderers in this book killed because they wanted something.

The Australian Institute of Criminology, through the National Homicide Monitoring Program (NHMP), has been scrutinising the trends in Australian homicide since 1989. The program analyses 'homicide incidents' in which one or more people are killed at the same place and time, from acts classified as murder or manslaughter.

In the 29 years to June 2018 there have been 8126 homicides in Australia, involving 9169 offenders – 7937 men and 1232 women. Homicides are assigned to categories defined by the type of offender: stranger, intimate partner, family, friend or acquaintance, or unknown other.

Don't be fooled by the category of 'stranger homicide', because it covers a multitude of sins. It simply means that the killer and victim were unknown to each other at the time of the incident. That might sound scary, but it relates more to male-on-male violence aggravated by alcohol, drugs or money, or during the course of another crime such as robbery, sexual assault or arson, than to death by random strangers – with the obvious exceptions, of course, of the too many women over those years who were murdered by (mostly) men they did not know – like Jill Meagher, Tracey Connelly, Anita Cobby, Eurydice Dixon, Sallie-Anne Huckstepp, Debbie Fream, Elizabeth Stevens and Natalie Russell … we'll stop now.

While, according to the NHMP data, men are more likely to die at the hands of a friend, acquaintance or stranger, the truth about murder in Australia is that it's rarely committed by strangers, workmates going 'postal', or twisted serial killers with a taste for fava beans.

Terrifyingly, most Australians are murdered by someone they know, and most likely by someone in their own family; male intimate partners pose the greatest risk to women.

Let's take 2017, in which 155 Australians died at the hands of other Australians. The gender breakdown of the victims was 42 women, 98 men and 11 children. So yes, more men died than women, but 103 of the culprits were men. Only 20 of the killers were women, and 32 were unknown – which covers unproven or unsolved.

The 2018 statistics show that of the 245 people who were murdered, 38 women died at the hands of 34 men, and 28 of those deaths were related to family violence. Three of the victims were allegedly killed by another woman, and one case remains unknown. And by November 2020 there had already been 200 murders: 48 women, 21 children and 131 men.

There are a lot of 'personality types' to look at in a book about murder, even when all but one of the cases involve family members or intimate partners. The one murder within these pages that doesn't quite fit that category was still 'a murder among friends' with a toxic personality as the ringleader.

Regardless of the motive or the identity of the victim or offender, or whether the crime is ultimately deemed murder or manslaughter, there is always one word for it: homicide.

Note: The statistics used here come from the National Homicide Monitoring Program, and the running tally recorded by The Red Heart Campaign. The Campaign is the only organisation in Australia that counts all deaths by violence, regardless of the victim or perpetrator's gender or relationship, as they happen.

We would like to acknowledge the ongoing and tireless work of the Campaign's volunteer researchers, Sherele Moody and Catherine Benson.

More information can be found at www.theredheartcampaign.org.

Chapter One

ABSOLUTE BASTARD

When Danny Deacon fronted court in the Northern Territory in 2016, charged with the murder of his girlfriend Carlie Sinclair, his legal team tried to press for manslaughter – on that tired old excuse of 'provocation'.

Deacon was going to jail regardless, because he'd confessed, but how long his sentence would be depended on the verdict of manslaughter versus murder.

Danny Deacon maintained that Carlie brought on her death by provoking him into violence.

Danny Deacon hit, then strangled, then buried his girlfriend in a lonely bush grave he'd prepared earlier.

Danny Deacon was – and likely still is – a violent man.

He buried the mother of his child in a hole he'd dug with an excavator a month before she provoked him.

When he buried her, wrapped in a tarp, their toddler was a few metres away in the car.

Nonetheless, it was provocation that Deacon's legal team ran with as the mitigating circumstances leading to the brutal death of their client's victim.

One of Danny Deacon's previous wives would've had a better claim – against *him* – for provocation. But she managed to escape their violent marriage before it was too late.

Carlie Sinclair didn't.

She was about to.

But she left her run too late.

CARLIE'S STORY – THROUGH OTHERS' EYES

Carlie Sinclair, a Christmas Day baby, grew up into an adventurous, outgoing and outdoorsy woman. Her family – mum Marlene, father Robert and brother Kristian – revelled in an active life, especially anything to do with the water. For her 21st birthday, in 1998, her mother gave her a scuba-diving course.

Carlie immediately fell in love with the sport and soon scored a job on a dive boat in the Whitsunday Islands, where she escorted tourists on explorations of the Great Barrier Reef.

It was there, in 2003, that she fell in love with fellow dive boat employee Danny Deacon. Their passion for each other opened up the possibility of making careers out of their shared loved of diving. They moved to Fremantle in Western Australia for specialist dive training.

Carlie was a natural and soon earned the necessary qualifications to secure a contract with a gas and oil explorer off the remote WA coast.

When that contract ended, the couple moved to Darwin, where Danny established a concreting business, Darwin Decorative Concrete. Carlie got a job at the Royal Darwin Hospital, working in the hyperbaric chamber.

The few hairline cracks in their relationship, partly from the anxiety of getting a new business up and running, were salved when the couple welcomed their first child into the world. On the first day of a brand-new year, 1 January 2011, Carlie Sinclair gave birth to a baby boy, Alexander, bringing her a joy she could not have imagined.

From the moment he was born, Alex became Carlie's reason for everything. After her disappearance two years later, her close friends, Zoe Lane and Kylie Powell, described Carlie as a loving and attentive mother; that Alex was everything to her; that he was her reason for getting up in the morning.

Her family and friends said she would never have left him, would never have just walked away and left the little boy she adored.

While it's not unusual for the pressure of building a business to cause problems at work and home, that stress also colours the changing dynamics of a relationship, one already altered by the new, albeit welcome and loved, addition to the family.

Carlie realised something had to be done to salvage her relationship with Danny, to keep their family together, so she quit her job at Royal Darwin to work with Danny instead. She gave up the job she loved, to support her partner in his business and to make a go of everything together.

It didn't help. There was too much wrong between them. Danny was controlling, and often jealous, and Carlie found she could barely communicate with him. The couple's relationship deteriorated to the point where, by October 2012, it had ceased being physical. Danny became convinced Carlie was seeing someone else; over the following six months, things irretrievably broke down.

Marlene Sinclair said the couple had been having trouble for about a year before Carlie disappeared, and during that time her daughter became less confident in herself.

As early as March 2013, Carlie confided in her friends about how she was scared of Danny, and really didn't want to be with him anymore. She also told her family that she wanted to leave but was worried how he would react.

'She was sad,' Mrs Sinclair said. 'She wanted to move to Brisbane. Her relationship had broken down and she just wanted to get away … But she wanted to leave Darwin the right way, and do it all properly, not just take off.'

Carlie's close friend and confidante, Claire Robinson, was well aware of the state of her friend's unhappy relationship with Danny. Carlie had told her things had broken down soon after Alex was born; that she and Danny were unhappy and fighting all the time, and she thought it was over.

Claire and Carlie's other Territory girlfriends, Zoe and Kylie, often told her it was time she thought about herself, and what was best for her and Alex. They were pleased when Carlie let them know she was taking the steps to leave and was looking for work in Queensland.

On her last visit to Brisbane, when she and Alex stayed with her parents, Carlie realised she needed the love and support only her family could give. With no trouble at all, she secured two jobs — at the Royal Brisbane and Women's Hospital (in their hyperbaric department) and at the Wesley Hospital.

Marlene Sinclair said her daughter was joyous at the prospect of being able to work in Brisbane, in her true profession.

Back in Darwin, Carlie spoke to solicitors about how best to separate from Danny, with custody of Alex, so she could legally move to Brisbane and take her toddler with her. She planned to get everything in place first, so she and Alex would be secure. And safe.

In the week before her disappearance, Carlie told her father, Robert Sinclair, she was preparing to show custody papers to Danny. She also began moving personal possessions, both hers and Alex's, to friends' houses.

'She was trying to move things bit by bit, so Danny wouldn't notice because she hadn't told him she was leaving yet,' Claire Robinson said. Despite the secrecy, Carlie 'was positive about the fact that she had a plan in place finally'.

While she may have been making plans to leave, she still had to cope with how bad things were at home. As early as February that year, some of her neighbours in the block of units also came to know things were not good.

Thomas and Carolyn Chapman, who lived in the unit below Carlie and Danny, had an agreed 'warning system' in place, to ensure Carlie felt safer in her own environment. Thomas said Carlie had told them sometime in February, about four months before her disappearance, that 'Dan pushed her across onto the lounge and crossed his finger across his throat'.

Though neither she nor her husband had witnessed or been told of any physical violence, Carolyn Chapman said that Danny Deacon 'controlled' Carlie, and Thomas said it was obvious the young woman was 'very, very scared of Dan'.

So, in March 2013 they made an arrangement that Carlie 'would knock three times on the floor or throw a bottle out onto the patio. I was to come up and stop the problem', said Thomas.

Although she never used their system, Carlie admitted to Carolyn that she was worried about the Chapmans going on holidays on 14 June.

Carlie told her, 'Guys, I'm happy that you're going on holidays but it's such a bad time for me now, I'd feel a lot safer if you were here.'

A few days before she disappeared, another neighbour in the complex, Robert Bain, noticed that Carlie seemed worried.

'She said that Danny had been an arsehole to her, and he

threatened her,' Mr Bain said. He gave Carlie his phone number so she could call him if she ever felt unsafe, but never heard from her.

On 12 June 2013, things became more urgent for the 35-year-old mother when concerned staff at Alex's day-care centre contacted Carlie to tell her Danny had just turned up and removed the boy from their care.

Claire Robinson said Carlie 'was really panicked, she thought she'd lost Alex'.

At first Danny denied taking Alex from day care and then, for several hours, refused to tell her where he was. When Danny finally rang, he apparently said: 'He's safe, that's all you need to know.'

In reality, according to Danny's workmate Dean Arnold (partner of Carlie's friend Zoe), that afternoon the two men were on a concreting job together. 'Danny would *never* answer her phone calls ... so obviously he rang her,' Dean said.

When Danny ended that call, he claimed that Carlie had just announced she was thinking of leaving him. 'Five minutes later he shot through, just before the concrete arrived for the job,' Dean said. 'He came back later with Alex.'

Danny then asked their client to look after his toddler, while the two men finished the concreting job.

When Carlie finally tracked Danny down, the police were called. They talked to both parents and checked on Alex's welfare. According to the attending officer, when Carlie was given permission to take custody of Alex, Danny began screaming at her, 'You're not taking my son anywhere.'

Zoe and Dean expressed their disgust at how Danny had hurt Carlie by his actions. 'Danny used Alex as a weapon against Carlie,' Zoe said, adding it was awful for a father to behave that way.

The last time Marlene Sinclair spoke to her daughter was on Monday 17 June 2013, when Carlie told her she was figuring out how she was going to tell Danny she was actually leaving.

The next day, 18 June, Carlie spoke to her brother for the last time. Kristian 'Kris' Sinclair said he and his sister were good mates and often talked on the phone.

He said they'd chatted earlier on that Tuesday evening. The last communication Kris ever had with his sister was a text message she sent to him at 9.42 pm the same night, which said:

Danny turned up at the yard with Alex in a pram???????? talk tomorrow big kiss.

A MISSING PERSON

The last known sighting of 35-year-old Carlie Sinclair was at the BP service station in Fannie Bay at 6.20 pm on 18 June. She was on her way to water the plants in the yard at the family concreting business in Parap. She'd left Alex at home with his father.

The last time anyone heard from Carlie Sinclair was the text message she sent her brother Kristian at 9.42 pm on 18 June.

On Wednesday 19 June 2013 Danny Deacon reported Carlie Sinclair missing; or, rather, he reported concern for her welfare. He phoned Darwin police, said he was worried about his girlfriend, admitted they'd had an argument the previous night and he hadn't seen her since. For nearly 12 minutes he overshared details of their relationship and the 'reason' he was worried: that she planned to run away with their son.

By the following Tuesday, 25 June, the Northern Territory Police had declared Carlie's disappearance a major crime. A team of detectives interviewed witnesses, viewed CCTV footage, conducted aerial and ground searches of the local area and organised information stands in Parap, to no avail. Despite an intensive, year-long investigation, police were unable to find her, or anyone responsible for her disappearance.

Twelve months later, on 18 June 2014, the then Northern Territory Chief Minister, Adam Giles, announced the government had approved a reward to help police in their search for the person or persons who may have taken the life of Carlie Sinclair.

'Around midnight on Tuesday, June 18 last year, police believe the young mum left her business address at number 209 Stuart Highway in Parap after an argument with her partner,' Mr Giles said.

'She left behind her personal belongings, her car and her young son. She has not contacted her family or friends since, which relatives say is completely out of character. Her bank accounts have not been touched since the day she was last seen ...'

DANNY'S STORY

What Danny Deacon told police

On 19 June 2013, the day after Carlie Sinclair was last seen, Danny Deacon rang the Northern Territory Police to report – something.

The call was recorded and lasted 11.38 minutes. Danny did most of the talking; the officer responded, for the most part, with 'uh-uh, yes, okay'.

Danny begins: 'I have just been speaking with an officer who basically recommended I call you ... it's about, well not a missing person as such, but someone's welfare. My partner and I had a bit of an argument I guess last night, and it's been going on a bit lately, and that's why I've been in contact with this particular officer. Last week I took my son out of day care because I pretty much thought my missus was going to take him away from me. Something's been going on that's making me realise she's going to leave.'

He pauses and says: 'I'm a bit out of breath.'

'Yeah, anyway, um last night she left, she was pretty drunk, we both were, and she's left the yard, and ah, the last I've seen her she's walking up the street. And like I say she was quite intoxicated. But, you know, she's all right when she's drunk, like she's not, she's not a soft touch either.

'But yeah, what I did, I walked home because I was too drunk. I, um, took my son in a pram home and I left the car at the yard with the keys and her phone and, ah, her purse.

'The only thing that she's come back for is her purse.

'So, um, I don't know what to do. It seems very strange, 'cause she is a very loving mother, she really is, um, like she dotes on him. But, um, then there's times that she, you know, she hates him as well, but that's just motherhood.'

Danny again says, without prompting, 'I don't know what to do. This is very, very strange. If you speak to any one of her friends, her mum, this would be considered very strange behaviour, for her to be gone from around midnight last night and still no sign of her.

'I'm about to go home, as soon as I'm off the phone to you, I'm gonna drive home and see if she's picked up her phone, or anything. She's not been answering it, and not returned my missed calls. I've only called three times. But um, I dunno, it's strange. It's strange behaviour.

'So ah, I dunno, my mum, she – she obviously reads too many bloody murder mysteries – and she's um, yeah, she's ah, paranoid and she wants me to just not wait. Two mates of mine said wait 48 hours before you go reporting anything. Mum's saying ignore that; don't worry about it; just do it.'

The officer asked Danny if he'd tried contacting any of her friends.

'Yeah, I've spoken to her *best* friend. And another one who is, um, they babysit for each other. I wouldn't say they were close friends, but they see eye to eye, you know, they're both mothers with kids round the same age. And she only lives around the corner. So, I've already made contact with both those two girls. The one who lives around the corner, I've asked her to look after Alex when and if she comes home tonight.

'So, ah, when Carlie comes home, I'm just gonna buzz Tabitha and she's gonna just zip around and grab Alex and take her back home; ah, take him back home, which is only just around the corner.

'So, I've lined that up so her and I can have it out and, um, do it sober this time; 'cause like I say, we had a few drinks last night.'

Danny then told the officer someone had advised him to go to Family Court. When asked if the court had heard from Carlie, Danny said, 'Um, I don't know, I haven't made contact yet.

'I've been a bit busy this morning. I had a lot of running around to do and, um, I was gonna get a mate to look after my son today, ah, 'cause I didn't want to leave him at day care because, yeah.'

The officer asks: 'What is your main concern at this point in time?'

Danny says: 'I'm gonna lose my son. That she's … I've got good reason to believe that she is gonna leave me. I've overheard conversations, that she doesn't know that I've overheard them. And I've confronted her with this and she'd denying it implicitly.'

The officer tells Danny that he doesn't think 'there's a huge amount that we, that police can do in relation to that at this stage'. He verifies Danny's name and phone number, asks for his partner's name and says: 'Right, so your concern at the moment is that you think she's going to come home and take the kids, or something like that.'

'Yeah, yeah, that is my primary concern. And I'm caught. I can't go to work 'cause, um, yeah, she, and um – as you can hear – I'm keeping him here with me.'

The officer then says: 'I thought you might have had some concerns about where she was.'

'Yeah, well,' says Danny, 'no-one knows and look I know she's seeing another fella. There are certain signs, and I'm not stupid.'

Danny then spends the next five minutes of the call talking about the bad state of his relationship with Carlie; that he knows she's having sex with someone else even while claiming he believes both of Carlie's friends — her best friend Claire and her not-very-close friend Tabitha — that they know nothing of an affair.

The officer asks about the previous police contact, a week or so earlier.

Danny explains he and Carlie had had an argument the Tuesday night before — at the yard again; he'd slept at work, then the next day, while on a job, he got a phone call from Carlie to say: 'I'm sick of this. It's over, I've had enough of you, I hate you.'

'And she's hung up on me,' he said. 'So, I'm constantly ringing her back and she's hanging up on me and she's not talking to me. And I said to Dean, my offsider, I said, "Mate, she's not talking to me. The only way I can make her talk to me is to go and get Alex."

'I did say I'm a concreter, I'm not the smartest bloke in the world, obviously I made a bad decision. I raced down to the day care and took him out. Yeah, apparently a very bad move. But at the end of the day, it sounded like she was about to get on a bloody plane.

'And this is my concern, like her and I are over, and we get it; I know she's a great person but her and I just aren't right anymore and that's the end of it.'

On being asked, he tells the officer that he's currently at the yard in Parap; he says he stayed at home the previous night, and that ever since the argument the week before he'd been 'sleeping in the spare room, which is the kid's playroom'.

Before ending the call, the officer advises Danny to contact the Family Court.

What Danny asked his friends

On 19 June, the day after Carlie was last seen, Danny Deacon rang his workmate Dean Arnold and asked if either he or his partner, Zoe Lane, could babysit his son that day. Neither friend was available to help out.

According to Danny, he needed a sitter because 'Carlie wasn't at home or he didn't know where she was'. Dean said, 'I thought it was a bit strange.'

What Danny told Kris Sinclair

On 20 June, Danny Deacon told Carlie's brother Kristian that he'd gone to the yard on the Tuesday – with Alex in the pram – to 'catch her out' with another man.

Kris said Danny told him he believed Carlie was having an affair, and that he'd planned to confront her that night in the yard they used for their business in Parap.

'He went to the yard to catch her out with this mystery person and they'd got into an argument … and Carlie had walked off,' Kris said.

A few days later, when Danny decided to elaborate on those events, he told Kris that Carlie had become aggressive towards him that night.

'He said he went to the bathroom to lock the gate and when he came back, Carlie was standing there with a star picket in her hand,' Kris said. And then, according to Danny, Carlie just 'slipped through the gate and left'.

What Danny told Claire Robinson

On 20 June 2013, Claire Robinson visited Danny to check on her missing friend's child. Danny spent time showing her a sheet that he claimed had been bundled up with $300,000 in cash and stashed in the back of a shipping container on his property. The alleged cash was missing.

According to Claire, Danny was sure the fact that the cash was gone meant that Carlie knew about his secret stashed life savings and it was she who'd taken it.

'I didn't believe it,' Claire later told the police, and the court. She said Carlie had often told her she was worried about money and having enough to feed her son.

What Danny told police who visited his home and work

On 25 June 2013, Danny Deacon gave three Darwin police officers a tour of the Stuart Park unit he shared with Carlie Sinclair. This official police visit was videoed by Detective Senior Constable Eric Curriez.

During the filming, Danny told police he had a gut feeling something was going on, and that a few of Ms Sinclair's things had gone missing.

'I, um, had a few things that I've seen over recent days that, to be honest, I've been ignoring and trying not to think of the worst of it,' he said.

'Since yesterday, ah, I just feel that I've got to let you guys know what I'm seeing and I just want to help. I'm feeling stronger and angrier and I just want you guys to see what I'm seeing.

'I'm not saying you guys aren't doing your job properly.'

Later that day the same police were shown around the yard of Danny's concreting business behind a tyre business on the Stuart Highway at Parap, about two kilometres from his home.

For the benefit of the camera, Danny indicated several objects and areas to the police, mentioned the $300,000 cash he alleged Carlie had taken, mentioned some bleach bottles, and noted that a blue tarpaulin and a shovel were missing. He also took the police between, and into, two shipping containers on the site.

PUBLIC APPEALS

On 25 June 2013, Northern Territory Police made the first of many appeals for public assistance – via Crime Stoppers NT, various news programs and even Facebook – to help with their investigations into the disappearance of Carlie Sinclair.

Crime Stoppers said: 'On the 18th June 2013, Miss Carlie Sinclair went missing from her premises at the rear of Beaurepaires on the Stuart Highway, Parap. If you have information regarding her sudden disappearance, please phone Crime Stoppers.'

On 25 June 2013, the Northern Territory's Channel 9 News coverage featured a large photo of Carlie and her son Alex, on a Crime Stoppers banner, and a mannequin dressed in clothes similar to those Carlie was last seen in.

The news report also included an appeal from Carlie's mother. An emotional Marlene Sinclair made a plea to her daughter: 'Carlie, if you can … s-see this, please call home.'

On 28 June 2013 the following appeal was posted on the NT Police Fire and Emergency Services' Facebook page, with a photo of Carlie at a football match, wearing a Brisbane Lions cap.

Working on information received from the public, Territory Response Group Officers and Detectives from the Crime Command have spent the morning combing an area south of Noonamah in an effort to locate evidence relating to the disappearance of missing woman Carlie Sinclair.

Police are thankful to the public for providing information to Crime Stoppers.

It is understood that Ms Sinclair, a mother of one, was last seen in the late hours of Tuesday 18 June, and Police are concerned for her welfare.

Carlie Sinclair is described to be of Caucasian appearance, solid build, with blonde hair which she wears in a ponytail. She was last seen wearing a black mini-skirt, a horizontal striped black and white top with sleeves and brown 'Havaianas' thongs.

Detectives will have a stall with a mannequin depicting clothing similar to those worn by Ms Sinclair when she was last seen, set up at the Parap Markets tomorrow, and urge anyone with any information on the whereabouts of Carlie to speak to Detectives at the stall, or call Crime Stoppers …

Your information could be vital in assisting Police locate Carlie Sinclair.

On 9 July 2013, an unemotional, subdued Danny Deacon also faced the cameras for Crime Stoppers.

'Carlie, if you can hear this, you need to know that we both miss you very much. Alex and I are struggling on a daily basis, we need you home. We need you home soon.'

THE NORTHERN TERRITORY POLICE FORCE (NTPF)

Darwin Metropolitan Command, with seven police stations, is the smallest of the command districts of the Northern Territory Police Force. The force's Northern and Southern Command districts cover the rest of the Territory. The police force is part of the Northern Territory Police, Fire and Emergency Services.

After Danny Deacon reported his partner missing, Darwin police soon verified that the last known public sighting of Carlie Sinclair was at the BP service station in Fannie Bay at 6.20 pm the previous night. They also confirmed she had texted her brother at 9.20 pm that same night with the words: *Danny turned up at the yard with Alex in a pram????????*

Danny told police Carlie had left him at the yard after an argument and walked off up the street – without her keys, phone or purse.

Detective Acting Sergeant Wade Jeremiah later said that Carlie's disappearance was quickly declared a major crime for several reasons, one being she had left behind personal items including a phone and purse, and because the last transaction on her bank accounts was on 18 June.

'We had already spoken to a number of people who said it was extremely unlikely that Ms Sinclair would leave her son ... for any significant amount of time,' he said.

On 28 June, in a statement recorded when Danny went to the Berrimah police station and asked to speak with someone, Danny claimed, 'I've got a horrible feeling like I've been set up.'

On 9 July, detectives formally interviewed Danny Deacon over the disappearance of Carlie Sinclair.

Detective Acting Sergeant Hayley O'Neill began the interview by informing Danny he was the prime suspect in the disappearance and alleged murder of Carlie. Sergeant O'Neill asked him how it was that Carlie had come to work for him.

Danny claimed Carlie had become unhappy working at a Darwin hospital, so he had offered her work. He agreed to pay her $1000 per week, sometimes in cash, but he also paid her 'as often as she needed'.

'What other income did Carlie have?' Sergeant O'Neill asked.

'Well, I found out recently she has been claiming welfare and, ah, getting the payments back from day care, apart from that I couldn't tell you,' Danny said.

'What did you find out about claiming welfare?' O'Neill asked.

'I've seen payments coming into her account on her statements,' he said.

Sergeant O'Neill asked Danny about an altercation he had with Carlie on 11 June, a week before her disappearance. Danny had already claimed Carlie had accused him of having an affair.

'I was at the yard and Carlie came to the yard with Alex. We were talking and my phone rang. When I finished that phone call, I rang back Lorelle, who is an assistant to me in Perth, and I was talking to her for quite a while ... then Carlie accuses me of sleeping with Lorelle.'

Sergeant O'Neill asked Danny to recount the exact details of the conversation.

'Basically, I came back, she pulled the phone out of my pocket to see who I was talking to,' Danny said. 'That's when she accused me of sleeping around. She has done it many times. Carlie was just a jealous person. She always has been.

'But as I found out ... people who are the most accusing are people you have got to watch the most. Carlie admitted to me that the last few boyfriends she was with, she slept around on them.

'So, yes, I did keep her on a short leash, especially when we were out drinking ... that's why I tend not to leave her on her own especially when we are out drinking.'

During the interview Danny also claimed Carlie had been violent towards him; that on one occasion she'd hit him around the head with a heavy torch. Several times during the interview Danny appeared agitated, and at one point asked, 'Do I need to go and get a solicitor?'

Operation Samburu

Despite having no body or any other physical evidence, the NTPF's Major Crime Squad began a murder investigation – codenamed Operation Samburu – into the disappearance of Carlie Sinclair. Police Commissioner John McRoberts later said that, although they kept an open mind, which was proper, they believed Carlie was the victim of foul play.

Teams of detectives interviewed witnesses, viewed CCTV footage and conducted aerial and ground searches of the local area, tracking through scrubland and bush, rechecking drains and doorknocking homes.

With no evidence to hold or charge him on, Danny Deacon soon left Darwin altogether and relocated to Perth with his son.

Carlie's birthday

Six months after she went missing, in the week before what would have been Carlie's 36th birthday, NTPF detectives made sure the community knew they were still working on the case.

Detective Sergeant Tony Henrys, head of Operation Samburu, said that, acting on information received early on in the investigation, detectives and members of the Territory Response Group searched bushland and water courses in the vicinity of Parap, Stuart Park and Berry Springs. A search warrant was also executed in Parap, with soil samples gathered.

'Police are also still seeking anyone who may have seen a white HiAce van or late model silver Toyota RAV4 around the Parap, Stuart Park, Cox Peninsular Road or Berry Springs area on the evening of June 18 or before midday the following day,' said Detective Sergeant Henrys at a press conference.

'Somebody knows something,' he said. 'Somebody has the vital piece of information that will help us piece together this suspicious disappearance, and find some justice for Carlie, her parents, and her three-year-old son, Alex.'

He noted that Alex would spend Christmas – which was also Carlie's birthday – without his mum.

TWELVE MONTHS MISSING

A reward and a new campaign

On 18 June 2014 – 12 months after she disappeared – the Northern Territory Government offered a $250,000 reward for information 'leading to the conviction of those responsible for the disappearance of Darwin mother, Carlie Sinclair in 2013'.

It was hoped the substantial reward would provide an incentive for someone to come forward with what they knew, saw or heard. The reward included a recommendation of indemnity from prosecution for any accomplice who gave information leading to a conviction – provided he or she did not actually commit the crime.

NT Chief Minister Adam Giles said the reward had been approved to help police in their search for 'the person or persons who may have taken the life of Ms Sinclair.'

'Around midnight on Tuesday June 18 last year, police believe the young mum left her business address at number 209 Stuart Highway in Parap after an argument with her partner,' Mr Giles said.

'She left behind her personal belongings, her car and her young son. She has not contacted her family or friends since, which relatives say is completely out of character. Her bank accounts have not been touched since the day she was last seen and police suspect she may have been murdered.

'A single piece of information, no matter how small, may hold the key to solving this crime,' Mr Giles said. 'Carlie Sinclair's family, particularly her young son, deserve answers about what happened to her and who was responsible.'

Also on 18 June 2014, while most Darwinians were home watching the second Rugby League State of Origin match on TV, NT Police were out in force unfurling enormous Crime Stoppers *What Happened to Carlie Sinclair?* bridge banners along main arterial routes. They also hammered 100 billboards featuring the words, *What Happened to Alex's Mum?* into nature strips around the city.

Police were also giving all drivers stopped for random breath tests a business card with Carlie's photo and the Crime Stoppers phone number. The campaign, which distributed 10,000 cards and 10,000 beer coasters, was designed to reinforce the Channel 9 News special *Unknown Territory*, which screened before the football.

Unknown Territory

On 18 June 2014, the anniversary of Carlie's disappearance, a TV news special called *Unknown Territory – the Carlie Sinclair Story* was aired on Channel 9, Darwin. Produced by Nine News presenter Jonathan Uptin, it featured re-enactments and interviews with Carlie's family and friends, and Danny Deacon. The four-month project was shot on a shoestring budget, taking Uptin and his senior cameraman Graham Morrison from Darwin to Perth and Brisbane.

Uptin said at the time that *Unknown Territory* was something he became emotionally invested in. 'It absorbed my life and I really want closure for the family. It sounds cliched but it's true.'

Uptin revealed in the special that Danny Deacon had moved to Perth, had limited communication with police, and had shown little interest in the case. Despite this, when Uptin approached him for an interview, he 'was obliging' and revealed he knew he was still the chief suspect but also claimed he was the victim.

When asked in the interview what really happened to Carlie, a now-bearded Danny Deacon said it was likely that Uptin knew more about what had happened to Carlie than he did. 'You'd be able to answer that better than me.'

Uptin said, 'I wish I could answer it and give the family some answers.'

Danny nodded, and said, 'Mm, we all would like some answers. Especially me.'

When Uptin asked if he had any answers, Danny said, 'Not really, I've told everyone everything that I know. And what more can I do? I'm sitting here feeling guilty for something that I haven't done.'

'Do you feel like a victim here?' Uptin asked him.

'I do feel like a victim, yeah, because I'm constantly being looked at like this,' Danny indicated the camera, 'thinking that I've done the worst thing that anyone can do to somebody – and that's a pretty awful feeling.'

Uptin asked Danny what his theory was. Danny said it didn't matter anymore what he thought.

'All we've gotta do is sit around and wait for the police to come up with something; or her feel guilty and come back; or if somebody's got a hold of her feel guilty and give her up. I don't know, there's so many scenarios I don't want to think of most of them. I like to think she's sitting on a boat somewhere, enjoying a quality beer every night and having a laugh at me.'

'You're the only one who believes that, Danny,' Uptin said.

'Yeah, I know, I know. But I know some things that a lot of people don't, as well.'

Danny claimed Carlie was a completely different mother at home than the front she put on out in public. He said she would shout and swear at Alex – 'when all he wanted was his mum'.

He also said he knew she was seeing another man and he 'was going there' – presumably the yard on the night she disappeared – 'to punch somebody'.

'That's what I was going to do. Because that's what I was expected to do.'

Uptin verified Danny was talking about the bloke she was having the affair with.

'Yeah,' Danny said. 'Because I can't hit her. But I can hit him. And that was basically what was on my mind. And he wasn't there, so all cool, there's my girl, let's have a drink. And, ah, we had a good night. We really did. Until the last 10 minutes.'

'Does that make it harder, the fact that she's disappeared?' Uptin asked.

'Yeah, yeah, I keep thinking about that. You know, I should've just stayed home and let it happen.'

Uptin asked Danny if he believed Carlie was still alive.

'It's getting harder to believe that,' Danny said. 'I still do, but it's getting harder to. I still hold some hope that her and I can have a life together. Because if this situation is out of her hands, she knows I'll fight tooth and nail for her.'

'What do you think happened?' Uptin asked.

Danny shrugged and said, 'I think a lot of things. But I still think that she's in Asia somewhere. That's what I think … She loved parts of it while we were over there. And she loves boats. She loves living on boats. I dunno. A lot of scenarios have gone through my head, the longer she's away the more I think that something has backfired … a few things just keep telling me that, yep, she's done some very careful planning.'

Uptin said, 'I can tell you this is now a homicide investigation. Do you want Carlie's killer caught and brought to justice?'

'If that is what's happened, yeah. But I still don't think that's what's happened.'

'Did you kill Carlie Sinclair?' Uptin asked.

'No. But it doesn't matter what I say. People are always gonna think I'm a liar, as far as that's concerned … But at the moment, the way I'm feeling, I just want her to show up – so all this can stop; all the accusing eyes and comments, and the so-called experts. That's what I want put to an end.'

Operation Samburu continues

A year on from her disappearance, four Northern Territory detectives continued to work full time on the baffling case: re-examining evidence, reinterviewing people, and poring over old statements.

By 17 June 2014, it was the best they could do in their efforts to bring closure to Carlie's family – her parents, Marlene and Robert, her brother Kristian, and three-and-a-half-year-old Alex.

Police suspected foul play and Danny Deacon remained the only suspect. Acting Commander Tony Fuller said Danny Deacon would 'remain a suspect in Ms Sinclair's disappearance until he's eliminated.

'He was the last person to see her and he was in a domestic

relationship with her,' Fuller said. While he would not comment on the couple's relationship, what evidence police had uncovered, or what lines of inquiry they were pursuing, Commander Fuller said there were no fresh leads.

He explained that, while building a case was difficult with no body and when the trail has gone cold, Operation Samburu detectives had ruled out suicide, and her devotion to Alex had all but ruled out the possibility she ran away.

'The mostly likely scenario is she met with foul play that night, by person or persons unknown to us at this stage,' Commander Fuller said.

'It gets taxing over time, but those officers are very committed, and they've only got one thing on their mind – that's to get answers for young Alex.'

NT Police and the Operation Samburu detectives may have publicly said that going over existing evidence and following leads from the new *What Happened to Carlie Sinclair?* campaign was 'the best they could do', but it wasn't by any means all they were doing.

BALI, THE EX-WIFE AND THE FEDS

Sometime around August–September 2013, expat Aussie Val Garner (a pseudonym, at her request) was sitting in her office upstairs in the spa she owned in Bali. Val, who'd been living in Bali since 2007, had an agreement with her staff that if the police ever turned up, they were to say she wasn't there. This precaution was about the Balinese police, who would only ever arrive unannounced for bribery purposes.

'So that day, when one of my staff rang to say the police were there, I told her off for telling them I was in the building but she said, "No, no, Australian police to see you."

'I had no idea why they were there but wasn't worried because my father was a policeman back in WA, so they don't scare me. I went downstairs, and there's these two cops in suits and I said, "G'day, boys, what do you need? Do you want to come through?"

'I took them into our hospitality area, we all sat down, and they opened the conversation with: "You used to be married to Danny Deacon?"

'When I said yes, their very next sentence was: "Would it surprise you to know that we are investigating him for murder?"

'I said, "No, not really."

'And they said: "Interesting, it seems everyone we talk to about him isn't surprised by that thought," to which I said, "Well, I thought it was only a matter of time. I was only married to him for six months, halfway through which I knew had to get out."

'Then they told me Danny was the prime suspect in his girlfriend's disappearance and probable murder.'

The officers showed Val a phone number, which she acknowledged had been hers until five years before, when she moved to Bali.

'They told me Danny had been calling that number up to seven times a day. I asked how they knew that, why he'd be ringing that number, and who he was talking to.

'They said they'd been tapping his phone. He kept getting the message that the number – *my old number* – was out of range. I told them it was more than out of range; I didn't even have the same phone.

'These Feds then told me that Danny had been insisting to, I don't know, them or other cops, that the only good relationship he'd ever had in his life was with me. And that he is like a father to my child.

'I said, "Well he's *not* like a father to my child. We only co-habited for the six months after we got married. He's part of the reason I'm living up here in Bali.

'They wanted to know more about Danny and why I thought he'd be capable of murder. And I said, "Because he was violent, and prone to escalating outbursts of anger."

'They asked if he had hurt me and I said no, but one time he had me up against a wall by my throat and another he chased me down the hallway with a knife. Besides all the mental stuff, I believed it was only a matter of time before he physically hurt me. I told them I was not an unintelligent woman; I knew I had to get out.'

When Val asked the Feds what had happened to Danny's girlfriend, they told her the bare minimum: that she was last seen at a petrol station; that it was unusual for her to have left her child, even though there were signs she'd been organising to leave him.'

'So, I said, "Well, you're the police, you sort it out."

'And they said, "We haven't got a body."

'So, naturally, I said, "Why are you here then?" And they said, "Would you testify to his character? Would you come to Darwin and testify about what he was like? He thinks you're the best relationship he ever had and he's constantly ringing your number. He's obsessed and seems to think you will vouch for him."

'My response was, "If you don't have a body, what good is anything I might have to say?" I told them I was not prepared to go to Darwin. I hadn't seen Danny in years and the last time I heard anything about him he was a dive instructor in Darwin.

'They said, "No, he's not a dive instructor anymore; they own a cement company. They lay cement foundations."

'I admit I couldn't help myself. I said, "Well there's a good way to hide a body."

'They persisted with stuff like, "Look, this is really important. We believe he's done it, we just don't have a body." They were there for about an hour and left with me saying if they wanted a statement, they could take it from me in Bali.'

Over the next few weeks Val received letters from senior detectives of the Northern Territory Police, as well as emails and a couple of phone calls, always asking her to go to Darwin as a witness. 'It started to get quite strange, so I tried to ignore it all.'

Val and Danny: the first time

'I owned a restaurant in Perth and Danny came to work there as a cook. The intensity of working in a kitchen was perfect for him. The adrenalin rush of getting all the food ready and out to customers quickly, and yelling at staff in the kitchen to make that happen, was his happy place.

'We started a relationship that was really intense and passionate, although we never lived together or anything. But Danny soon became very controlling. He was younger than me, so I thought it was all about that. One day in the restaurant, however, my brother nearly punched him because his behaviour to me was so wrong. It soon became too much and I told Danny to stay away from me.

'When I realised Danny had these massive anger issues, I asked people he knew and they said, "Oh yeah, he solves everything with his fist."

'They told me he'd get in uncontrollable rages that were hard to stop. And that he was always befriending like-minded blokes; the ones who believed, like he did, that women pushed men to their natural instinct, which was violence.'

When Val broke things off with Danny, he headed for Australia's east coast, telling her, 'I can't live in the same state as you, if we're not together; I love you too much.'

Val and Danny: the second time

Val met a new man, the month after Danny left Western Australia, and was soon pregnant. Her son Scott was born in 1995, but the relationship with the child's father lasted only another nine months. Just over three years later, when Scott was four, Danny returned to Perth briefly to cater for a social event.

'My girlfriend had offered to fly him to Perth from Newcastle to cater her 40th birthday party in 2001. Apparently the first thing he asked when he landed was, "Where is Val?"

'So, there was all this socialising going on and nearly everyone in our circle commented on how Danny seemed like changed man. And to me, Danny was charming and all "I've changed, I've realised I made mistakes, I can't live without you. You are the most important thing in my life".

'And I was conned.'

Unbeknownst to Val at first, Danny also believed that Scott was his child. He'd 'counted back' to one last night of passion, after they'd broken up, and just before Danny left Perth for Newcastle.

'The interesting thing about that notion of Danny's,' Val said, 'is that I'd been told I couldn't have kids. So, the whole time Danny and I were together – both times – we never used protection.

'And yet along comes a new relationship and bam – within three or four weeks I'm pregnant. So, on his return Danny assumed Scott was his and that I'd I lied to the incoming guy about my pregnancy.'

In 2001 when Danny and Val got together again, she was 39 and Danny was 30.

'The big question, in retrospect, was why the fuck did I let him back into my life?

'Why? Because I was a single mother with a very sick child. I was doing it tough; I couldn't work, and financially I was up shit creek. I needed help.

'Why? Because Danny's timing was perfect, and his undeniable charm got him most of the things he wanted.

'Why? Because I bought his story that he had changed. He really did seem to be a different, better man. It'd been nearly four years since we'd seen each other. And people can change, right? And he maintained that facade right up until we got married. He held it all together until "I do" and then he didn't.

'We got married in Bali because a girlfriend and I had already booked a holiday there. Suddenly a dozen friends and family members also booked trips to be there for our wedding.

'Thinking back now, I know why it was easy for him to maintain the good bloke facade in the lead-up to our wedding. It was because I was in Perth and he'd gone back to his job in Newcastle. So, at the start we were actually on opposite sides of the country. He flew to Bali from the east coast and I flew from the west.

'And, of course, Bali with the wedding and all our friends was all fun and games. He was great; the charming life of the party, always telling people how much he loved me. After Bali we flew home to our own states, then I flew to Newcastle to spend two weeks with him there while he finished up his job, then we both drove to Perth. We renovated an old fish and chip shop and opened an up-market takeaway food place in Perth. Danny also did a cake-decorating course.'

Much to Val's horror, it was only a month or so 'before things went to shit. His behaviour reverted to the controlling, suspicious, angry Danny I'd known all those years before.

'It was almost the moment we were back in Perth that it started again. It was like he just couldn't hold onto it any longer. It started small, with the usual: always wanting to know where I was going, who I was with, what I was doing; then increased and increased to the first time he shoved me up against a wall by my throat. He'd do things like move the furniture around all the time so when I'd come home from working late, I couldn't go to bed straightaway because I couldn't get to it. It was all control, control. And I knew it.

'The takeaway concept of our place was so that Danny could do the job he enjoyed without working ridiculous restaurant hours. But I'd be out somewhere with friends and he'd ring wanting me to get things for him. It was only ever about controlling where I was. If he knew I was at home, he wouldn't do it.

'Once I was out with family, including an aunt I hadn't seen since the 1970s. She was visiting from the US and, as she was also a restaurateur, we were having a great time talking about our shared passions. And Danny couldn't stand it, knowing I was out without him, surrounded by people who loved me, and he wasn't there to play.

'So, he rang me and said, "I need lettuce." I said, "Well there's an IGA just down the street, go there and buy lettuce." And he said, "I don't want *that* lettuce. I want you to come here and then go and buy me some lettuce."

'I told him to go get his own lettuce. So then, as he probably figured my aunt had heard the exchange, that evening when he joined us out for dinner as planned, he spent most of the night charming her. He laid it on really thick, as he always did in public, being the life of the party and telling her how much he admired and loved me.

'When we were leaving the restaurant, my aunt said to me, "Wow, that boy certainly loves you, there can be no doubt about that, but I'd watch yourself with him."

'At home he was mostly unbearable. I'd come home and find all of Scott's toys in the garbage bins out the front of the house. Every toy. I'd ask him, "What the hell is going on here?" And he'd say, "He doesn't deserve them. He doesn't appreciate how hard you worked to buy them for him. So, I'm throwing them all out."

'This was pure control. He hated that Scott – a toddler – was getting more attention than him.

'To make my life easier, I used to invite *his* friends over most weekends to keep him company and away from me and Scott. They'd all smoke dope – a lot of dope – and drink and do blokey things together.

'But I knew I had to get out, even before the most frightening incidents.

'One day he came home from somewhere he'd been with my son – who was nearly five by then. Scott told me that "Danny very angry, Mummy". Knowing that Danny was a shocker when it came to road rage, I told Scott to go off to his room.

'And Danny's all "Nah, nah, I just swore at a guy when he cut me off. It was nothing".

'But I talked with Scott because he was clearly upset by it. My five-year-old told me he saw Danny punch the guy through the window of his car.

'I of course brought it up with Danny, who admitted, "Well, he fucking deserved it," and then told me the guy had cut him off. So Danny sped around him, pulled up in front to stop him, got out of his car, went to the other driver's window and tapped on it to get him to wind the window down and just punched him. He told him, "That'll teach you, you prick," then got back into his car with Scott and drove off.

'Imagine doing anything like that with a kid in the car. But then, let's talk about *his* mother and the affect she had on him. She was apparently a controlling bitch of a woman but couldn't handle Danny once his father had taken off. He was still a kid, about six maybe, when she gave him to an uncle, or a man she referred to as his uncle, to raise. This guy was a long-haul truck driver and Danny lived a boys' own adventure with this guy, driving around the country, until the Education Department found out and made sure he went home so he could go to school.

'His mother got into a very abusive relationship for about four years from when Danny was 10. That guy ended up thumping his mother. But Danny told me that he understood why the guy hit his mother: "because she was a pain in the arse".

'And yet, Danny has a scar over his eye from the time when, as a grown man, he tracked his father down in Melbourne. His father said a few derogatory things about Danny's mother and they got into a fight. Danny told *me* he was "defending" his mother, but his father clocked him in the face. He never saw him again.'

Val and Danny tried counselling, but Danny stormed out of the first session, shoving furniture out of the way as he left, claiming that because the counsellor was also a woman it meant everything was stacked against him. The counsellor said to Val afterwards, 'The purpose of counselling isn't always to save a relationship. Are you safe?' When another session was made, this time with a male counsellor, Danny simply didn't turn up.

'The final straw was the time he chased me through the house with a knife. I believe my neighbour accidentally saved my life that day. It was pure luck that, as I was running down the hall past the front door to get away from him, Diane knocked on it.

'And Danny – calm as a cucumber – stopped, put the knife in the back of his chef's pants, opened the door, and with a big smile said, "G'day, Diane, how are you going?"

'She said, "Hi, I've brought this cooked chicken and some orange juice for Val because I hear she's sick and might not be able to get out to the shop."

'And Danny says, "Oh, how lovely of you, Diane, that's fantastic. Yeah, she isn't well, so you can't come in, but I'll take that. Thanks."

'Meanwhile, I scrambled down the hall, grabbed my car keys, picked up my son – all the way saying *shhh* – and went out through the laundry door at the back and down the side of the house. By the time I got to the front, Diane had left, and Danny was inside hunting for me. I just threw my stuff in the car and did a runner.

'And then I got help. I got help from my father, who was still alive then, although I never gave him the full story because he would've killed Danny. I just told him I needed to get him out of the house and I need help to do it; there's reasons I don't want to go into, they're private, but Danny has to go.

'So, with my father's background support, I told Danny he had to get out. He stayed for about three days and then left. So, Scott and I went back to the house. I told Danny not to come back; that I didn't want to see him again.'

Val had already been looking at ways to get out of the marriage without violence, but knew she also had to get out of the cafe as well.

'Danny wasn't very bright in the business sense, so I'd started planting ideas about how bad the cafe was doing. It *was* failing, but not nearly as badly as I made Danny believe. I had to manipulate my way out, but I sold the business out from under him – all the while making him believe it was for his benefit. I mean I was losing our business too, but I was determined to make it look like I was doing everything to look after him. He took that and disappeared into the ether.

'Except for one day. I hadn't changed the locks because I thought he'd gone; left the state. This day I was expecting a delivery of a desk but had told the delivery guys to leave it on the veranda. I was in the shower when I heard noises inside the house. As Scott wasn't home, my first thought was someone had broken in. I wrapped a towel around me and stood looking down the hall, to see if anyone was in the front of the house so I could decide whether to run or not.

'And there's Danny, in the lounge room. I said, "What the hell are you doing in the house?" And he said, "I've told you, you can't live without me. I'm putting together this desk."

'I told him I hadn't asked him to put the desk together and that I didn't want him in my house.

'He said, "You can't see, Val, this is a classic example, *you* can't put this together. How would you put this together? I'm going to do this for you."

'And I'm now screaming at him to get the fuck out of my house. And he's all Mr Charming, Mr Gorgeous: "I'm just helping you. Why is it that you can't accept people's help? Just let me finish putting the desk together and then I'll go."

'I said, "You're not welcome here. I'm going to change the locks, you psychopath."

'Then his mood just slipped – and he ran straight at me, with the side of his neck bulging like a bloody frill-necked lizard. He pushed me up against the wall, got right in my face and screamed, "You need me. You can't live without me."

Val realised she had to de-escalate the situation and admits now she doesn't remember exactly what she said, but she calmed him down. She then told him she had to get dressed because she had a meeting to get to.

'He stepped back and I went and got dressed. When I came out, he'd gone. Then I changed all the locks.'

Bali: the Feds return

'Two or three months after that first visit, one of those two Federal officers, who was apparently "on holiday in Bali", came to see me in person again,' Val said. 'He rocked up to my spa in his board shorts with his mate, a different cop, and said, "We're up here on holiday, and we just thought we'd drop in for another discussion. To see if maybe you might change your mind and come to Darwin."

'I said, "Guys I just don't get it, if you haven't got a body and you haven't got any evidence, how's my testimony that he was violent years ago going to make any difference?"

'They told me Danny had gone back to Perth. They'd checked all the cement jobs he done since Carlie had disappeared, with some sort of machinery that looks through cement, and they were still tapping his phone and his mother's phone. Apparently, he was still ringing me; still completely obsessed with me. And then came the real reason for the visit. "Would you, perhaps, participate in a bit of a sting? You know, go to Perth, bump into Danny, tell him you were wrong to break up with him and suggest you both try again.

'My response: "No bloody way, you've *got* to be joking."

'They said, "We'd pay for your flight, pay for your motel," – *motel*, the big spenders! – "and we'll protect you."

'And I said, "How would you protect me? He must know I'm in Bali – I'm all over the internet with my business. It's probably why he keeps ringing that old phone number, assuming I'm overseas, out of range – but he rings in case I come home for a visit and use it again. And why are you so sure it's him? You've told me nothing. Yes, he's a violent arsehole, but why are you so sure he's a murderer?"

'That's when they told me they had blood evidence from a car or van he owned. And it's proven to be her blood.'

Val again refused to participate. 'I got a couple more letters from them after, but for some reason I got really uneasy about it all, because the pressure from them was strangely intense. I rang a criminal barrister friend of my sister's in Melbourne for advice; I mostly wanted to know if they could *force* me to testify.

'After I told him everything he said, "Under no circumstances should you go anywhere near it. They think you're involved, Val. My sixth sense is they believe somehow you and Danny got back together again and this is all part of the plan."

This was not the response Val had expected. 'Thinking back, I suppose Danny's obsession with me, and the delusion that I'd vouch for him, came from how I conned him when we separated. I used the law, the taxation office, the insolvent trading rules to do it, and kept telling him how I was getting *him* out of all that by selling the place without him carrying any debt. And wasn't I a fabulous person always thinking about him?

'It's how I got him to sign the papers to hand the restaurant over to the guy who'd been working for us. We had debt – it was a debt in my name for us to start the business; but the business was in his name. I didn't want to carry that debt with him for another 10 years; I'd never have gotten rid of him.'

Val says she later discovered that in-between the two television appearances Danny made regarding his missing girlfriend, he contacted all *her* family friends with a cheery, 'Hi, it's Danny here.'

Val said, 'And they were like: "It's been like seven years, why are you ringing us?" And he said, "Well, you may have seen me in the press or the TV, I just wanted you to know it's all a big mistake; I'm being wrongly accused; I can't believe it's got to this; I don't know want to do; I'm in Perth now from Darwin, do you wanna catch up?"

'One friend said, "Sure, give us your number we'll organise something," but never did. He rang my cousin, my brother, my brother-in-law. He never rang the women though, only the men. He didn't ring my sister. My brother-in-law told him, "Danny, I don't know why you're ringing me. Lose my number." And my brother told him never to call again.'

The Federal and Northern Territory Police eventually left Val alone.

'They did tell me, when they were talking the whole "sting thing", that they believed Danny's ego was such that if any bloke was clever enough to befriend him on the basis of his low opinion of women then he'd feel comfortable and safe.

'They'd heard he said things like, "Thank god women have got vaginas or we wouldn't talk to them."'

And that very approach was partly how police got him to confess.

While Val refused to take part in any kind of sting designed to get on Danny Deacon's good side to get information, it *was* ultimately a sting of another kind that took him down.

DANNY DEACON JOINS A CRIMINAL GANG

After several interviews in which Danny denied any involvement in his girlfriend's disappearance – including one in which he suggested Carlie had tried to set him up to make it *look* like he had murdered her – NT police realised they needed a back door to find out what really happened on 18 June 2013. And it was obvious the only way to get the truth out of Danny Deacon was to pander to his masculinity and 'boys' club' mindset.

According to the court transcripts (Deacon V the Queen – in the NT Criminal Court of Appeal, delivered 11 October 2019 after appeal hearings in February and August 2015), NT police conducted an undercover operation against Danny Deacon using 'what is colloquially referred to as the "Mr Big" methodology.'

'The use of this methodology is typically reserved for murder investigations where traditional investigative techniques have reached an impasse. The technique involves creating a fictitious crime group comprised of covert police operatives and luring the target into the group. The group members form social bonds with the target and gain his or her confidence through the inclusion of the target in a criminal enterprise relationship. The basic premise of the methodology is that suspects are likely to incriminate themselves if there is a perceived benefit for them and they feel safe doing so.'

Dispensing with the strict legal-speak, in August 2014 undercover police officers made contact with Danny 'using a subterfuge'. One undercover cop in particular established a rapport with Danny and befriended him, but over the next month the other undercover guys also gained his confidence. Danny was soon willingly taking part in the activities of this fabricated gang of criminals.

Talk about an ego boost for a man already wanted for murder.

From August to 16 December that year, Danny took part in 33 tasks or jobs that were designed 'to test his commitment' to the group. Most of the scenarios involved fictitious criminal activity designed to make Danny believe he was playing with his new mates in a fair dinkum criminal enterprise. Danny was paid cash for the things he did for them, to foster that belief, although there was in fact no illegal activity.

Danny's role involved things like picking up and counting money or acting as a lookout. Over the months his involvement was increased to make him feel more connected to the group.

During October 2014, for instance, he received seven payments of $200. In November he got another seven payments of $200, three of $250 and one of $500; and in December he got one of $50, five lots of $200, one of $400 and one of $600, plus travel and other benefits. The undercover police used the payments as positive reinforcement of his bond with their gang, and an incentive to continue to work with them.

While working together and socialising, the scenarios were designed to make Danny believe his new mates had 'power' by reason of the gang's links to corrupt law enforcement officers. Early on, in particular, they randomly chatted about having the ability to get incriminating evidence destroyed.

Eventually Danny was told that to become a proper part of the gang, he had to get the approval of their – as yet unmet – fictitious 'Boss', the Mr Big of the methodology. This Boss naturally expected trust, loyalty and honesty from his minions. Danny was finally given his chance to enter the inner – or upper – circle of the gang in a Perth hotel room on 17 December 2014.

The meeting with the Boss, obviously an undercover operative but also controller of the whole police operation, was – as the court transcript describes – 'the culmination of hundreds of hours of artifice, deceit and the contrived criminal interactions'.

The deal, from Danny's perspective, was to get the Boss's approval to take part in two big upcoming jobs. The objective from the undercover police perspective was to get Danny to tell the truth about Carlie Sinclair's murder, and to get evidence to corroborate any admissions of guilt.

The Boss told Danny his group was professional, careful and well connected. He said he wanted Danny on the team, and he'd get a new car if they let him in officially, but Danny really needed to get the 'shit up in Darwin' sorted out in case it came back to bite him and thereby hurt their activities.

The Boss gave him the choice to leave if he didn't want to talk about 'that shit', but Danny obligingly rolled out the same story he'd been telling for over a year. The Boss reminded Danny how important things like trust and honesty were to him. He assured Danny it wouldn't be the first time one of his blokes had a problem that needed solving.

The Boss told Danny that, according to inside info he'd obtained from a (corrupt) police contact he had in Darwin, the word was Danny had a very real problem that needed fixing before he could be allowed to take part in any future jobs with them. The Boss also implied how important it was for Danny to eliminate any possible problems he had in Darwin, because his son needed a father.

Danny tried to get an idea from the Boss whether police up there actually knew for sure that Carlie was dead. When the Boss acknowledged a body hadn't been found yet, Danny saw no reason to change his story. He raised his theory that Carlie had stolen money from his business and was living somewhere in Asia.

The Boss, then playing the Big Boss card, laid down the law by implying the only way Danny would get a permanent place in his group was to tell him the real story so they could deal with any possible fallout for him – in order to protect all of them.

The Boss resorted to an interview technique known as 'minimisation'. To build on the common bond of misogyny his undercover crew had already used to secure Danny's trust, the Boss admitted he didn't care at all what had happened to the woman – except for how it might affect him. He put Carlie down and made derogatory comments about women in general.

Things went back and forth for a while, with Danny at one stage even claiming he knew 'how to dispose of a body' but not admitting he had, and the Boss revealing a number of lucrative jobs were on hold because Danny's part in them depended entirely on his Darwin problem being resolved once and for all. The Boss assured Danny he had the money and other means to help him, whereon Danny insisted the cops had nothing on him. The Boss countered with the intel from his cop-on-the-side that police would soon be coming after Danny for murder.

For a brief time, Danny became suspicious and even asked if the whole thing, the group and the meeting, was a 'set-up'. He pointed out he'd only known his new friends for a few months and raised the possibility that the Boss was a cop.

The Boss feigned anger and threatened to pull the plug on Danny's connection to them unless he drew him a map of where he'd buried the body.

And that was it. Clearly desperate not to lose the criminal brotherhood he'd been enjoying for five months, Danny Deacon drew a map of where he had buried the body of Carlie Sinclair.

The Boss – feigning approval – asked for all the details, so Danny proudly told him and his crew how he'd organised and carried out the murder of his girlfriend. He told them he'd punched her in the head, which made her unconscious. Then he 'choked her out', wrapped her body in plastic and a tarpaulin and put her in the boot of her own car, where he left her overnight. The next morning, he took Carlie's body out into the bush. He buried the mother of his child two metres down in a hole he'd dug a month before with an excavator.

Officially a member of the group, and with a promise from the Boss that he would help Danny ensure the body would never be found, Danny went off to lunch with his good mate in the gang.

A couple of days later Danny Deacon returned to Darwin and, in the company of blokes he still believed were fellow gang members, the murderer led the undercover cops straight to the grave of Carlie Sinclair.

NT POLICE: WE KNOW WHERE CARLIE IS

That same day – 19 December 2014 – NT Police Commissioner John McRoberts fronted the Darwin media with the news that 'as a result of a man being seen in the Berry Springs area, he has been arrested and we are now holding him in custody until the results are known of a comprehensive crime scene analysis, which is currently underway.

'Based on all the evidence that has been compiled, based on the fact that we now have a man in custody, based on the fact that we now have what is clearly a gravesite at Berry Springs, we are very confident that we have solved the mystery surrounding the disappearance of Ms Sinclair,' he said.

'We are very confident that we know where Carlie is. Although it will take us some hours – possibly not even until tomorrow – to be able to tell her family that we have in fact confirmed her identity and where she is.'

Commissioner McRoberts told the assembled media they would be escorted to that crime scene where they'd be able to see the efforts of their forensic officers.

'I need to make it very clear that the team of detectives that have been involved in this were steely in their determination, they were professional in everything they did, purely because they were not satisfied that Miss Sinclair had simply disappeared.'

Commissioner McRoberts said his Northern Territory Police had assistance and support from Queensland Police, Western Australia Police and the Australian Federal Police, and specialist advice from the FBI in the US 'because we would not leave any stone unturned', he said.

NT Police Scene of Crime officers, led by three forensic experts, carried out a comprehensive analysis of the alleged gravesite in bush about 60 kilometres from Darwin. Earthmoving equipment was brought in to assist with the process of excavating the area of interest in Berry Springs. As the site was characterised by heavy vegetation, the Northern Territory Fire and Rescue Service helped clear some of the problematic foliage by a burning process. The meticulous process was conducted as quickly as possible but with the utmost consideration to avoid compromising any potential evidence.

Danny Deacon was arrested and charged with murder on 19 December and, during the course of a formal police interview four days later, confessed to killing Carlie Sinclair.

THE TRIAL

Danny Jack Deacon went on trial for the murder of Carlie Sinclair on 10 August 2016. The trial involved around 80 witnesses and lasted four weeks.

He had already led the undercover sting team to Carlie's grave and, on his arrest, confessed to NT police, as well as to fellow inmates while on remand in prison in Darwin. When it came to trial, however, Danny pleaded not guilty. He admitted killing her but asserted he had done so under provocation.

In his opening, Crown Prosecutor Paul Usher told the court that in May 2013, Danny had taken an excavator out to the bush site and dug a two-metre-deep grave in which to bury Ms Sinclair 'when the time came'.

'The Crown says that the accused killed Carlie Sinclair in a secluded area by hitting her in the head and causing her to fall to the ground and probably lose consciousness,' he said.

'Later the accused strangled her until she was dead using a rag to avoid leaving any mark on her throat. Before she died, she bled from an unknown injury. The accused wrapped her body up in a blue tarpaulin and tied it with rope. [Deacon] then wrapped her body and the rag in another layer of material and secured it with more rope. He moved the deceased's wrapped body into the boot of her RAV4 vehicle that was in the yard ... and went home with their son.'

Mr Usher told the court Danny 'then disposed of Ms Sinclair's body in accordance with his plan. On the morning of June 19, 2013, Deacon drove the RAV4 to a property on Mulgara Road in Berry Springs with the body in the boot of the car.'

Deacon then buried the body 'quickly while [their son] waited in the car', he said.

What the court was told

The jury was shown three videos filmed by Detective Senior Constable Eric Curriez on 25 June 2013, when police responded to the report that Carlie Sinclair was missing. One video was at her home in Stuart Park, the other two at Danny's concreting business in Parap. One featured Danny pointing out things that were suspiciously missing – a shovel, a tarpaulin.

When Senior Crown Prosecutor Mary Chalmers played the third video, she pointed out the area between the two shipping containers where police believed Carlie was killed.

Detective Acting Sergeant Wade Jeremiah showed the court a rubber car mat found under a pie warmer in the couple's food van in the yard at Parap, which he said had tested positive for Carlie's blood. The jurors were also escorted to the basement of the Supreme Court to see her RAV4.

Dean Arnold, Danny's concreting offsider, testified that Danny had told him in May 2013 (a month before the murder) that he was heading to Berry Springs to dig a tree root. When Dean offered to do it for him, because it was out of Deacon's way, Danny insisted he do it himself, which Dean thought was 'strange'.

Dean and his partner Zoe Lane also testified that Danny had contacted them on 19 June, the day after Carlie was last seen, and asked them to look after Alex for a few hours. He told them he needed a sitter because 'Carlie wasn't at home; he didn't know where she was'. Neither were available to help out.

Adam Hicks, a prisoner being held on remand in the Darwin Correctional Centre at Holtze, 22 kilometres from Darwin, in December 2014 – at the same time as the accused – told the court about a conversation he had with Danny Deacon a couple of days after his arrest.

Hicks said Danny told him and two other prisoners that Carlie had swung a star picket at him on the night she died. 'He said he saw it coming and ducked, turned around and punched her in the head really hard,' Hicks testified.

'She was unconscious on the ground. Then he took the body inside the shed and wrapped it in a tarp ... He said after a while Carlie had come semi-conscious again. Danny said he "placed his hand around her throat and choked her out until she was lifeless"'.

Hicks said Danny told the men, 'He then placed the body in the back of the car … and he had driven the body to dispose of it in the hole he dug two weeks before.'

The prosecutor asked Hicks whether Deacon said anyone else was nearby when he buried Ms Sinclair. Mr Hicks said: 'Yes, his boy. He was in the car.'

The jury was shown the video recording of the police interview between Danny and two NT Major Crime detectives on 23 December 2014, in which he told them he apologised to Carlie and told her he loved her – as he strangled her.

What Danny told the detectives

'I was apologising, talking to her, telling her that I love her and it was all for Alex,' Danny said in the interview. 'I know it was making excuses to someone who couldn't hear me, but it was just what came out of me.'

Danny declared he was immediately suicidal after he killed Ms Sinclair. 'I wanted to kill myself. If I had a gun at the time I would have,' he told the detectives.

'I snapped. I didn't think I was going to do it that night. For some reason in my head I thought I might be putting two people in a bloody hole,' he said.

Danny told the detectives he hit Carlie on the temple and she collapsed to the ground. 'She just sat down like' – Danny hit the table to demonstrate – 'a sound I will never forget'.

Danny said he then straddled Carlie. 'I knew she was out cold and I could feel her breathing. I just said, "Finish it, finish it, finish it." I finished it. Honestly, guys, I just didn't want her to suffer.

'I went and grabbed that tarp and wrapped her up in that and used the rope from my pull-up bar to bunny wrap her. I treated her in as much respect as I can, when I hit her and she went down, I paused because I couldn't believe I'd done it.

'I dug that hole when I was very angry and I heard she was looking for work.'

In his original statements to police, after Carlie went missing, he said he'd just decided at 7.30 am that next day to take a drive with Alex. He told police he'd planned to take his son to friends in the rural Acacia Hills area so he and Carlie could talk privately later when she showed up.

The alleged trip to Acacia Hills, however, was simply a believable reason for him to be in the nearby area of Berry Springs, should he ever have to explain his whereabouts that morning. But those friends, Dean Arnold and Zoe Lane, had already told him on the phone they couldn't help. Nevertheless, Danny still headed south on the Stuart Highway, later claiming – to explain the time away – that he and Alex stopped at a parking area on Cox Peninsula Road, where he and Alex kicked a ball for a while.

So yes, he'd wanted to dump his toddler with Dean and Zoe but in reality, Danny Deacon *had* to take two-year-old Alex along when he buried Carlie because he couldn't get a sitter.

As it turned out, having Alex with him provided good cover; after all, who would suspect a man out driving with his toddler would be up to anything bad? He was filmed driving Carlie's silver Toyota RAV4 into the United petrol station in Noonamah, where he put petrol in the car and then headed inside, carrying Alex, to pay. It was 9.17 am on 19 June.

In the police interview played to the court, Danny said he hoped he'd be filmed by CCTV that day. 'Just to look like I didn't have a care in the world ... it's the old smoke and mirrors.'

A traffic camera from the corner of Woolner Road and the Stuart Highway in Parap showed the RAV4 back at Danny's Parap business yard property by 11.20 am the same day.

The 52-kilometre drive to bush site in Mulgara Road, Berry Springs, with the brief stop in Noonamah at 9.17 am to be filmed while getting petrol, would have taken Danny about 45 minutes. To be back in Parap by 11.20 meant Danny had, at the most, one hour in which to dispose of Carlie's body.

The court heard Danny tell the arresting detectives that he put towels over the windows of the car so his son could not see him burying his mother. The boy was 'in his car seat, strapped in so he couldn't get out', Danny said.

'I kept him in the car so he couldn't see; he was crying his eyes out because he couldn't see what Dad was up to.'

The verdict

On 9 September 2016, after four days of deliberation at the end of the four-week trial, the jury returned a majority guilty verdict. In the

Northern Territory, a murder conviction attracts a mandatory life sentence with a minimum 20-year non-parole period. Danny was given a non-parole period of 21 years and six months.

His defence of not guilty because he was provoked did not wash with anyone.

Justice Peter Barr rejected Danny's explanation that he lost control after being provoked by Carlie, and called him 'untruthful, cunning and manipulative'.

'You engaged in a detailed and calculated planning prior to the killing, and a complex cover-up after the event,' Justice Barr said.

'You intentionally deprived your son of his mother's love, care and guidance. You killed the deceased specifically to ensure that she would have no role in your son's upbringing,' he said.

The Sinclairs spoke to the media afterwards. Carlie's brother, Kristian, welcomed Justice Barr's rejection of Danny's provocation defence.

'I think everybody saw straight through it, so the fact that's been pointed out in court to Danny's face, he's been caught lying again, brilliant,' he said.

Kris and Carlie's mother Marlene wore white ribbons – the symbol of the anti–domestic violence movement – on their lapels, and said they planned to turn their attention to advocating against domestic violence.

'Carlie was such a strong, lovely young woman, who just got tied up with the wrong person. And unfortunately, that happens around the country. We've got to fight now to stop that,' Marlene Sinclair said.

She urged parents to act on any signs of domestic violence in their children's relationships. 'If they see even an inkling of trouble that all's not well, investigate it really thoroughly because you never know, it could be another Danny Deacon out there.'

The appeals

Both sides appealed against the verdict in 2017 and it took more than two years for the judges in each case to reach a decision.

Danny Deacon appealed (in February and August) on the basis that his confessions to the undercover police shouldn't have been admitted into evidence because the jury could not have understood whether or not his confession had been influenced by 'oppressive conduct' on the part of the fictitious Boss of the criminal gang. In other words, that Danny was intimidated into telling the truth.

The Crown appealed (in February) on the basis that the 21.5-year non-parole period of Danny Deacon's life sentence was manifestly inadequate given the seriousness of the offence, the high degree of planning involved, the elaborate concealment of the crime and the lack of remorse.

Decisions relating to both appeals were handed down on 11 October 2019. Both were dismissed.

☠ ☠ ☠

Danny Deacon's particular – though hardly unique – brand of toxic masculinity not only resulted in the untimely and vicious death of Carlie Sinclair, but it also took him to jail for life. He could, quite possibly, have got away with murder except for the twisted ego that drives men like him. The undercover detectives conned him into joining their boys' club, their criminal gang, their cohort of misogynists, by stoking that ego and pandering to the lowest, ugliest parts of his personality.

Danny Deacon was a bastard who honestly believed his women couldn't live without him, or were to blame for making him angry.

But any man who thinks women can push him to violence simply loves an excuse to *be* violent towards women.

Chapter Two

NOT ONE SCINTILLA OF REMORSE

When news reports revealed that 47-year-old mother Karen Ristevski had disappeared from her Avondale Heights home on 29 June 2016, many Melburnians undoubtedly assumed the worst.

Many suspected, when her husband, Borce Ristevski, filed a missing person's report the following day, that she was already dead.

And many of those many undoubtedly suspected that 52-year-old Ristevski was to blame.

The police suspected so too.

After all, Ristevski had confessed to police that he and his wife had argued about the previous day's takings from their boutique store, Bella Bleu. What he didn't say was that their Taylors Lakes shop was haemorrhaging money and they were in a serious financial crisis.

He said Karen had then left their million-dollar family home to 'go and clear her head'.

Karen, he said, had left the house on foot, rather than in her luxury black Mercedes sports car. It wasn't unusual, he'd said; she'd done it more than once before but usually returned an hour or so later.

For days, weeks and months after his wife's disappearance, Ristevski would have the police believe that if she had met with foul play, it must have been at somebody else's hands.

That didn't ring true to police.

It didn't ring true to the Melbourne public either. What, after all, was the likelihood that a woman who'd just argued with her husband would soon after be preyed upon by a stranger?

Police no doubt asked the same question.

Given that Karen's mobile phone had been switched off, that she hadn't used her credit card, contacted her daughter or any other

46

family members, or appeared at her Taylors Lakes boutique in the days following her disappearance, police undoubtedly assumed that she was dead.

Melburnians kept their collective fingers crossed that the attractive Kiwi would be found safe and well, but as days passed with no confirmed sightings and no sign of her despite an exhaustive search of the neighbourhood, including the adjacent Maribyrnong River, speculation was rife that she was, indeed, a homicide victim.

The fact that police had unearthed no alternative suspects – and the well-established fact that the vast majority of murders are committed by someone known to the victim – meant all eyes were on Borce Ristevski.

In fact, Ristevski was always the police's only suspect.

They thought he'd done it; they just couldn't prove it.

With no body, no murder weapon, no signs of blood on the home's pristine white carpet, they had little to go on. With nothing but Ristevski's account of what had transpired, police were stymied unless Karen's body was found … or Ristevski confessed.

But that wasn't going to happen. At least, not any time soon.

Instead, Ristevski lied.

He lied to police. He lied to his daughter, Sarah. He lied to the general public.

When questioned by police in the days and weeks after 29 June, he changed his version of events several times. Ristevski initially told police that after Karen had walked out of the house, he had a shower and stayed home. He later said he'd gone out on a shift for Uber in the afternoon and later had dinner with his parents, telling them that Karen was 'at the shop'.

At a press conference at Avondale Heights police station, three days after Karen's disappearance, Ristevski and Sarah pleaded for information about Karen's whereabouts, saying they were desperate for her return.

Sarah, who had turned 21 three weeks before her mother vanished, said she wanted to know her mother was safe. 'I just want my mum to come home. It's not like her to miss work as well. It's not like her.'

Ristevski said that the last thing his wife had said to him was, 'I'm going to go and clear my head'. 'She has always walked back in the door after calming down. And this time we've got concern and that's why we made the report. It is distressing for all the family. Without the knowing is the hardest part — not knowing where she is or what we can do to actually get her back.'

That was it. No tears. No anguish. No 'I love you, darling; please come home'.

Ristevski was, as in almost all later public appearances, deadpan. The fact that he gave no hands-on help in the search for his wife also demonstrated an apparent lack of concern for her absence. That apathy was manifest in the fact that in the 24 hours after she 'left' their home, Ristevski did not ring her to ascertain her whereabouts, nor did he ring their shop to ask if she was there, nor did he ring any family member to say she was gone. His phone records would later show that he *never* tried to ring Karen *at all,* in the months that she was still regarded as a 'missing person'. The fact that his phone was switched off between 11.09 am and 12.51 pm on 29 June, and Karen's phone was switched off from 11.40 am that day, would later prove telling in the police's prosecution case.

When interviewed by Detective Graham Hamilton on 4 July, Ristevski gave three different versions of his movements after Karen left the house. He admitted having driven Karen's black Mercedes to get petrol at about 10.30 am, then later said that the fuel gauge was faulty and that, in fact, the car had a full petrol tank. He then said he intended to go to the shop at Watergardens Shopping Centre, but instead went well past. In the same interview, three hours later, he changed his story, saying he'd driven almost to Gisborne, taking the Gisborne turn-off from the Calder Freeway before crossing the overpass and travelling back to Melbourne. The following day, he changed this again, saying he had turned at Organ Pipes Road and returned to Melbourne.

During these interviews he contradicted himself on several other points: that Karen had walked out the front door; that she'd left through the garage; that she'd gone upstairs after the argument; that he'd been home all day doing bookwork; that he'd gone Uber driving in the afternoon. The discrepancies in Ristevski's stories were later borne out by phone records and CCTV footage.

In later police interviews, Ristevski refused to comment – surely the actions of a man not wanting to further incriminate himself.

At a second press gathering at Avondale Heights' Canning Reserve two weeks later, Ristevski said less still. In fact, he said nothing, leaving Karen's aunt, Patricia Grey, to tell reporters that Ristevski was 'too distressed to comment right now'. It transpired that Ristevski was reluctant to attend, but had been coerced by his lawyer on advice from police.

Unlike notorious wife-killers John Sharpe (see Crocodile Tears, page 93) and Gerard Baden-Clay, who made television appeals for information about their missing wives, Ristevski was silent, stoic and tearless.

When Channel 7 reporter Cameron Baud asked Ristevski the question everyone wanted to know – 'Borce, did you kill Karen?' – Ristevski stared mutely, turned and walked away. It was Ms Grey who responded, 'That's really not appropriate at the moment. This is about Karen. This is not about anything else. It's about finding Karen.'

Ristevski simply didn't react the way an innocent person accused of murder would react. He didn't vehemently defend himself.

Almost three years later, Cameron Baud revealed in a news report that he had drawn the same conclusion. He had expected an innocent man's answer to that question would have been something along the lines of, 'Of course not, what a ridiculous question!'

'He didn't even open his mouth to tell me where I could jam my question. One of the aspects of this case which has been burned into my brain is the way that Borce didn't say a single word during the many times when I and other members of the media attempted to speak with him. Even on the occasions when I managed to take him by surprise, he didn't utter a single peep. That is remarkable, possibly unnatural, self-restraint.

'I've been reporting for 27 years and I've dealt with some of the best and the worst members of society, including when double murderer John Sharpe cried his crocodile tears about the disappearance of his wife and daughter. At points during that interview he was breathing so heavily it seemed he was going to hyperventilate.

'A complete contrast to Borce's unflinching stoicism,' Baud said.

Around the same time, Borce Ristevski's brother, Vasko, told the media that police had interviewed 'somebody else from Avondale Heights'.

This was disputed by a Victoria Police spokesperson, who said, 'Only one 52-year-old man has been interviewed after Mrs Ristevski's disappearance at present.'

Vasko Ristevski said his sister-in-law's disappearance was out of character and he begged her to contact the family. He said his brother was 'feeling awful' and could hardly talk.

'Give us a ring and let us know you are alive. It is heartbreaking. I can hardly sleep at night. I wake up at 2 am … it's a nightmare,' Vasko said.

A month after Karen's disappearance, police were still treating it as a missing person's case and had not revealed whether they had any suspects. They had, by then, set up an information caravan in Avondale Heights displaying a dummy dressed in a black blazer and jeans and carrying a gold handbag, according to Ristevski's description of what Karen had last been wearing. They also handed out information leaflets in Milleara Road and conducted a doorknock of neighbours in the vicinity of the Ristevskis' Oakley Drive home, gleaning information that Ristevski had questioned his immediate neighbours about whether they had CCTV footage of the day his wife went missing.

Was that the behaviour of a man earnestly trying to determine where his wife had gone – because he *cared*? Or was it that of a man hell bent on covering his own tracks? Interestingly, although the Ristevskis had their own security cameras, they weren't working at the time.

Around this time, Ristevski's son from a previous relationship, Anthony Rickard, told police about tensions and conflict within the family and said he believed his stepmother had run away. He said his father's marriage was 'fake' and that the couple had stayed together for money and image, and for Sarah's sake, but that Karen had always planned to leave Borce when Sarah turned 21.

Rickard later claimed he had been having an affair with Karen Ristevski. Such claims were never established.

A month later, Vasko Ristevski made the astonishing claim that Karen was alive and well and had most probably fled to China or the US under a false passport.

The *Age* newspaper reported Vasko saying, 'I reckon she's run away. That's my feeling, what with all the rumours going on. I don't think she'll come back; I reckon she's gone for good.'

Throughout the rest of 2016, according to victim impact statements later revealed in court, Ristevski made no meaningful effort to locate Karen and spent much time 'ranting and raving' to family members about the investigations and making angry calls to them demanding they stop talking to the police or media.

Months passed, and police inquiries were coming up with nothing, but in December 2016, following tip-offs, police searched properties at Toolern Vale and Gisborne, both between 32 and 40 kilometres, or an hour to 90 minutes' return drive, north-west of Avondale Heights. They found nothing.

☠ ☠ ☠

Finally, on Monday 20 February 2017, human remains were discovered in scrubland off Loch Road in Macedon Regional Park, some 52 kilometres from Karen's home. Two horticulturalists had stumbled open the body, laid between two logs and covered with branches, about 66 metres from the roadside. Twenty-four hours later, police confirmed that the decomposed body was Karen.

Two plain-clothes detectives visited the Ristevski home at around 5 pm on 21 February, to break the news to the family.

Her cause of death could not be established by autopsy.

Two weeks later, on 6 March, hundreds of mourners packed St John's Uniting Church in Essendon to farewell Karen. After the funeral service, Sarah Ristevski, carrying a photograph of her mother, led the procession from the church. Behind her, Borce Ristevski (maintaining his charade of innocence) and Karen's brother, Stephen Williams, were among the six pallbearers who carried Karen's coffin to the waiting hearse.

In a victim impact statement to the Supreme Court in Melbourne in March 2019, Stephen Williams said that on the day of the funeral, he suspected Ristevski had killed Karen. 'It was so difficult to lead my sister's casket out of the church, knowing who was leading on the other side.'

Ristevski's son did not attend the funeral, saying he was too emotional. In a Facebook post, he wrote; 'Don't want to go in, can't explain it. I apologise Karen this is my way I would say goodbye but I know one thing, you'll be a part of me for the rest of my life. RIP, the good in you far outweighs the bad. I remember and will never forget ya.'

☠ ☠ ☠

Almost six months passed. Then, on 31 August 2017, police re-created the route Karen's Mercedes-Benz SLK coupe took – according to CCTV footage – on the day she was last seen, as a further public appeal for information.

It might have appeared that detectives didn't suspect Ristevski, but in fact they had been gathering crucial evidence against him. They were certain that Karen's body had been in the boot of her car when Ristevski drove it out of their garage that morning.

And Ristevski, carrying on as the poor victim relying on his family and friends for comfort, must surely have been wondering when the handcuffs would lock on him.

Finally, they did.

At 7.20 am on 13 December 2017, 18 months after Karen disappeared, detectives from the Missing Persons Squad swooped on Ristevski's home and charged him with her murder.

For many, it was a 'no kidding' moment.

Still, Ristevski did not confess.

He appeared briefly in the Melbourne Magistrates' Court later that morning, saying nothing other than to confirm his name.

His lawyer, Rob Stary, told the court that Ristevski would plead not guilty to his wife's murder.

Prosecutor Andrew Tinny QC asked the court for 12 weeks to serve a brief of evidence on Ristevski's lawyers – longer than the usual 10 weeks – because of the ongoing work that needed to be done.

Ristevski was remanded in custody to re-appear in April 2018.

In a statement after the hearing, Karen's brother Stephen said Ristevski's arrest, after a 'long 18 months', had left him emotional.

'Today has been a surprisingly emotional day, one in which I have patiently waited to arrive. It is in no way a celebration but just another stage in bringing my beautiful sister Karen the justice she so deserves.'

☠ ☠ ☠

But Borce Ristevski had one thing in his favour. The fact that Karen's body was in such an advanced state of decomposition when eventually found meant that no cause of death could be established. Aside from an irregularity with Karen's hyoid bone (a bone in the neck between the chin and thyroid cartilage), which could have been due to blunt force trauma, strangulation or post-mortem interference from animals, her body showed no sign of fatal injuries.

Hence, the likelihood that Borce would be found guilty of 'intentionally' killing Karen – murdering her – was unlikely. Prosecutors would never be able to prove that this otherwise 'loving husband' who had no background of domestic violence had *intended* to kill his wife.

In April 2018, Ristevski appeared via video link to the Melbourne Magistrates' Court, at which time his defence team advised it was still wading through 22,000 pages of evidence, including transcripts of recorded phone calls.

Those phone transcripts would later show that on many occasions, Ristevski warned – or begged – family members, including his daughter, not to speak to police. Evidently, he didn't know his phone was bugged, otherwise he would not have told his daughter and a friend that he hadn't told police about his purported movements the day Karen disappeared ... unless this was a means to create an alibi – at least to his family and friends – for that morning.

On 21 December 2016, he told Sarah and a friend, Arthur Veloukas, that on the morning of 29 June he 'went to get shisha' (hookah tobacco) at Lalor, but didn't tell police that because he didn't know if it was legal.

A month later, in a recorded call with Sarah, Sarah said, 'You did not tell them [the police] where you went.' Ristevski responded, 'What's that got to do with the fact they haven't looked anywhere else? They don't give a fuck.'

On 30 January 2017, he rang Arthur Veloukas and told him to 'make sure you don't repeat anything', then rang another friend, Tony Andonios, and said, 'Make sure you don't say anything ... don't let – tell 'em anythin' that I spoke to you about. Nothing at all.'

☠ ☠ ☠

A two-week committal hearing, to determine whether there was enough evidence for Ristevski to stand trial for murder, began before

Magistrate Suzanne Cameron at Melbourne Magistrates' Court on 16 July 2018.

Prosecutor Matt Fisher summarised the case, detailing the Ristevskis' dire financial circumstances and the many inconsistences in Borce Ristevski's versions of events.

The Bella Bleu boutique had lost more than $320,000 over four years and the Ristevskis also had several loans and a credit-card debt of more than $80,000.

'Sales coming in did not cover their expenses. It is alleged the financial predicament was very serious,' Mr Fisher said.

Among the discrepancies in Ristevski's account, Mr Fisher said, was that he'd initially told police that he'd gone Uber driving in the afternoon of Karen's disappearance, but had later said he couldn't access the ride-sharing app on his phone so he drove around for 30 minutes but collected no passengers.

Mr Fisher told the court that two horticulturalists found Karen's remains. 'They were drilling into the base of a pine tree when they both smelled an odour.' Though otherwise fully clothed, she was not wearing shoes or socks.

Among those called to give evidence at the committal hearing was Ristevski's son, Anthony Rickard. But Rickard wanted none of it. In fact, he had been dodging police from the Missing Persons Squad for two months as they tried to serve him a witness summons.

They'd finally caught up with him the day before the committal began, arresting the 34-year-old at Diggers Rest on outstanding warrants, including failing to answer a bail charge. Rickard himself appeared at Melbourne Magistrates' Court that day, charged with failing to appear on a bench warrant issued the previous December after he'd failed to appear earlier still on charges of breaching an intervention order and threatening serious injury.

Police told that court hearing that Rickard was arrested in a midnight raid at the home of a woman and her 14-year-old daughter – all of whom had pretended not to be at home, despite police observing them at the residence. Once transported to Melbourne West police station, he was served with the witness summons, after saying he refused to give evidence against Ristevski at court. Rickard was remanded in custody.

The first person to give evidence at the committal hearing,

pathologist Melanie Archer, said she could not say exactly when Karen's body was moved to Mount Macedon.

Given that she had remained virtually silent in the previous 12 months, and given that her father had been charged with her mother's murder, Sarah Ristevski's testimony was perhaps the most anticipated.

But though she scarcely looked at her father, she appeared reluctant to portray him as anything but a loving husband and father, which later led to media speculation that she was either an accomplice in the crime or under the 'coercive control' of her father.

Sarah told the court that although her parents had occasional trivial disagreements, her father was the 'calming influence' in her parents' relationship and that her mother was 'more prone to getting worked up'.

'I didn't grow up in a household where there were a lot of arguments. Mum would get annoyed. She had the same personality as me. Dad was always the calm one. He would calm us down.'

In response to defence lawyer David Hallowes SC's question, 'Did you ever see him being aggressive towards your mum?', Sarah replied, 'Never.'

Among those who testified at the hearing, Victoria Police forensic accountant Gerard Curtin said he had 'no idea' why Borce Ristevski had set up a second company to receive funds from the struggling Bella Bleu store in the months before Karen disappeared.

Mr Curtin told the court that the shop had serious cash flow issues and could not cover rent, wages and stock. He said Bella Bleu was originally owned by Warrant Brands, but that in December 2015, Ristevski formed a company called Envirovision – which became effective two days after Karen's disappearance – naming himself as director and his daughter as stakeholder – with no reference to Karen's involvement. He said he had 'absolutely no idea' why Ristevski had done that. He described the Ristevskis as being in a dire financial state, having refinanced their home with loans totalling $750,000 in 2013 and having reduced those loans by only $8000 over the next three years.

The defence team told the court that since Karen Ristevski had no life insurance policy, her husband stood to gain nothing financially from her death.

Nearing the end of the committal, Ristevski's lawyers argued that the case against him was circumstantial and asked for the murder charge to be downgraded to manslaughter.

But although agreeing the evidence was circumstantial, Magistrate Cameron ruled that the prosecution's evidence, particularly as it related to Ristevski's behaviour after his wife's disappearance, was sufficient to show murderous intent.

'I must take the prosecution case at its highest.

'Given the nature, extent and duration of the post-offence conduct, I'm of the view that it would be open to a jury, properly instructed, to be satisfied that the accused caused the death of Karen Ristevski and at the time had a murderous intent,' Magistrate Cameron said, before committing Ristevski to stand trial for murder.

On 10 September 2018, Ristevski made a written offer to the prosecution to plead guilty to manslaughter. It was rejected on the grounds that Ristevski was not prepared to disclose how or why he killed his wife.

☠ ☠ ☠

Borce Ristevski's trial for murder was set to start on 13 March 2019; however, in an extraordinary eleventh-hour twist – at the pre-trial hearing and jury empanelment on the eve of what was set to be a five-week trial – prosecutors reluctantly withdrew the murder charge and Ristevski instead pleaded guilty to the lesser charge of manslaughter.

Although prosecutors argued that murderous intent could be proved, Justice Christopher Beale's pre-trial ruling – that evidence about Ristevski's conduct after her death could not be used to prove murderous intent – effectively kiboshed the prosecution case.

It meant prosecutors could not tell a jury any details of Ristevski's efforts in withholding information and covering his tracks after the crime.

In response to the bombshell ruling, Chief Crown Prosecutor Brendan Kissane QC told Justice Beale that the prosecution would need more time before proceeding.

After a short adjournment, Mr Kissane said a new indictment, with one charge of manslaughter, would be filed.

At this time, Ristevski's lawyer, David Hallowes SC, told the court that Ristevski would plead guilty to that charge. He told the hearing there was no evidence of murderous intent and that Karen's death had been a 'spontaneous' killing.

However, despite the fact that Ristevski had ultimately confessed to killing his wife, he never admitted why – or how – he had done it. It did, however, confirm that he had been lying from day one.

Prosecutors likened the case to that of Brisbane's Gerald Baden-Clay, who killed his wife, Allison, in 2012, then dumped her body and denied any involvement. Baden-Clay was found guilty of murder in 2014, but his charge was downgraded on appeal when his lawyers argued he could have unintentionally killed his wife. A later appeal to the High Court saw the murder charge reinstated.

The prosecutors argued that if Ristevski had *unintentionally* killed Karen, he would have raised the alarm, not 'bundle her into the boot, drive to a remote area, conceal the body and lie about the circumstances of his wife's disappearance to family, friends and investigators'. They said it should be for a jury to decide whether Ristevski's behaviour meant he had murdered Karen, not for a trial judge to interfere with a jury's role of deciding the facts.

However, Ristevski's lawyers argued the lack of evidence of motive, physical altercation or any ascertainable cause of death distinguished his case from Baden-Clay. Baden-Clay, they said, had been having an affair and also had scratches on his face, which suggested a physical struggle with his wife, whereas there was no known motive for Ristevski to kill his wife. His behaviour after killing her, they said, was consistent with a 'panicked reaction'.

In support of his ruling, Justice Beale, said:

> The accused submitted that his post-offence conduct, if proved, could not be said to be out of proportion to the level of culpability involved in a manslaughter by an unlawful and dangerous act.
>
> The accused highlighted:
>
> (a) the lack of any evidence of motive;
>
> (b) the lack of any history of violence from the accused towards his wife;
>
> (c) the close relationship between the accused and his daughter, Sarah Ristevski;

(d) the evidence regarding the finances of the Ristevskis, which in
the accused's submission could not sensibly lead to an inference
of murderous intent rather than a lesser intent. The accused
submitted that the financial situation of the Ristevskis was likely
to deteriorate if Karen Ristevski was killed given that she was in
effect the 'heartbeat' of the 'Bella Bleu' clothing business which
they operated. Her importance to that business was a motive for
the accused not to kill her;

(e) the absence of any evidence regarding a physical confrontation
between the accused and his wife, including no witnesses
hearing any 'yelling and screaming' on the morning of 29 June
2016; and

(f) the general lack of any evidence going to premeditation in this
case, supporting the inference that the accused's conduct was
spontaneous and that his post-offence conduct was consistent
with a panicked reaction. For example, the accused did not switch
his phone off until 11.09 am on 29 June 2016, 26 minutes after he
had been driving his wife's car and he did not switch off his wife's
phone until 11.40 am. Further, there was photographic evidence
of a couple of shovels left in the garage, which did not appear to
have been used in any effort to bury Karen Ristevski.

Ristevski was remanded in custody to reappear for a plea hearing
two weeks later. On 18 April 2019, Justice Beale handed down his
sentence – nine years' imprisonment with a non-parole period of six
years. He noted that Ristevski had already served 491 days in pre-
sentence detention.

Justice Beale told Ristevski, 'Although, by your plea of guilty to
manslaughter, you have finally accepted responsibility for killing
Karen, you have not revealed how or why you killed your wife. You
may have turned off the road of deceit but you have not taken the
high road of full and frank disclosure consistent with true remorse.
This explains in large part why the discount for your plea of guilty
will be less than you might otherwise expect.'

Among other things, Justice Beale said, 'Within a very short time of
killing Karen, you put her body into the boot of her own car and then
drove from the house. You left the house at about 10.43 am in search
of a location to dispose of Karen and conceal her body. This search
ultimately led you to isolated bushland in Loch Road, Macedon.

'When Karen's body was eventually discovered after eight months, and she was finally given a proper funeral and burial, you acted as a pallbearer, playing the part of the innocent, grieving widower. The pretence – the rank deceit – only ended a few weeks ago when you pleaded guilty to manslaughter, which carries a maximum penalty of 20 years' imprisonment.'

Justice Beale noted that victim impact statements had been provided by Karen's brother, Stephen Williams, her former sister-in-law, Kerry Williams, her nephew, Lachlan Williams, her aunts, Patricia Gray and Marguerite Knight, her uncle, Gregory Knight and her cousins, Stephen Richardson, Lisa Gray and Nevada Knight.

He then said, 'What am I to make of the fact that no victim statement was provided by your daughter, Sarah? It does not mean, of course, that she is not a victim. Indeed, after your wife, she is your principal victim, as Sarah and her mother were very close. Out of love for you, no doubt, Sarah has declined the invitation to make a victim impact statement and has provided you instead with a glowing character reference. I mean no criticism of Sarah. Anyone with a modicum of compassion must understand that her predicament is an agonising one. Regrettably, the sentence I must pass on you will add to her grief.'

In reference to the other statements, Justice Beale observed that Ristevski's 'protracted post-offence conduct has, according to Marguerite Knight, "compounded the sheer grief" of Karen's family'.

'Your disposal and concealment of Karen's body in Macedon resulted in family members not only having to cope with the anguish of her inexplicable disappearance, but also with the fact that her remains were significantly decomposed when she was found, eight months after her disappearance. For example, Marguerite Knight explains that "being advised that Karen was in such a decomposed state haunts my heart", and Kerry Williams explains that "even to this day, the hardest part to understand is how he left Karen out there, the way he did, to the elements".'

Justice Beale said a constant source of anger and disbelief was Ristevski's participation in Karen's funeral. 'You not only comforted so many in the family when you secretly knew that you were the cause of their grief, but you also carried your wife's casket in the knowledge that you killed her. Kerry Williams explains: "The audacity he showed that day was difficult to watch and I will never forget that he had the nerve to do this all while knowing exactly that he was the cause ... of all of our pain."'

In determining Ristevski's sentence, Justice Beale said it had been necessary to decide whether the crime should be regarded as a low-, mid- or upper-range example of the offence of manslaughter:

> Ultimately, the view that I have arrived at is that I have insufficient information to say whether your offence is a mid- or upper-range example of manslaughter, although it is clearly not a low-range example of manslaughter because of the aggravating domestic violence aspect. Without knowing the level and duration of the violence perpetrated by you which caused your wife's death, I simply cannot say whether your offending was mid or upper range. I do not regard your silence as to how you killed your wife as providing a sufficiently firm basis for drawing the inference that yours must have been an upper-range example of the offence of manslaughter. Whilst the community and the courts rightly abhor domestic violence, it is simplistic to suppose that all domestic violence manslaughter cases necessarily fall into the upper range on the spectrum of seriousness for manslaughter. It takes little imagination to think of circumstances where a domestic violence manslaughter – for example, one involving a momentary loss of control and a comparatively low level of violence – could not reasonably be viewed as an upper-range example of the offence of manslaughter.
>
> There are, however, several things I do know about your offence, as distinct from your post-offence conduct, which, as I have already indicated, elevate the objective gravity of your offence above the low range:
>
> (a) first, this is a serious case of domestic violence – notwithstanding its isolated character – because it resulted in your wife's death;
>
> (b) second, Karen was not only your wife – she was, as the prosecutor described her and you accepted, the "devoted mother" of your daughter Sarah, with whom she was very close;
>
> (c) third, Karen was killed by you by an unlawful and dangerous act in her own home, a place which should have been a sanctuary for her; and
>
> (d) fourth, your wife was 47 years of age and, in the ordinary course of events, should have lived for many more years.

Although Sarah Ristevski did not lodge a victim impact statement, she did, along with four others, provide a character reference. Sarah described her father as 'loving, caring, sympathetic, protective and charismatic'.

'Sarah is not alone in the depiction of you as a loving father and husband,' Justice Beale said. 'The other references suggest much the same. They also depict you as a loving uncle and godfather. Collectively, the references show you to have been a person of good character, well liked and involved in your local community, including as a player and coach in both football and cricket.'

In reference to Ristevski's plea of guilty, Justice Beale noted that it did not indicate remorse, given his secrecy about how and why he killed his wife.

'As for your prospects of rehabilitation, I find, on the balance of probabilities, that they are good, given your lack of criminal antecedents and the unchallenged character references.'

Just hours after Ristevski's sentencing, Karen's childhood best friend, Sam, told *The Today Show* that when she first heard the news of Karen's disappearance, she had 'a gut feeling' that Ristevski had killed her. After hearing that police had been searching around Toolern Vale, Sam said she and her sister took the initiative to also search.

'... each weekend we would meet in Bacchus Marsh and drive between Toolern Vale and Mount Macedon ... we actually went everywhere looking for her. Water catchments, hillsides, mountains, but we really didn't believe she had just been left without being covered.

'In Macedon,' Sam said tearfully, 'my sister said, "I can smell something," and I said, don't worry, it's probably just a kangaroo. Later on, we found that's where she was found.'

Sam described her friend as 'beautiful, shy, attractive and naive ... so much life and energy and sweetness'.

'I can't believe manslaughter is a fair charge. Borce controlled how Karen died, controlled where she went and that her body wasn't looked after. Now, he is controlling that he is able to have a lighter sentence, which I find incredibly unfair.'

There's almost no doubt that Sam, along with everyone else who had been long awaiting the sentence, did *not* find the sentence fair.

Most of all, the Director of Public Prosecutions (DPP) did not find it fair. In fact, in a notice dated 13 May 2019, the DPP appealed to the Supreme Court of Victoria Court of Appeal against the head sentence and non-parole period on a single ground – that they were 'manifestly inadequate'.

The six 'particulars' subjoined to the ground were:

> The learned sentencing judge:
> (a) failed to fix a sentence commensurate with the circumstances of the offending, giving too much weight to the lack of information about the unlawful and dangerous act;
> (b) failed to have sufficient regard to significant aggravating features when determining the nature and the objective gravity of the offending (cf [compared to] the circumstances of the killing), particularly in the context of family violence and the breach of trust;
> (c) failed to have sufficient regard to the impact of the Respondent's offending on the victims;
> (d) failed to give sufficient weight to the principles of general deterrence, specific deterrence, denunciation and just punishment;
> (e) failed to have sufficient regard to the maximum penalty for the offence; and
> (f) placed too much weight on the matters in mitigation, particularly in light of the lack of remorse, including the Respondent's plea of guilty and prospects of rehabilitation.

The appeal was considered by Chief Justice Anne Ferguson, and justices Simon Whelan and Phillip Priest, and their decision handed down on 6 December 2019.

Ristevski appeared via video link from prison for the resentencing in the Supreme Court and the judgement was live streamed online.

Although the three judges agreed that the original sentence was inadequate, they were not in total agreement about the duration of the sentence to be re-imposed, with Justice Priest suggesting a lower sentence than Ferguson and Whelan.

In delivering the determination, Chief Justice Ferguson said, 'When looked at in this way, it may be appreciated that the head sentence and non-parole period imposed simply are not adequate to reflect the seriousness of the respondent's offence. Plainly, in my view, the sentence imposed on the respondent was far too low to reflect the needs of general deterrence, denunciation and just punishment. This

Court's intervention is required to ensure that proper sentencing standards are maintained.'

Justice Ferguson went on to say that Ristevski's conduct revealed 'an astonishing lack of remorse'.

'Remorse is a mitigating factor to be taken into account where it is present. Conversely, a lack of remorse is not an aggravating feature. To this day, the respondent has shown not one scintilla of remorse. He has subjected those affected by the death to the most awful state of the unknown.'

The Court of Appeal concluded that the appeal should be allowed and the sentence first imposed be set aside. The judges imposed a new sentence of 13 years, with a non-parole period of 10 years.

Appearing via video link from prison, and sitting with his hands crossed in front of him, Borce Ristevski looked shocked when Chief Justice Ferguson increased his sentence.

Given that, at the time, he had already served almost two years in prison, Ristevski will be eligible to apply for parole in 2027.

☠ ☠ ☠

In the years since her mother's death, Sarah Ristevski has remained an enigma. Other than brief appearances shortly after Karen's disappearance, Sarah remained silent and supportive of her father. Clearly, she still loves him – even though he killed her mother.

The Australian public had likened her stony face and calm, stoic attitude with that of Lindy Chamberlain (wrongfully imprisoned for the murder of her daughter, Azaria) and Joanne Lees (suspected of involvement in the disappearance and suspected murder of Peter Falconio).

But one would ask, how is a person expected to behave in such circumstances? People wanted to know how she could possibly continue to defend her father. But she was a victim too. And, no doubt, she was grieving.

When her mother vanished, all Sarah Ristevski had left to cling to was her father. She loved her mother, but she loved her father too. He had always protected her. She had asked him, more than once, whether he'd done it and was apparently satisfied with his answer.

It's unlikely that anybody could understand the mental conflict and anguish she must have felt when her father finally confessed.

The nation's eyes were on the 24-year-old when she appeared in a *60 Minutes* interview with Liz Hayes on 16 February 2020.

On the night her mother didn't come home, Sarah said she was 'kind of all over the place ... and didn't sleep very well. It was raining and I just didn't know where she could have been'.

In the days following, she said she felt 'like we were just zombies ... paused in that day ... trapped in a nightmare'.

Sarah told Liz Hayes that in the months after her mother's disappearance, she was 'trying to put up somewhat of a front ... put a guard up'.

'There was media outside the house all day, every day ... I didn't want to leave the house.'

When asked how she reacted when police told her and her father that her mother's body had been found, she replied, '... we hugged each other and Dad said, "It's going to be okay."'

No. It wasn't.

☠ ☠ ☠

The Ristevskis' Avondale Heights home went on the market, with a price guide of $1.2–$1.3 million, in March 2020 – the same week that new Victorian legislation stipulated that real-estate agents and vendors must disclose any material facts about properties for sale, including whether they have been the site of a murder, used as a meth lab, or had flammable cladding or asbestos. Prior to that, vendors only needed to disclose such information when asked.

Chapter Three

AN AMBIGUOUS FREEDOM

Zialloh Abrahimzadeh was a hard-working man who was determined to save his family from a life of persecution in the Middle East by escaping to Australia. On the surface, it seemed this man wanted for his family the freedom that a life in Australia promised. After settling his wife and three children in Adelaide, the Afghani lawyer continued to work hard, establishing a pizza bar, driving taxis and helping other Middle Eastern refugees to settle into a new life in Australia.

He created a new life for his family – but he never gave them the opportunity to enjoy it.

In public he was a caring man; a courageous, determined, hard-working and supportive man.

But at home, Zialloh Abrahimzadeh was a tyrant. The life he provided for his family in Australia was a terrifying, violent and iron-fisted existence. His family lived in constant fear of his physical and verbal abuse. He had accused his wife, Zahra, of adding to the family's financial burden by refusing to sell a house in Iran. His constant threats and violence towards Zahra escalated to crisis point, causing her to make the brave move of leaving their own household and hiding their children from him. She then took the even braver step of initiating divorce proceedings.

To Abrahimzadeh, that was an act of defiance designed only to humiliate him.

He wanted revenge – the children and Zahra were certain of that. But did he want to exact his revenge in private and then plead innocence? No. Zialloh Abrahimzadeh stabbed his wife Zahra to death in front of 300 people, including one of his daughters – and *then* tried to plead innocence.

As far as Abrahimzadeh was concerned, he *was* innocent of murder.

Had Zialloh Abrahimzadeh killed his wife in certain Muslim countries – his homeland of Afghanistan or his erstwhile place of residence, Iran, for example – his actions may have been condoned under sharia law, especially since she had defied, or dishonoured him.

But Zialloh Abrahimzadeh killed his wife in Australia and thereby became subject to Australian law, which defines his action as murder. Once he realised this major cultural difference, he changed his plea from 'not guilty' to 'guilty', then tried to convince the court that he hadn't *intended* to murder his wife.

Abrahimzadeh told the Supreme Court of South Australia that prior to stabbing his wife eight times at a Persian New Year's Eve gathering at the Adelaide Convention Centre on 21 March 2010, he didn't realise he was carrying a knife.

The fact that Abrahimzadeh would not ordinarily have attended such a function, since he was Afghani, and somehow managed to gain a seat at his wife's very table, despite her having taken out a restraining order against him, also lent little credibility to his insistence that his actions were not premeditated.

To add insult to injury, he also tried to lay the blame for killing his wife at her own feet.

☠ ☠ ☠

Zialloh Abrahimzadeh was born in Afghanistan and studied law, but never really had the opportunity to practise it. At the age of 23, he moved to Iran to escape communist persecution following Russia's invasion of Afghanistan. He worked illegally as a labourer and tailor in Iran, but was periodically interned and deported to Afghanistan. The continuing political upheaval in Afghanistan made it difficult for him to earn a living there, so he continued to risk returning to Iran to eke out a living, which he supplemented by selling goods on the black market.

While in Iran in 1983, he met and later married Zahra. Four years later their first child, a daughter, Atena, was born in Afghanistan and two years later their son, Arman, was born. Their third child, Anita, was born in 1997, soon after the family arrived in Australia with identity documents Abrahimzadeh had obtained during a risky visit back to Afghanistan at the time of the Taliban takeover. He was detained during that visit and, while others detained with him were summarily executed, he was released (it's not known why).

Once in Australia, Zialloh and Zahra took out a substantial loan to establish a pizza bar and he supplemented their income driving taxis. He worked tirelessly as a caseworker for the Migrant Resource Centre of South Australia and established language schools for the young children of new arrivals to this country. He earned the appreciation of many refugees who settled in Adelaide, many of whom praised the care and concern he had shown to them in written references and character testimony presented to his sentencing hearing.

But that was Abrahimzadeh's public persona, which was in stark contrast to the hostility and violence he bore against his wife and children.

At Abrahimzadeh's trial in early 2012, prosecutor Sandi McDonald described the 57-year-old as a controlling and domineering man who regularly resorted to verbal abuse and violence.

'For years, Abrahimzadeh had used his anger, his fists, his feet and his belt to punish and control his wife and, at times, his family. This is the case of a man who lost control of his family and, as a consequence, hunted his wife down to punish her and make her pay the consequences of her actions,' Ms McDonald said.

She said he was controlling and domineering and regularly resorted to verbal abuse and to violence.

His own children testified in court to his bursts of abuse and violence, painting a grim picture of home life under his tyrannical rule. His son, Arman, said Abrahimzadeh would slap and punch his mother and sisters, or whip them with belts, if they disobeyed his rules. The assaults on Zahra increased after she returned from visiting Iran in 2007.

'He was very well respected in the community; people would say, "Your father is a gentleman." But obviously, they did not know about what happened behind closed doors. For my mother, there was nothing much to do … if you have got a bully over your head, beating you up, you just sit there and cry,' Arman told the court. He said that, in 2007, Abrahimzadeh admitted having 'another wife' and, in 2009, became so angry during an argument that he went to find a knife.

'My father was shouting, "I will kill you, I will kill you all ... I just can't live like this anymore. This is a prison. I will burn the house down, I will kill you all,"' Arman said.

After that incident, Zahra and the children left their home and hid in a motel and community shelters before finding alternative accommodation, the location of which they kept secret from Abrahimzadeh.

Abrahimzadeh's eldest daughter, Atena, also told of her father's violent behaviour, describing him as an abusive and aggressive man. She said he burned her fingers when she bit her nails. When she talked to boys, he broke a cordless phone antenna across her neck, whipped her with a belt for an hour and smothered her with a pillow.

'He said, "I would rather kill you and go to jail than have you ruin my reputation,"' she said.

He had also said he was not a man if he did not teach his family a lesson and he swore on the Koran that he would kill them. The court heard that at one time, in 2000, he dragged Zahra by the hair and pushed her into a window. She cut her hand and, as she lay bleeding and unconscious on the floor, he kicked her – in front of the children.

On 21 March 2010, Zahra, Atena and Arman's girlfriend attended the Persian New Year's function at the Adelaide Convention Centre. When Zahra bought the ticket, she had requested that she be seated at a table with other women only. She certainly was not expecting her estranged husband to appear. Considering that she had taken out a restraining order against him, following his threats to her during access visits with the children, she was stunned to see him take up a seat at her table 20 minutes after she had arrived. While it may have been a coincidence, since his ticket was bought from a grocery store, his decision to take his seat at the table and to remain at the convention centre at all was ominous.

Zahra became upset when Abrahimzadeh sat down; she asked him to leave and he walked away from the table. He eventually sat at another table. During the evening, Abrahimzadeh spoke to Atena and asked her to tell Zahra to discontinue the divorce proceedings. When he then asked Atena to arrange for him to talk to Zahra in private, Atena became frightened. She arranged for security guards to escort her and her mother to their car. But before they left, Atena left her mother to join others on the dance floor.

At that moment, Abrahimzadeh rushed at Zahra's table brandishing a knife that he had hidden in the inside pocket of his jacket. He stabbed Zahra eight times in the back and, according to witnesses, would undoubtedly have continued had he not been restrained by several other guests.

Atena, who was 23 at the time of the murder, told the court during her father's trial two years later that her mother was scared when she saw him arrive at the function and security staff had been asked to move him. She said she had turned and saw her mother on the floor and her father, with a knife in his hand, being restrained by up to 10 people.

'He was just calm, there was no shame, no anger. I was screaming, "You killed her," and holding on to his jacket because I wanted to make sure he was caught. But he was not even trying to get away,' Atena said.

At the trial before Justice John Sulan, Abrahimzadeh stared at the ceiling on several occasions while his children praised their mother and detailed how his actions had devastated their lives.

In a statement to the court, Atena described what life had been like for her beloved late mother.

'Growing up, I witnessed my mum get verbally and physically abused by Zio. It bothered me that I couldn't do much to protect her. After the separation in 2009 we all feared for our safety. We knew Zio would not rest until he took revenge on us for leaving him. We led secret lives and up until today have not disclosed our whereabouts to friends. Mum continued studying English. She was regaining the confidence to go out. She started to see what life was supposed to be like, a life without abuse, threats and fear.

'My mum was finally free and was living life; however, Zio took that away from her and cut her life short. On March 21 2010 my worst nightmare came true. Right before my eyes, my mother was stabbed by a man I used to call Dad. I watched Mum bleed to death and there was nothing I could do to save her life. Instead, I screamed and yelled helplessly. Zio's selfish act destroyed my life. It's not fair that due to the actions of a selfish man, his children have to suffer. I have been robbed of my mother, my youth and my freedom. I long for the times when she comes into my dreams, that's the only time I can see her, hear her and talk to her.'

Atena's younger sister, Anita, was just 12 when her father murdered her mother. Her heart-wrenching statement to the court told of her loss of innocence.

'My mum was a beautiful, kind and brave person. When my mum passed away, everything changed. When I see my friends with their mums it made me emotional and it still does. I miss her so much. There are so many things I miss about her – her food, she was the best cook; her voice, it was so soft; and her smile, it was just so beautiful. But most of all I miss her hugs and kisses.'

Arman told the court that his mother never had the chance to become a grandmother or to find true happiness. He said not a single second passed when he didn't think about his mother or wonder what life would be like or what she would be doing if she were still alive.

'Your cowardly thoughts and actions resulted in her death but her legacy as a brave and courageous lady and a loving and caring mother lives on,' Arman said to his father in front of the court.

'Life as I knew it is over. I am now one of my little sister's guardians.

'There are so many things I can never do again. I can never say to Mum how much I love her and miss her, and if I do the response is a long and never-ending silence.

'I tell her I miss her then I close my eyes and pretend she is still with us. I've seen my mother in my nightmares. I've seen her getting stabbed as she is kicking and screaming for help.'

The defence and prosecution broached the issue of premeditation at length, after Abrahimzadeh had tried to explain how he had come to have a knife in his jacket when he entered the convention centre that night. He testified that he had kept the knife in his car for protection after an incident in which he was assaulted while driving a taxi. He said that he had sold his car the day before and had placed the knife in his jacket, but didn't notice that it was still there when he put his jacket on, on the morning of 21 March. He testified that he didn't realise it was there until part-way through the night. He also testified that he was hallucinating at the time; believing that his youngest daughter, Anita, was being hurt by 'dark, ugly men'.

'I reached the dark men, they reached me and we were all fighting together, then someone grabbed my wrist and said, "You've killed, you've killed." It was Atena. I could not believe what I did ... I would never hurt anything, even an ant,' Abrahimzadeh told the court.

Addressing the court in Farsi and translated by an interpreter, he blamed Zahra for their marital problems. He fought back tears as he described how their relationship had changed since moving their family from Iran to Australia.

'After [my family] became independent, they became Australian citizens and they were collecting Centrelink money, my wife changed. She used to promise to do things and she never did ... other people influenced her and she would break her promises. She was involved with a few bad women, and I really didn't like that she was involved with them.'

He denied having an affair with a woman named by his children, describing her as just 'a very good friend'.

Justice Sulan rejected Abrahimzadeh's claim that when he stabbed Zahra he was hallucinating about Anita being attacked by 'dark, ugly men'.

'That was, in my view, fanciful. I am satisfied, beyond reasonable doubt, that your act was premeditated and deliberate,' he said.

At his sentencing hearing on 19 April 2012, Justice Sulan said Abrahimzadeh 'projected a double life'. He said the Persian community considered him a kind, gentle and helpful man, but while at home, he was violent and 'obsessed' with the house the couple had owned in Iran. He said Abrahimzadeh was convinced that Zahra and her relatives were blocking the sale of the house and denying him money.

'You believed she was responsible for the break-up of your marriage, the financial difficulties you were in. You took action because she continued to disobey your demands that she not proceed with the divorce. I accept you were distressed by the family situation. That may go toward explaining your conduct, but it can never excuse it,' Justice Sulan said.

'You came to the function with a knife and the intention to attack your wife. You were motivated by the fact you had lost control of your family, in particular your wife.'

Justice Sulan rejected Abrahimzadeh's evidence and found beyond reasonable doubt that he knowingly brought the knife with him with the intention of using it.

He said that because of Zahra's death, Atena and Arman had been forced to assume adult roles and guardianship of 14-year-old Anita, at a time when they 'should be enjoying their lives'.

'Your three children have demonstrated courage and dignity in the face of the tragedy that has befallen them,' Justice Sulan said.

He said Abrahimzadeh's continual denials of his children's claims demonstrated that he lacked remorse for his crime and showed no regret for the misery he caused to his family. He said a letter Abrahimzadeh sent to Arman clearly showed his lack of remorse.

'It demonstrates how you are completely self-absorbed and fail to have any regret for the misery you have caused to your family,' Justice Sulan said.

In the letter, made public at the trial, Abrahimzadeh told Arman he 'deplored enemies who laid the foundation' for Zahra's murder. He said he believed he was also a victim and asked Arman to judge him fairly.

'I condemn those who put wealth and materialism ahead of integrity, principles and dignity,' the letter stated. He then blamed Zahra and the children for driving him 'towards insanity' by denying him most of the equity in their former house in Iran. 'How much do you think the body and mind of a human being can tolerate? How long can a human being live with fear and anxiety, and with no security?'

In the one-and-a-half-page letter, Abrahimzadeh listed all the family's possessions and stated he would 'not allow anybody to take what is rightfully ours'.

'When someone is trying to destroy you in any possible way, you would defend yourself and sometimes, this defence results in the destruction of the opposing party. I think I am also a victim of what happened.'

Justice Sulan sentenced Abrahimzadeh to life imprisonment with a 26-year non-parole period. He said he had reduced the non-parole period by 12 months because Abrahimzadeh had pleaded guilty in the middle of his trial. Abrahimzadeh applied for permission to appeal before a single judge of the Supreme Court of South Australia, but was refused.

In September 2012, he then renewed his application to the Full Court of the Supreme Court (usually a bench of three judges) to have the sentence reduced. The application listed three grounds of appeal:

(1) *whether the sentencing judge erred in finding that the offence was premeditated*

(2) *whether the sentencing judge erred in not taking into account, or not giving sufficient weight to, the applicant's contributions to the community and his cultural background*

(3) *whether the sentencing judge erred by giving too much weight to the applicant's lack of contrition.*

Appearing before Chief Justice Chris Kourakis, Justice Malcolm Blue and Justice Tim Stanley for Abrahimzadeh, Stephen Apps told the court that the sentencing judge, Justice Sulan, had not given enough weight to the issue of premeditation.

'Mr Abrahimzadeh seemed to do very little thinking and very little planning. If he wanted to kill her, why not walk up to her and kill her, one might think. He went there with a view to talk with his wife and then when she refused and over the evening, then he lost control.'

In court, prosecutor Jim Pearce QC described Abrahimzadeh's actions as akin to 'cold-blooded murder'. He said he arrived at the function with a knife, which he intended to use to kill his estranged wife.

'He sat there for some hours keeping watch on the deceased and when she picked up to leave, he made his move. He made his move and it was a brutal and sudden move.'

Referring to the previously mentioned letter from Abrahimzadeh to his family, Mr Pearce said Abrahimzadeh's comment, 'Do you think I deserve to suffer this much punishment because I married an Iranian woman?' dispelled any suggestion of contrition or remorse.

In their findings, Chief Justice Kourakis and Justices Blue and Stanley said that Justice Sulan found that Abrahimzadeh's conduct was premeditated and deliberate. 'The evidence overwhelmingly supports that conclusion.'

The transcript of their finding states (in part):

> *First, the applicant had a motive to harm his wife. He had been deeply and obsessively hostile and violent to his wife for many years. In the year leading up to the murder, he had become angry that his wife had left him and that she had initiated divorce proceedings.*
>
> *Secondly, statements made by the applicant at the time of the attack, and in a letter to his children after his arrest, showed that he was*

overwhelmed by a hatred towards his wife for what he perceived were the wrongs and dishonour she had done him.

Thirdly, the applicant had attended another Persian festival just days before. The inference which can be drawn from that evidence is that he was stalking his wife.

The justices held that 'there was sufficient evidence for a finding that the offence was premeditated and no reason was established to interfere with the sentencing Judge's finding; the sentencing Judge referred to both the applicant's community contributions and his cultural background and therefore, no error was established; and the sentencing Judge did not err in finding the applicant was not remorseful and therefore, no error was established'.

The court refused Abrahimzadeh permission to appeal his sentence. Barring any future successful appeals, Abrahimzadeh will remain in prison until 2036.

For his children, the sentence will be much longer.

But while some victims of crime might prefer to hide from public view, Arman Abrahimzadeh has been empowered by it.

So traumatised by his mother's brutal murder and a lifetime of family abuse from his father, Arman, now 33, has made it his life's work to fight against domestic violence.

This young man has become an inspiration to other young people and has received many accolades for his endeavours. In 2015, he, along with his sisters Atena and Anita, founded the Zahra Foundation Australia, a not-for-profit organisation committed to supporting and assisting women and children affected by domestic and family violence by empowering them and providing pathways towards economic independence.

When they established the foundation, they ensured in its constitution that a member of the family would be on the board at all times.

'Atena started on the board first, for a year or two,' Arman said, 'but it can get quite heavy; quite draining, and so we swap. But my wife [Genevieve] is about to go on the board,' Arman said in August 2020.

Arman was named the Allan Sloane Young Citizen of the Year in 2015, South Australia's Young Australian of the Year in 2016 and the 2017 City of Charles Sturt Young Citizen of the Year.

He was awarded an OAM in 2018 and has been a City of Adelaide councillor since November 2018. He is also an ambassador for the White Ribbon Campaign in Australia and Our Watch Australia

Arman Abrahimzadeh tells the story of his father's brutality to anyone who will listen, but most pertinently, to prison inmates and police cadets.

Between 2013 and 2018, he made several visits to prisons and to police cadets. He tells police cadets to pay close attention to domestic violence cases so they don't have the chance to escalate.

'I paint a good picture of what a domestic violence case might sound like, might look like. In my case, my dad worked in the community, was very well known, he didn't have any prior convictions, he was an educated man – a lawyer by background. It essentially took 12 months for the situation to escalate and get as bad as it was. I try to paint that picture and get them to look what type of questions to ask, and how to look at a family dynamic, and also to look at it through a cultural lens.'

He adopts a different tack when talking to prisoners.

'The majority, not all, but a majority have grown up in violent homes or they've been victims of domestic violence themselves. I try to use that to make them realise that just because they've been through that themselves, it doesn't mean that's a reason to copy what they've seen. They need to break that cycle. It's hard when you're constantly surrounded by it; it sort of becomes the normal way of life. But I try to get them to change their shoes. The other thing I ask them is if you have a wife or daughter, how would you feel if someone did that to them,' Arman said.

'I want men to stop and think about their actions, and the consequences of those actions … and if I can do that, perhaps we might be able to stop some types of crimes.'

At one of these talks, in March 2018, Arman spoke to 60 prisoners at Mobilong Prison in Murray Bridge, South Australia. He told them about his father's cruelty in the years leading up to that fateful night. His father, he said, held his family in contempt, despite his public persona as a caring family man.

'I was "the idiot" or "idiot boy". My sister, she was "the useless one", and my mother, he called her "the donkey".'

He gave a graphic account of how his father murdered his mother –

in front of 300 people – then continued to claim that he, rather than his wife, was the victim.

When one prisoner asked him whether he still saw his father, Arman answered 'no', emphatically.

Asked why his father had behaved that way, Arman answered, 'Because no-one stopped him.'

Arman was, however, taken aback when one of the prisoners commented, 'I'm from a Persian background too. I was there that night your mother was killed. My family had nightmares about it too.'

Arman told a reporter afterwards that the man's comment shocked him. 'To be honest, I started to get a little bit defensive because I wasn't sure where he was going. But he just wanted to say sorry. It shows that what happened to my mum affected many other people as well.'

Arman and Genevieve's first child, Raphael Christopher Azadeh-Lewis, was born on 24 August 2020. Arman is definite that his child's upbringing will be vastly different from his own. 'My family life wasn't exactly a nice environment. So I will certainly reflect on that in how I raise my own children.'

When asked whether he fears the day his father is released from prison, Arman says, 'I'm not sure.'

He hasn't seen his father since the appeal hearing in 2012.

'If he gets out and leaves us alone, that's one thing. But if he doesn't, we'll cross that bridge when we come to it.'

Arman did intimate that the milestones of getting married and having his first child have prompted him to consider visiting his father. 'It's been on my mind for a little while. I think maybe I do want to go and chat to him. Maybe get some closure.'

Chapter Four

UNPROTECTED BY THE SYSTEM

Olga Baraquio Neubert knew her life was in danger.

Her estranged husband Klaus had been stalking her for months after she left him for another man. She had endured several unexpected confrontations with him, both in Tasmania and the United States. She'd asked for help through her solicitor; had sought a restraining order from police; had done everything a frightened woman should do to protect herself.

But nobody helped. Tasmanian police did not think her situation warranted intervention.

Olga's situation was doomed to become yet another domestic violence case with a tragic outcome, because Klaus Dieter Neubert was determined that his wife – his possession – should pay for betraying him.

☠ ☠ ☠

Attractive Filipina Olga Neubert had no particular reason to believe that she was in imminent danger on 14 May 2015. The 37-year-old was enjoying a day out with her friend Josephine Cooper in the suburbs of Hobart. The two women had visited a friend in the south-western suburb of Kingston, and had then travelled north to Moonah to do some grocery shopping. They were on their way home to the outer eastern suburb of Rokeby, travelling along Risdon Road in New Town towards the Brooker Highway, which would ultimately take them across the Tasman Bridge to their destination.

It was around 3.30 pm and the volume of traffic approaching a red light at the Brooker Highway meant that Olga's silver Peugeot hatchback was well back in the queue, just short of the intersection of Risdon Road and Albert Road. While they waited for the traffic to move, no doubt chatting about their outing, a black car suddenly cut in front of them. In a split second, Klaus Neubert appeared at the driver-side window brandishing a sawn-off vintage rifle. Josephine saw the gun first and began screaming and shouting, but before Olga could react, he fired a shot through the closed window, shattering it and showering them with broken glass. The bullet passed through Olga's right shoulder and entered the skin behind her right ear before exiting her head above her ear.

The car lurched forward, but Neubert followed. He wasn't done yet.

In a panic, and seeing blood coming from the right side of Olga's head, Josephine reached over and placed the back of her hand on Olga's ear in a desperate bid to stem the blood flow and to protect her from another shot. She had no idea who this man was and was undoubtedly acting on adrenaline. She begged him to not to shoot again. But he placed the barrel of the gun against her palm and fired – through her hand into Olga's head.

In that split second, Josephine saw flame from the gun barrel, heard the deafening bang, felt instant pain in her hand and most probably saw her friend's agony. The bullet, after passing through Josephine's hand and blowing off two of her fingers, had penetrated the lower right side of Olga's head and exited her skull behind her left ear.

Perhaps from an involuntary movement by Olga, the car lurched again onto the footpath and hit a safety barrier over a creek below. Josephine, in a desperate bid to get away from the gunman, opened the passenger door and got out, but slipped down the embankment into the creek.

William Yabsley, who was three of four car lengths behind, witnessed the shooting and was first on the scene. Though Neubert was still holding the gun, Yabsley bravely got out of his vehicle and approached Neubert. As he did, Neubert placed the gun under his own chin and pulled the trigger. But nothing happened. Neubert's suicide bid failed. With no thought for his own safety, Yabsley seized the weapon from Neubert and threw in into the creek.

Fortunately, two paramedics were close by and Olga was rushed to Royal Hobart Hospital, but she died soon after arrival. In the intervening time until police arrived, Josephine remained in the creek – freezing cold, wet and with a profusely bleeding and mashed right hand, along with an injury to her left hand from the fall.

The police took Neubert into custody and charged him with murder, causing grievous bodily harm (to Josephine Cooper), and a range of firearms offences including possessing a firearm without a licence, possessing a shortened firearm and possessing a loaded firearm in a public place.

Shortly afterwards, Detective Inspector Ian Whish-Wilson described Olga's murder as 'a brutal and tragic event' and he applauded William Yabsley's actions in disarming Neubert as 'an extremely brave act'.

☠ ☠ ☠

Olga grew up in the Philippines and was just 18 when she met Klaus Neubert, a German-born Australian citizen who was twice her age. The couple decided to move to Australia and were married here on 4 December 1997. In 2000, they moved to Tasmania and bought a house at Lymington in the Huon Valley, 56 kilometres south-east of Hobart. They had no children, but their life appeared to be a happy one until April 2014, when Olga told her husband she intended to leave him.

Despite this, the couple travelled to Massachusetts in the USA in September 2014, to sell their boat, the *Catriona 11*, which was registered in Olga's name. However, on 5 September while in Boston, Olga told Neubert that she was leaving him for another man. She subsequently moved onboard a nearby boat, the *Gypsy Spirit*, with a man named Eric Harvey.

But Neubert would have none of it.

On several occasions, Neubert took to a rowboat and, usually at night, circled the *Gypsy Spirit,* yelling out to Olga and threatening to commit suicide. On 23 September his behaviour escalated to the point that police were called to the harbour. Olga told the police about Neubert's repeated harassment and said that on one occasion, he had grabbed her arm. He had also sent her a letter in which he claimed to have 'lost his honour' through her behaviour.

Neubert was taken into custody, and a local judge issued a 14-day

Abuse Prevention Order and directed Neubert to undergo a mental health evaluation.

Neubert left the USA on 8 October and, after spending some time in Germany, returned to Tasmania on 21 October. Olga had returned to Tasmania a few days earlier and had immediately sought legal advice from a family law specialist. She removed her personal effects from their Lymington home and moved in with a friend in Rokeby. Proceedings under the Family Law Act began shortly afterwards.

Finding his home empty of Olga's possessions, Neubert started to look for her and even reported her to police as a missing person. Police were able to contact Olga and ensure her safety but did not reveal her location to Neubert.

On 17 March 2015, Olga and Neubert attended a conciliation conference, under the direction of the Federal Circuit Court, to try to resolve the distribution of their property but could not reach an agreement. A month later, on 14 April, the estranged couple attended a further court appearance at which, according to Olga's solicitor, she was 'clearly uncomfortable' in Neubert's presence.

What nobody knew at the time was that Neubert was travelling to these hearings with an 1873 sawn-off, lever-action Winchester repeater rifle in his boot, ostensibly with the intention of shooting himself – in front of his wife – at the court.

Five days later, Olga drove to a park in Sandy Bay to attend the birthday party of a fellow Philippines expatriate. She did not expect to see Neubert there, as it was unlikely that he had been invited, and was apparently shocked when she saw him. Without getting the opportunity to wish her friend a happy birthday, she decided to leave to avoid a potentially embarrassing scene. But as she attempted to drive out of the park's only exit point, Neubert appeared in front of her car and, according to witnesses, asked to talk to her but she responded, 'Not without lawyers.' She tooted her horn at him but he failed to move and, instead, spread himself on the bonnet and grabbed her side rear-view mirror, in an attempt to prevent her leaving. She reversed the car to try to throw him off the bonnet, and several passers-by told him to get off. When he finally did, she drove around him and sped off.

Two days later, and three weeks before she was murdered, Olga told her solicitor about the episode at the party and asked what could be done to protect herself. She was then referred to a junior solicitor of the same firm who advised that yes, she could apply for a restraining order, but that allowing for the time required to draw up a family violence order, file it in the magistrates court, serve the respondent and then convince a magistrate that such an order was warranted, it could take a month or two to come into effect. The solicitor advised Olga that if she wanted immediate protection from her husband, she should go to the police, who had the power to make an immediate police family violence order (FVO), and show them the copy of the American intervention order.

Obviously still shaken by the confrontation with Neubert, Olga took the solicitor's advice and went to the Bellerive police station later that day. She apparently spoke to a police officer for about 15 minutes, indicating that she was afraid her husband's aggressive behaviour might escalate, but was told that her situation did not satisfy the provisions for the police to issue a police FVO. The officer did, however, furnish Olga with an application form for an order.

The failure of the police in providing more prompt action would later become the subject of a coronial inquiry.

☠ ☠ ☠

Klaus Neubert appeared in the Hobart Supreme Court via video link from Risdon Prison on 18 April 2016, charged with murdering his wife. He pleaded not guilty. Chief Justice Alan Blow remanded Neubert in custody to reappear on 6 June 2016.

Neubert stood trial before Tasmanian Supreme Court Justice Michael Brett in February 2017. Neubert was represented by barristers Todd Kovacic and Jessica Sawyer, and maintained his plea of not guilty.

How Neubert could have pleaded not guilty when he had committed the crime in broad daylight, in front of many witnesses, was beyond comprehension. Despite the fact that Neubert had been carrying the firearm in his car for at least three weeks prior to the murder, it was claimed in court that he had seen his wife's car by chance and had followed her that day. His lawyer attempted to convince the jury that Neubert's intention was to shoot himself in front of Olga because he was upset that their marriage had come to an end.

The trial ran for some three weeks, during which about 30 witnesses, including those who intervened on the day of the murder, testified.

The Director of Public Prosecutions, Daryl Coates, told the trial that Neubert was humiliated and enraged when his marriage broke down and described the outcome of Neubert's despair as 'a very tragic and sad case'.

He told the court that when Olga launched divorce proceedings, she refused to make contact with Neubert, but had lodged a family court application for a temporary payment of $50,000.

Mr Coates said that, in response, Neubert offered a 'kind and generous' $650,000 settlement but Olga refused it.

'The accused was angry and distressed with his wife who would not talk to him and who he could not find, and was frustrated with the court proceedings. The accused killed Mrs Neubert because she left him for another man. She would not talk to him, he felt humiliated … and she would not settle the Family Court proceedings,' Mr Coates said.

Citing a police statement given by Neubert after the shooting, Mr Coates said Neubert believed the legal system was unfair.

'He had the rifle in his car because he planned to shoot himself and was mindful to do it in front of the Family Court,' Mr Coates said.

Neubert claimed in court that he had no recollection of the events surrounding the shooting.

The jury took just two hours to find Neubert guilty of murdering Olga and guilty of inflicting grievous bodily harm to Josephine Ramos Cooper. Neubert showed no reaction when the jury delivered its unanimous verdict.

Neubert appeared for sentencing on 22 May 2017, and again sat expressionless as Justice Brett sentenced him to 25 years' imprisonment, with a non-parole period of 15 years.

Justice Brett said Neubert had made the decision to kill Olga because of his inability to accept the breakdown of his marriage and stemmed from his belief that as his wife, Olga was his 'possession'. He said Neubert had shown no real remorse for his crimes.

'In a calm and purposeful manner, you walked towards her car and fired repeatedly into her vehicle. You brutally executed her in a public area in front of many onlookers.

'You committed these selfish, brutal and callous crimes because you had no other way of exerting control over your wife.

'I am satisfied that you had, well before this day, formed a plan to murder your wife and then kill yourself.'

On the lesser charge of causing grievous bodily harm to Josephine Cooper, Neubert was sentenced to three years' imprisonment, with a non-parole period of 18 months.

Given that Neubert was 75 years old when sentenced, Justice Brett pointed out that he would be 'a very advanced age when you become eligible for parole'.

☠ ☠ ☠

Between the murder and the sentencing, Josephine Cooper took legal action to sue Neubert for $2.4 million in damages, claiming she was unable to work because of the injuries to her hand and accompanying psychological injury. She claimed damages and aggravated damages against Neubert for trespass, negligent trespass and negligence.

Her hearing before Justice Stephen Estcourt took place the week before Neubert's sentencing hearing.

Justice Estcourt told the hearing, 'The plaintiff must succeed in her claim in trespass in the form of an intentional battery, notwithstanding that the defendant gave evidence that he did not intend to hurt her. Given that the plaintiff engaged the defendant's eyes with her own and asked him not to shoot, and given that the defendant caused direct physical contact with the plaintiff's right hand with the gun and by the bullet discharged from it, I do not need to consider whether the facts of the case might also fulfil the requirements of a cause of action in negligence.

'I reject the defendant's evidence that he had no intention to hurt the plaintiff. The objective features of the shooting are to the contrary, and on his own admission he has no memory of the event.'

In an affidavit to the court, Josephine outlined what had happened on the day of the shooting, the trauma of the aftermath, and how it had affected her life since. She said that when she arrived at the emergency department at Royal Hobart hospital she was in 'a terrible condition'.

'I was in terrible pain from my injured right and left hands, crying and screaming, scared, looking for Olga, shouting incoherently, covered in blood – both mine and Olga's – soaking wet from being in the creek, cold, covered in dirt and mud, my hair was matted, my glasses and shoes were missing.

'I was told by the staff in the emergency department that I would need emergency surgery on my right hand. My left hand was also treated for a fractured ring finger. I believe that my left ring finger was fractured in the process of escaping the vehicle after I was shot or when I fell down in the creek below.' When Neubert fired the gun through her hand, Josephine's middle and ring fingers were severed at the base, the top joint of her little finger was severed and her thumb was fractured.

Josephine said that following her surgery, she spent four weeks in the hospital's 'hand ward', during which time her estranged husband Tom visited every day, especially to help feed her because both her hands were bandaged. She then spent two weeks in the hospital's psychiatric ward because she was 'too scared, anxious and terrified to go outside the front door'.

'The psychiatric ward was a terrible place with other patients who were truly "crazy", causing all sorts of problems such as shouting, fighting and acting strangely. It was very unpleasant for me.'

In the two years following the shooting, Josephine underwent regular physiotherapy for her hand, along with psychological counselling.

Josephine had loved her job as a housekeeping assistant at Calvary Health Care, but after the shooting she was unable to return to work. She's now on a disability support pension. Her injuries had a profound and permanent impact on her ability to function properly, making ordinary daily chores – like preparing food, driving and personal care – extremely difficult.

Justice Estcourt found, 'The plaintiff's current symptoms are said to include reduced functional use of right hand, impaired sleep patterns, increased anxiety, including fear of traffic and crowds of people and post-traumatic stress disorder. The physical and psychological sequelae are claimed to be permanent and such as to prevent the plaintiff from ever enjoying a normal life.'

Forensic psychiatrist Dr Michael Evenhuis told the inquiry that after assessing Josephine in September 2015, he believed the incident was 'sufficiently harrowing in nature to give rise to post-traumatic symptoms in an individual without psychological vulnerabilities'.

He said Josephine's initial stress reaction had progressed to a post-traumatic stress disorder (PTSD), that she was frustrated at the loss of functioning in her right hand, and that her absence from the workplace and fearfulness had contributed to a degree of social isolation.

In the context of determining damages, Justice Estcourt referred to Neubert's actions on the day of the shooting.

'As to the manner and circumstances of the defendant's wrongdoing I accept, as I have already alluded to, the plaintiff's unchallenged evidence that she fixed the defendant's gaze and asked him not to fire the rifle which he was holding against the palm of her right hand as she sought to shield her friend's head with that hand. The defendant could have desisted, but he fired nonetheless, shooting through the plaintiff's hand and into her friend's head, killing her, if indeed she was not already dead from the first shot the defendant had discharged into her head through the car window.

'I reject out of hand that the defendant did not intend to injure the plaintiff. He did so as a necessary means to the end of killing his wife, the plaintiff's friend. In doing so he not only grievously injured the plaintiff, but forced her by what he did to witness her friend's atrocious murder.'

Justice Estcourt ultimately awarded Josephine Ramos Cooper $2,312,284.20 in compensation.

☠ ☠ ☠

A coronial investigation into Olga Neubert's death, conducted in July 2020, concluded that while Tasmania Police's refusal to issue an FVO against Klaus Neubert did not *cause* Olga's death, it did leave her 'unprotected by a system designed to protect her'.

A magistrate, at the time, could have made such an order whether or not they were satisfied a person had committed, or may commit, family violence.

According to Coroner Simon Cooper, there was nothing to stop an application for an FVO under either the *Family Violence Act 2004* or the *Justices Act 1959* being granted. He noted that while it may take some time to obtain an FVO, it wasn't always the case.

'The power exists – and existed at the time of Mrs Neubert's death – for a magistrate to make an interim family violence order, at any stage in the proceedings,' Mr Cooper said. He added the granting of an interim restraint order could also have been issued at any time; that these are also frequently made on an urgent, interim basis.

Perhaps the greatest failure in Olga's inability to get an FVO against her estranged and threatening husband was Klaus Neubert's unhindered access to a lethal weapon.

Mr Cooper said that '... had an order under the *Family Violence Act 2004* been made protecting Mrs Neubert from her husband it would certainly have contained an order requiring him to surrender his firearms'.

'At the risk of repetition, both powers existed at the time of Mrs Neubert's death,' he said.

The coroner observed that an internal review of the case by Tasmania Police had concluded that the officer from whom Olga Neubert sought assistance had not breached any departmental policies.

However, Mr Cooper stated: 'With respect, I cannot accept that this is a reasonable conclusion in the circumstances. Even without the benefit of hindsight, it should have been obvious that she was particularly vulnerable. She had already been to her solicitors and provided them with considerable evidence, but instead had been sent to the police. Police actually had extra evidence, but the officer involved chose not to look for it.'

'I accept that Tasmania Police's inaction (and the legal advice she received) did not cause Mrs Neubert's death.

'However, I consider it necessary to comment that both led to a situation where she was unprotected by a system designed to protect people such as Mrs Neubert.'

Chapter Five

MUMMY LOVES YOU

Thursday 25 November 2010 was just like any other day for 22-year-old Gemma Gaye Killeen. The pretty young mother had nothing pressing to do. She slept in after a late night out, cleaned at her mother's house, sunbathed, strolled around a shopping centre, had a manicure, left her toddler son to drown at a nearby marina, updated her Facebook page and ...

Yes, that's right. As though it was a usual thing to do, Gemma Killeen deliberately placed her 22-month-old son, Kayden, at the water's edge, or maybe even drowned him, at Hillarys Boat Harbour, north of Perth.

An hour after the self-absorbed young woman claimed that he had been abducted, the little boy was found floating face-down in the water two kilometres away from where she had raised the alarm.

Why did she do this? To get attention from the baby's father, with whom she'd had an argument and who had failed to respond to her text messages during the day. But what the young woman hadn't counted on in her half-baked plan was that her movements would be picked up on a closed-circuit surveillance camera – thereby destroying her callous charade.

☠ ☠ ☠

Many young parents struggle to balance their working and social lives with their parental duties. Most cope somehow, but Gemma Killeen still enjoyed late nights out partying with friends and she still wanted to live the life she had enjoyed when she first met the father of her child, Eddie Wetere. It seemed Kayden, whose full name was

Te Rerenga Kayden Ashley Wetere, was a hindrance to her lifestyle. One can only guess at the frame of mind she must have been in, to use her son as bait in a premeditated drama aimed at either punishing her de facto partner or eliciting his sympathy.

Gemma Killeen always maintained that she didn't intend for Kayden to die – but he died just the same.

Her actions would later be described by her sentencing judge as 'selfish and immature'.

☠ ☠ ☠

Eddie Wetere kissed his son, Kayden, goodbye at about 6.45 am before leaving for work on that fateful day, not realising he would never see him alive again. He left Killeen asleep in the spare room – to which she'd been relegated after arriving at his home at 2 am after a night out. The pair had argued. Apparently, it wasn't the first time.

When Killeen got up later in the morning and bundled up Kayden to go to her mother's place, probably even she didn't know what the day would bring. But as the day wore on, Killeen started thinking about how her life was panning out. Having a baby was a big responsibility – one she maybe wasn't really ready for. And things with Eddie just weren't how they used to be. Nothing was perfect anymore.

So, after enjoying a laze in the sun at her mother's for a while, Killeen decided to go shopping, have her nails done and maybe buy a new dress. She strapped Kayden into the car seat in her blue Holden Nova and headed for Whitford City Shopping Centre at Hillarys.

At about 5 pm, after finishing her shopping and beauty treatments, she sent a text message to Wetere asking what time he'd finish work. She got no reply and texted three more times between then and about 5.26 pm.

When she got no response to any of the texts, she drove to Hillarys Boat Harbour, a trendy tourist precinct with restaurants, shops and services for boaties and pleasure-seekers, and parked at the north-side car park, which was almost deserted save for two other parked cars. Between 5.35 pm and 5.43 pm, Killeen got out of her car and walked around for a few moments, returning to her car when another car entered the car park and the driver got out to use the public toilet. Once the coast was clear, Killeen removed Kayden from his car seat and carried him down to the water, climbing over the rocks to get there, and placed him either in the water or close to its edge.

Grainy CCTV footage, later shown in court, showed her car entering the car park, and Killeen taking her son out of the car and carrying him towards the water and returning to her car empty-handed. What she actually did with Kayden once she got to the water was not captured on film. But it was eight minutes of her life that she would live to regret.

Killeen then drove to the harbour's southern car park. She called Wetere again and then sent him a text message saying it was urgent. She also rang his mother, who didn't answer the call, before calling her own mother, claiming that she had lost Kayden. She then walked into the shopping centre's newsagency, where she told the assistant that her baby had been taken from his stroller.

Killeen shed crocodile tears as she tried to convince those first at the scene that a stranger had abducted her child from his stroller while she was momentarily distracted. Her mother, Sheryl, and other family members quickly arrived on the scene and Killeen seemed to revel in the attention, particularly when a distraught Wetere arrived to help search for his son.

By 6 pm, police were on the scene and they, along with Killeen's family members, frantically searched the area around the southern car park – initially believing her story that Kayden had been abducted. But they were, of course, looking in the wrong place. At about 6.25 pm, a couple taking their evening walk along the water's edge at the north car park spotted what they thought was a doll floating face down in the water. When they realised it was actually a child, the man dived in and pulled Kayden's body from the water. Despite the efforts of bystanders and paramedics to revive him, he was pronounced dead on arrival at hospital.

Far from appearing to be the distraught mother, within a few hours of the tragedy Killeen found time to update her Facebook status with a childish message: 'R.I.P my lil angel mummy loves adOres yOuhh so much LOve yOuhh my baby'.

It wasn't very convincing.

Just a few hours later, she was charged with murder. Police had viewed the footage from the CCTV camera – it was damning evidence.

Killeen appeared in Joondalup Magistrates Court the following day, charged with the murder of Te Rerenga Kayden Ashley Wetere. She was shielded from public view by two security guards as her lawyer, Seamus Rafferty, advised that she would not apply for bail. He requested that forensic psychiatrist Dr Adam Brett examine a police video record of interview with Killeen as she was dealing with mental health issues.

Killeen's Facebook message may not have been heartfelt, but the many messages of condolences and support posted on Eddie Wetere's Facebook page within hours of Kayden's death certainly were. Many of these were from Wetere's whanau (a Maori's extended family) and the grieving for little Kayden began in earnest in both Perth and in Wetere's homeland of New Zealand. Among the messages was one from Kayden's grandfather, Harold Byrne: 'Hey son. U b strong. Dad and maria wil Always b their 4 U. R.I.P KAYDEN. Luv u son'.

Several members of Wetere's family flew from New Zealand to Perth for Kayden's funeral, or tangi, about 11 days after his death. Around 300 people, including small children from Kayden's playgroup, Jelly Bean Child Care, gathered at the Pinnaroo Valley Chapel in Padbury to remember the little boy.

☠ ☠ ☠

Killeen initially wanted to plead not guilty to murdering Kayden, but when she appeared in Stirling Gardens Magistrates Court a month after the event, prosecutors argued it was too early for her to enter the plea. They told the court they needed more time to prepare the case against her and it was not yet known what evidence would be presented. She was remanded in custody, reappearing in court in June 2011 to plead not guilty to one charge of murder.

Meanwhile, Eddie Wetere was still trying to come to terms with the loss of his son. It was reported that he had taken up a job in a Western Australian mine to get away from things and clear his head.

When Killeen ultimately appeared in court on 3 February 2012, she had changed her plea to guilty of felony murder, which meant she took responsibility for her son's death but had not meant for it to happen. Dressed all in black and sobbing quietly, she was almost inaudible as she said the word 'guilty' at her plea hearing before Western Australian Supreme Court Justice Lindy Jenkins.

The pretty young woman who had always appeared bright-eyed on her Facebook page looked drawn and broken at her sentencing hearing before Justice Stephen Hall in May 2012.

Justice Hall told Killeen that she had robbed an innocent child of his life, and had left a father without his son and two families without a grandson and nephew. He said she would be 'forever blighted' by her decisions on that day, even if she hadn't intended to kill or harm her son. He said it was beyond belief that she could have left her son by the water and driven off without succumbing to her motherly instincts to go back and rescue him.

'You placed him by the water's edge, which is seriously aggravating. You remained there in the car park for a further two minutes. You left him in life-threatening danger. There were moments in which you could have saved your son. Even if your judgement was clouded by anger, it was in those moments that you could have changed the course of the outcome. That you could do such a thing to a 22-month-old child only beggars belief. As a parent it is your duty to care and protect him from harm. He trusted you to care for him. It's difficult to understand the confusion and fear when he realised he had been left alone,' Justice Hall told Killeen.

'I have concluded that your actions were impulsive and stemmed from your anger following your failed attempts to contact Mr Wetere in the time shortly before the events in question. However, even though no significant planning was involved, your actions were nonetheless deliberate and you did not seek to prevent the consequences, despite opportunities to do so,' Justice Hall said.

'It is very difficult to understand what your thought processes were at the time you placed Kayden on the rocks by the water's edge. As you well knew, he was only 22 months old and could not swim. As you must also have known, there was no-one close by who you could reasonably have expected to rescue him … he was dependent upon you to care for and protect him. That you not only failed to protect him but deliberately placed him in danger is the most serious abrogation of a parent's duty that can be imagined.'

Justice Hall no doubt echoed the thoughts of many when he said: 'Even if you had made an impulsive decision to do something so terrible, even if your judgement was momentarily clouded by anger, it was in those moments that you remained in the car park that you had a chance to change the course of events. It is at such a time that one would expect the love of a mother for her child and the desire to protect her child from danger to rise up and overwhelm any other feelings. That did not happen. Rather, you got into your car and drove away.

'Your conduct is at odds with one of society's most dearly held values, the strength and unconditional nature of a mother's love. I can only conclude that you were overcome with selfishness due to your self-absorption and lack of maturity.

'You were so self-absorbed that you could think only of trying to obtain attention by creating a drama.'

Justice Hall sentenced Gemma Gaye Killeen to life imprisonment, with a 13-year minimum. The sentence was backdated to 25 November 2010 – the day she let her innocent and helpless son die.

Chapter Six

CROCODILE TEARS

In late May 2004, John Sharpe stood at the door of his house in the Victorian bayside suburb of Mornington and begged his estranged wife to come home.

Anna Kemp's family back in New Zealand believed she was missing, so authorities on both sides of the Tasman had been alerted.

John Sharpe said Anna had left him in March, for another man; that she'd just walked out and taken their daughter Gracie with her. But, as no-one but him had heard from her in two months, her family and friends had become increasingly worried.

So John Sharpe stood at his front door, flanked by his own parents, and asked his wife to come home, or at least let people know that she was safe.

Anna Kemp's family and friends said her disappearance was not only out of character but also highly unlikely, given that she was five months pregnant.

Detective Senior Sergeant Steve Waddell, of the Victoria Police Missing Persons' Squad, said they considered Anna Kemp's disappearance to be suspicious. 'We're very concerned that the potential is there for a chilling outcome.'

The whole time that John Sharpe stood tearfully addressing the TV cameras, pleading for Anna to contact someone, anyone, and not to cut him off from his daughter, he knew exactly where they both were.

Victorian police, alerted by the New Zealand police who'd been contacted by Anna's family in Dunedin, put out an APB and did everything they could to locate her and Gracie. Meanwhile, John Sharpe didn't tell them what he knew, even though he knew everything.

When John Sharpe told the media he'd spoken to Anna just the week before, he was lying. When he expressed concern for his daughter Gracie, saying, 'She's just a beautiful little girl, I just want to see my daughter,' he knew it wasn't possible.

This bland, unassuming, invisible man knew – without a shadow of a doubt – that his wife Anna and their daughter Gracie would never come home alive.

As he continued his charade for the TV cameras, he knew exactly where they both were because he'd put them there; he'd discarded them like they were nothing.

As he wept and shook and lied, this cold and callous man stood outside the very home in which he'd killed his two-year-old child and pregnant wife. He cried and lied, only metres from where he'd buried Anna's body for a time in a shallow grave.

Probably few people in the state of Victoria, however, were fooled by John Sharpe's performance. There was something decidedly unconvincing about him; something dubious; something not quite right. And although Victoria Police let him front the media, in the vain hope that Anna *was* still alive, they already feared the worst. They too felt that something was awry, and they already had John Myles Sharpe in their sights.

A worried mother, her Catholic priest and a determined Kiwi police officer had set in train the investigation that brought John Sharpe's shocking actions to light and his plan completely undone.

Two months earlier, in response to messages for his wife on their answering machine, Sharpe had called his mother-in-law in New Zealand to tell her he didn't know exactly where Anna was, so he couldn't get her to call back. She had left him the previous Tuesday, he said, for another man.

Lilia Gebler did not believe this of her daughter; she would never do such a thing. Anna was of strong moral character, and she was pregnant.

Sharpe rang Lilia in Dunedin three times on that weekend in March. At the time of his first call, on 26 March, Anna was already dead. He rang again the following day to tell Lilia that Anna said she'd be home the next day to collect Gracie.

By the time he rang New Zealand again, on Sunday 29 March – to say Anna had come and gone and taken Gracie away with her – his wife was buried in the backyard, and he'd just taken his daughter's life as well.

Back in Dunedin, Lilia Gebler talked to her parish priest about her concerns. She thought it ridiculous that Anna had run off with another man, and it did not explain why her daughter had missed making her weekly phone call home.

John Myles Sharpe murdered his wife and child in March 2004. He then lay a false trail to convince Anna's friends in Mornington and her family and friends in Dunedin that she was still alive weeks after he'd first buried her in the backyard; he then he lied to the police, and an entire community united in its concern for a missing mother and child.

☠ ☠ ☠

Anna's brother Gerald always believed she had married beneath herself; that she'd settled for less, because it was better than nothing. He reckons that because she'd hit her thirties without meeting Mr Right, that she basically opted for Mr Okay. She chose stability over passion; safety rather than excitement. Gerald said his sister had a practical approach to life. She was a good Catholic girl who wanted to get married, so she finally chose the boring guy from work. All she wanted in the end was a guy 'with a half-reasonable job, who cared for her'.

Anna Marie Kemp met John Myles Sharpe in the Commonwealth Bank in Mentone where they both worked as tellers; she was 31 and he was 27. He'd lived and worked his entire adult life within 25 kilometres of his childhood home; she had spread her wings and left New Zealand for a new life in Australia. They were married in 1994; their first child came along eight years later.

Gracie Louise Sharpe was born on 13 August 2002 – a Friday; notable also because it marked the retirement, after 17 years, of the 35-year-old John Sharpe from the Commonwealth Bank. Encouraged by Anna to try something different, something new, John had bought a half-share in a conveyancing firm with an older friend. The long-term plan was to buy his business partner out on his retirement.

Gracie, like many newborns, hadn't slept well or fed easily and she'd cried a lot. Her restlessness, though, had a lot to do with a congenital abnormality in her hips. The tiny baby had to wear a corrective harness for her first three months of life. Anna was a doting mother who adored her child, but in those first few months she too had trouble sleeping, and with coping virtually on her own with her daughter's condition. Desperate for sleep, for help, and for an understanding ear, she had three separate in-patient admissions in a maternity unit.

Her husband, who by now Anna realised was incredibly childish and self-centred, wasn't much help at all, and often visited his mother just to whinge about his irritable and demanding wife.

As Gracie's health improved, Anna too settled back into a normal routine. Gracie later started at a childcare centre, where she made friends and impressed the staff with her happy and alert nature.

After living in a few places around the Mornington Peninsula for the first eight years of their marriage, John and Anna bought a two-storey weatherboard house in Prince Street, Mornington – barely two kilometres from his parents.

Not long before he and his family moved into their new home in Prince Street, John Sharpe – for no apparent reason and with no prior interest in water sports or fishing – bought a spear gun and, oddly, a second spear. He paid cash for it.

Less than a year later Anna was pregnant again, and her husband was not happy about it. He wasn't good with change; he wasn't good with too much responsibility; he wasn't good with stress – of any kind.

John Sharpe was born in Mornington in 1967; went to school locally and didn't pass his Year 12 exams; took a job in a bank close to home and stayed there for 17 years; married a woman with whom he worked; had a child he never really wanted; and, at the age of 36, moved into his new home, a stone's throw from his mum and dad. He clearly didn't like change. The psychiatric and psychological experts who examined John Sharpe in the weeks after his arrest described him variously as socially inept, dependent and isolated, with inappropriate social skills and few friends.

On Tuesday 23 March 2004, John Myles Sharpe decided to change his life.

That evening, he and Anna had had an argument about – something – Sharpe couldn't remember what exactly. They went to bed, together, some time between 9 and 10 pm. She went to sleep, he did not.

Sharpe lay beside his sleeping wife, brooding about his unhappy marriage and entertaining thoughts of killing Anna. Some time during that night he got out of bed, went to the garage and retrieved the spear gun and both spears. He loaded the weapon, returned to the bedroom and, from a distance of a few centimetres, shot his still-sleeping wife in the temple.

Anna did not stop breathing, so her husband loaded the second spear, aimed at the same area and shot her again. The second spear killed her.

Sharpe covered Anna Kemp with towels so he wouldn't have to see her that way, closed the bedroom door on his way out of the room, and went downstairs to sleep on a sofa bed.

Gracie slept through the night in another room.

The next day, 24 March, Sharpe took Gracie to childcare and picked her up at the normal time. He told a TV serviceman, who turned up for a visit scheduled by Anna, not to go upstairs as his wife was sick.

On Wednesday evening, Sharpe dug a hole in the backyard and tried to remove the spears from his wife's head. He couldn't get them out so he unscrewed their shafts and left the embedded spear heads where they were. He pulled his wife and the bed sheets onto a plastic tarpaulin and dragged her body downstairs. Then he buried Anna Kemp in a shallow grave.

The next day, Sharpe kept Gracie home from childcare and set about creating his fiction that his wife had been having an affair. He contacted two of Anna's friends and told them she had left him, but could be contacted on her mobile phone. It didn't occur to him that, on so many levels, this was an unusual thing for him to do.

He took Gracie to childcare the following day, only to inform the staff that he and his wife had separated, so it would be his daughter's last time there. It was that night, Friday 26 March, that Sharpe made the first of the calls to his mother-in-law in New Zealand.

Sometime during those few days, he also paid another visit to Sport Phillip Marine and bought another spear. He had Gracie with him at the time.

By Saturday night, when Sharpe returned a phone call to Anna's brother in New Zealand, he was starting to wonder if his scheme was going to work. Gerald wanted to know the whereabouts of his sister, and reinforced how worried their mother was.

Sharpe repeated the lie he'd told Lilia; that Anna had said she was returning for Gracie the next day.

That same evening, Saturday 27 March, Sharpe put Gracie to sleep in her cot and then drank several of glasses of whisky and Coke to numb his senses. Using the same spear gun he'd used to kill his wife, and the newly acquired spear he'd bought in the company of his two-year-old, John Myles Sharpe covered his eyes and fired the spear gun at her head.

Sharpe left Gracie there overnight. The next morning, he wrapped her body in garbage bags and a tarpaulin and bound her with black duct tape. He disposed of her body at the Mornington refuse transfer station, along with the spear gun, the spears, and some of her clothes and toys.

It was also on Sunday that Sharpe rang Lilia Gebler, for the third time. He told her that Anna had returned for Gracie as she'd said she would; that they had left in a taxi, and that Gracie was now with her in 'a bigger and better place'.

☠ ☠ ☠

Meanwhile, back in Dunedin, even Father Tony Harrison was starting to worry when, by Monday 29 March, his friend and parishioner Lilia Gebler had still not heard from Anna.

Another unusual happening that day was an email Gerald's younger brother Joe received, allegedly written by their sister and sent from her email address. It said:

> Please print this and give it to mum. I don't know if mum or Gerald has told you but I've left John & taken Gracie with me. It's been a loveless marriage for a long time with no passion or real feelings of affection. Mum has known this was likely to happen for a while. John is very dutiful if you know what I mean but that's about it. He really only cares about his work and doing things around the house. He doesn't show me any intimacy and is almost like a robot that just exists in its own little world. This has led me to look elsewhere for love and I have found it.
>
> There is a wonderful guy who loves Gracie and me and he is the father of the new baby.
>
> I want to make it clear mum that although I haven't rung you, I am not angry with you or trying to punish you.

There was no way I could tell you the night before I finally left because John could hear our whole conversation and it wouldn't have been right for him to find out by overhearing us talk about it.

Gracie is fine and was thrilled to see me when I came to collect her. It was a magic moment and she was clinging to me like a monkey and laughing saying mama.

I hope you can all rest easy now you've read this and I'm sorry that I've told a few white lies in the past few months in relation to how stressed I am and how full on Gracie is. Please respect my wish for privacy and take comfort in the fact that I'm about to enjoy life like I never have before. Love always.

Understandably, instead of allaying the family's fears, John Sharpe's fabricated email only made things worse. Father Harrison asked Joe to send the email to him at St Joseph's Cathedral in Dunedin, whereon he and Lilia contacted Constable John Woodhouse to file a missing persons' report on Anna Marie Kemp.

It was Tuesday 30 March – one week since anyone but John Sharpe had seen Anna and, as Constable Woodhouse said, 'When a priest asks for you help, you don't say no.'

One of the constable's colleagues placed a call to the Sharpe residence in Mornington but like most callers, he only got the answering machine. John Sharpe returned his call, however, and reassured him that Anna was fine; she'd simply left him for someone else the previous week. He gave the detective Anna's mobile number.

Anna Kemp of course did not return the detective's message, or ring her mother as he had suggested.

Constable Woodhouse gathered all the available information and contacted Interpol, but was told that what he had wasn't enough to go on – yet. He was advised to conduct his own investigation, and if he was still worried to get back to them or the Australian authorities.

'You have to go through the correct channels,' Constable Woodhouse said. He couldn't just ring up and just say a mother in New Zealand was worried because she hadn't heard from her daughter for a week.

What he did do, by phone from Dunedin, was ring all the taxi companies that Anna might have used on the day she was supposed to have collected her daughter. 'None of the firms that operate in that area had any record of a collection from the Prince Street house,' he said, and 'that just didn't add up'.

Despite his suspicions, the case was put on the backburner on 10 April, after Gerald Kemp also received an email from his 'sister'.

☠ ☠ ☠

Back in beautiful bayside Mornington, John Sharpe was finding it harder and harder to maintain the charade he had invented. Apart from writing emails from his murdered wife to her worried family, he also used her mobile phone to ring 'home', and he used her credit card to make cash withdrawals from an ATM in Chelsea, where he claimed she had gone to live.

On Monday 29 March, Sharpe drove to Bunnings in nearby Frankston and bought two poly tarps, a roll of duct tape and an electric chainsaw. A day or so later he dug up his wife's body and used the chainsaw to cut it into three pieces. He wrapped those in the poly tarp and disposed of them, along with the chainsaw, at the Mornington transfer station, from where he knew they would be taken to a landfill site elsewhere on the peninsula.

Over the succeeding days and weeks, he also disposed of the bloodstained mattress from his bedroom and a variety of Gracie's things, by taking them to the transfer station.

He wrote letters 'from Anna' to her friends, telling them 'she needed space'. He sent flowers and a card, from Anna, to Lilia Gebler for Mother's Day in May and for her birthday.

☠ ☠ ☠

In mid-May when some of Anna's friends in Australia contacted her mother in Dunedin to express their concerns, Constable John Woodhouse took up the case again. Soon he had enough to go through those correct channels, via the New Zealand police liaison officer in Canberra to the Missing Persons Squad of Victoria Police.

His file landed on the desk of Detective Sergeant Shane Brundell, who agreed with Woodhouse that from all reports Anna's disappearance was totally out of character for 'a responsible lady, a responsible mother and wife who was also pregnant'.

On 20 May police finally visited the house in Prince Street, to talk to Sharpe in person. In his official statement that day, John Sharpe repeated his story about his wife's affair; he said that the baby she was carrying belonged to this other man, and claimed that he didn't know exactly where in Chelsea she was living with him, but she had been back several times to collect clothing and personal belongings. Sergeant Mark Kennedy, who took his statement, later described Sharpe that day as matter-of-fact and not very emotional.

Sergeant Kennedy said that Sharpe stated, 'I don't really care where Anna is, I just want to know where Gracie is.'

Unconvinced by the husband's version of events, police began watching Sharpe and soon saw him searching for something hidden in bushes near a public toilet block in Mornington. He removed what looked like a credit card and then replaced the bag in the bushes. Officers retrieved the blue plastic bag and found that it contained Anna's Kemp's mobile phone and credit cards.

According to Detective Sergeant Brundell, it was then that the Missing Persons Squad began to firmly believe that Anna had met with foul play and that John Sharpe was a prime suspect in her disappearance.

On 26 May, Sharpe gave the first of his TV performances begging his wife to come home. He even clutched a mobile phone in his hand as if he actually expected Anna to ring him, there and then, while he was on national television.

Sergeant Kennedy said there was a striking difference in Sharpe's demeanour between his police interview on 20 May and the doorstep media interview when he spoke about wanting his missing family to come home.

'I thought he was acting, pretending to be a concerned, emotional father and husband terribly worried about them.'

Kennedy said later that he wished he had a dollar for every person who said to him, 'This bloke's acting, he doesn't look truthful'.

On 10 June John Sharpe gave a second, longer and recorded police interview in which he stuck to his story that Anna had left him on 23 March.

On 22 June, three months after he killed Anna Kemp, police arrested John Myles Sharpe. He was interviewed twice that day. In the first, he maintained the elaborate lie he'd concocted, but after speaking with his family, he was interviewed again and finally admitted to both murders.

He made a full and detailed confession as to how he had killed his wife and daughter, and how he'd disposed of their bodies. He claimed he'd murdered Anna to end a loveless marriage and four days later killed Gracie in an 'act of irrational bloody madness'.

Brundell and Kennedy, two seasoned police officers, were shocked not just by what John Sharpe had done, but also the dispassionate way in which he confessed.

Sergeant Kennedy said he was dumbfounded that anyone could do that to their own child. Detective Sergeant Brundell said the matter-of-fact way Sharpe 'detailed those circumstances – it was cold, it was chilling. It was something I had never experienced before in relation to homicide interviews; something I hope I never have to go through again'.

For the Victorian police involved in the case, however, there was worse still to come. With only an idea of where to start looking, they began the awful and daunting task of searching for the remains of Anna and Gracie.

Dunedin police officer Constable Woodhouse said, 'That was a harrowing time for the family. The news that Anna and Gracie had been placed in a refuse tip was horrendous.'

☠ ☠ ☠

The rubbish from the refuse transfer station where Sharpe had discarded his wife and child was regularly taken to a huge landfill site at Tuerong, in the middle of the otherwise beautiful Mornington Peninsula. The site had a three-tonne minimum, which precluded tipping by domestic users, but the solid waste from local councils and industry included asbestos and other hazardous waste and chemicals.

The site's records included specific dump sites and delivery dates, so police were able to narrow their search of the 13-hectare landfill to a still-large area of 2500 square metres and to a depth of two metres.

Police volunteered to help look for the bodies. It was late June, and it was cold, wet and windy but officers stepped forward to join the search, all of them prepared to work overtime if necessary, to find Anna and Gracie and bring closure for their family in New Zealand.

'Everything got covered in mud,' Sergeant Kennedy said. Searchers wore gumboots, protective coveralls and masks to safeguard them from the asbestos, but the gear only made the odious task more difficult. And it just kept raining; on and off for nearly three weeks it rained on thousands of tonnes of rubbish, and on the heads of the determined police officers.

By mid-July they had unearthed all of Anna's remains. And then finally Gracie's body was found. Watched by their relieved co-searchers, Sergeant Mark Kennedy and Detective Sergeant Shane Brundell carried her out of the tip, to wait for the undertaker.

John Sharpe appeared via video link from Barwon Prison for the committal hearing at the Melbourne Magistrates' Court in November 2004. He reserved his plea on the charges of murdering his 41-year-old pregnant wife and two-year-old daughter pending psychiatric assessment.

Deputy Chief Magistrate Dan Muling denied a police application to prevent the media from accessing details of the case prior to any trial. He said there was nothing to warrant the suppression of the details, but added the material would be 'gruesome, repugnant and very distressing' for family members and the public.

Sharpe was ordered to appear before the Supreme Court in February 2005, again appearing only by video link from prison. He sat with his head bowed as the charges were read, then Justice Bernard Teague asked how he pleaded.

John Myles Sharpe paused for a moment and then said, 'Guilty'.

At his Victorian Supreme Court sentencing on 5 August 2005, Justice Bernard Bongiorno explained the purpose of his sentencing remarks. The first purpose, he said, was so that John Sharpe would fully understand the reasons for the sentence the Court was about to impose upon him.

'The second purpose is so that the community which you have grievously injured and in whose name you will be imprisoned may be informed of the full extent of your offending and of the details of the sentence imposed upon you according to the law of this state. As your plea of guilty has obviated the necessity for a trial, it is important that the details of these crimes be placed on the public record even though, as your counsel has properly conceded, they are perhaps, for many, too awful to contemplate.'

Justice Bongiorno recounted that Sharpe and his wife had purchased a house in Prince Street, Mornington in September 2003, and in about November Anna became pregnant again. He said Sharpe later told police investigators that this pregnancy came as a surprise to him.

Addressing the prisoner, Justice Bongiorno said, 'Some time before you moved to Prince Street with Anna and Gracie you purchased a high-powered spear gun from a sports shop known as Sport Phillip Marine in Mornington. Although the actual date of this purchase is unknown, it is clear that it was in your possession prior to 6 February 2004, that is to say some six and a half weeks before it was used to murder your wife and daughter. Although the spear gun was usually sold with one spear, you bought a second spear at the same time as you purchased the gun. You paid cash for this transaction, leaving no trace of its having occurred.

'After you bought the spear gun, you kept it at your then home at Spinnaker Rise, Mornington, where, on at least one occasion, you test fired it in the backyard in order to become familiar with its operation. You had never been interested in spear fishing and had no apparent use for this powerful weapon. You later told investigators that you were having thoughts of killing your wife at the time you purchased it, and that that was why you had done so. Shortly after purchasing the spear gun, you moved to your new home in Prince Street.

'On the evening of 19 March 2004, a female friend of your wife stayed the night in your new home. She noticed nothing untoward in your relationship with your wife and subsequently described her as having appeared happy.

'On Sunday 21 March 2004, you, Anna and Gracie went on the Mornington to Moorooduc steam train with other members of your family for a picnic to celebrate a nephew's birthday. Again, nothing untoward in your behaviour or that of your wife was noticed by any of the many people present.'

Justice Bongiorno said that Anna took Gracie to her childcare centre in Mornington on the following day, telephoned her mother in New Zealand that morning, and picked Gracie up at noon. Anna gave no indication to the centre's staff or her mother that anything was wrong. On the Monday afternoon, she arranged to meet a friend on the following Friday, 26 March, and noted this appointment on a calendar. At around 8.30 that evening, another friend rang Anna at home and had a long, and apparently normal, conversation with her.

'The following day, at about 2.00 pm, Anna phoned her private health insurance fund and inquired as to adding her unborn baby to her health cover,' Justice Bongiorno said to Sharpe.

'That mundane matter of personal business was the last known interaction between your wife and another adult human being, apart from you, before her death.'

Justice Bongiorno explained that the only account of the events immediately surrounding the death of Anna and Gracie came from what John Sharpe eventually told police investigators.

'That the most important parts of your account are true may be confidently accepted even if there may be some doubt about matters of detail. It is with some concern that I recount these events but, for the reasons already advanced, it is important that they be placed on the public record,' he said.

Justice Bongiorno then detailed what Sharpe told police about how he killed his wife, observing, 'During this whole dreadful episode Gracie was asleep in another room.

'The next day, you attempted to remove the spears from your wife's head. Being unable to do so, you unscrewed their shafts leaving the spear heads embedded where they were. You later buried your wife's body in a shallow grave in the backyard and commenced to act out an increasingly elaborate charade to cover your participation in this crime. This deception lasted for three months until you finally confessed to police on 22 June.

'The story you invented to explain Anna's disappearance involved a pretence that she had left you for another man. To add verisimilitude to it you engaged in activities, many of which were extremely callous, to mislead others, particularly your wife's family, as to the truth.'

This charade, Justice Bongiorno explained, included telling Anna's family, mother and friends that she had left without Gracie, but would return home to collect her on the following Sunday.

'In fact, as you later told police, from the moment you killed your wife you began to have thoughts that you would have to kill Gracie to maintain your facade of innocence with respect to Anna's murder.

'Indeed, at some time between your wife's death and the time you actually killed your daughter, you took her with you to Sport Phillip Marine whilst you purchased another spear for the spear gun. There could have been only one reason for that purchase, which was carried out in circumstances of unspeakable callousness.'

Justice Bongiorno, having already stated his concern with having to repeat details of Sharpe's actions so they could be placed on the public record, said that, according to Sharpe's own account, on the evening of 27 March Sharpe put Gracie to sleep in her cot, '… then drank a number of glasses of whisky and Coke to numb your senses to enable you to carry out your intention of killing your own baby daughter. At about 9.00 or 10.00 pm, you retrieved the spear gun from the garage and loaded it with the newly acquired spear. You went to Gracie's bedroom where she slept in her cot and fired the spear gun at her head. You may have closed your eyes before you did so. The spear struck her head on the left side and penetrated her skull. But Gracie did not die. She screamed loudly with the spear still embedded in her skull. You told police that you then went downstairs and retrieved the two spear shafts which you had removed from your wife's head earlier that week. You returned to Gracie's bedroom and, using the spear gun, fired these two steel rods into her head; but even these further assaults did not achieve your purpose, so you pulled the first spear from your daughter's head and fired it again. Only then did this defenceless child die.

'You returned to Gracie's bedroom the next morning and pulled the spears from her head whilst holding a towel in front of your face, as you could not bear to look upon the child you had so cruelly killed. You wrapped her body in garbage bags and a tarpaulin and bound her with black duct tape. You then disposed of her body at the Mornington refuse transfer station, discarding at the same time the spear gun, the spears and some of her clothes and toys,' he said.

'Over the following week you systematically disposed of various items of property associated with Gracie by taking them to the transfer station. Thus, you continued the deception you had already begun and which you maintained over succeeding weeks to create and maintain the impression that your wife had left and had subsequently taken Gracie with her.

'On the day you disposed of Gracie's body you phoned your mother-in-law and told her that Gracie was now with Anna in a "bigger and better place".'

Justice Bongiorno explained how Anna's family's concern had prompted New Zealand police to ask Victoria Police to look into the apparent disappearance of Anna Kemp and her daughter, Gracie. But when police from Mornington went to Sharpe's home on 20 May, he told them his wife had left on 23 March, returned to collect Gracie the following weekend, and that he believed they were living in the Chelsea area but did not know the actual address.

Sharpe also claimed in this statement that he and his wife had experienced marital disharmony for some time before she left and that eventually she told him that she wanted to separate and that there was another man to whom she was pregnant. The judge said that this conversation had occurred on the Tuesday after the family outing on the steam train.

'This day was, of course, as you later confessed, the day you killed your wife,' Justice Bongiorno said.

'Covert surveillance of your activities by police over subsequent days led to their observing you retrieving a credit card from a plastic bag hidden in bushes near a toilet block in Mornington. You were also observed discarding possibly incriminating material in a garbage bin at Mount Martha, a bayside beach not far away.

'In late May you allowed yourself to be interviewed on television more than once. These interviews were widely broadcast and reported in newspapers. You spoke about the disappearance of your wife and daughter, expressed concern for Gracie and said that you had spoken to Anna about a week earlier. You denied to journalists that you had harmed either of them. Thus, you extended the fraud you had already perpetrated on Anna's family and friends to the wider Victorian community.'

Justice Bongiorno said that in Sharpe's second interview with police, after confessing on 22 June, he said his marriage was unhappy, and that his wife was controlling and moody.

'You claimed,' he said to Sharpe, 'she came between you and your family and siblings and prevented you from seeing them as often as you would have liked. Whether such claims have any truth or not now matters not at all. Anna cannot deny them. They provide neither justification nor excuse for anything that you have done.

'Over a period of three weeks late in June and July 2004, an extensive search of a landfill site on the Mornington Peninsula where refuse from the Mornington transfer station was dumped was undertaken by a large number of police and other searchers. The remains of both Anna and Gracie were found and subsequent pathology examination at the Victorian Institute of Forensic Medicine largely corroborated your confession as to how they died and how you disposed of their bodies.'

During the sentencing hearing, Justice Bongiorno described John Sharpe's family background as unremarkable. He said his parents were alive, as were his four older sisters and a younger brother. None had any criminal or antisocial histories, and his parents, now retired, were shopkeepers in Mornington.

The opinions of two specialists were presented to give some idea of John Sharpe's personality. Justice Bongiorno explained that the purpose of psychological and psychiatric assessment was not to seek to excuse criminal behaviour, but rather to provide a sentencing court with as much relevant information as possible to carry out its task of imposing an appropriate sentence.

Forensic psychiatrist Dr Lester Walton examined Sharpe twice while he was on remand. He described him as being socially inept, dependent, passive, and a retiring individual who was unable or reluctant to confront problems.

Dr Walton believed that Sharpe perceived irresolvable difficulties in his family situation and reached the conclusion that the only solution to these difficulties was to kill Anna, and subsequently, Gracie. He thought that although most of his actions since committing the crimes suggested the opposite, Sharpe had made some expressions of remorse within the limits imposed by his underlying personality.

Dr Walton offered the opinion that these killings were 'irrational', although he could find no evidence that Sharpe was suffering from any frank psychiatric illness.

Justice Bongiorno noted that he presumed that by 'irrational', Dr Walton meant that Sharpe considered the killing of his wife and, later, his child were the only options he could see to relieve a state of desperation he considered himself to be in.

The judge said to Sharpe, 'As evidence of this irrationality, Dr Walton recounts your speaking of feeling "threatened" by your daughter – a situation which is, of course, objectively absurd.'

Mr Ian Joblin, a forensic clinical psychologist, formed an opinion of John Sharpe based on two examinations, information from his family and the case documentation.

He considered Sharpe to be an inadequate, isolated and withdrawn individual, with few appropriate social skills and few friends. He thought he was dependent on his parents and lacked the psychological resources to cope with the stressors in his life, his marriage, the arrival of a child and his career change from employed bank officer to being self-employed businessman.

Mr Joblin felt that the difficulties that Gracie had experienced in her early months and Anna's announcement that she was pregnant again caused Sharpe to attribute his own difficulties to her.

It was his view that Sharpe's behaviour in attempting to divert suspicion from himself regarding Anna Kemp's death was that *that* behaviour became virtually an intellectual exercise for him.

Justice Bongiorno told John Sharpe that if psychological and psychiatric assessments enabled a court to reach a firm conclusion as to why a particular offence had been committed, it was in a better position to impose a just sentence.

'In your case,' he said, 'the assessments of Dr Walton and Mr Joblin lead to a conclusion that you were not suffering from any psychiatric illness or any identifiable psychological abnormality at the time you committed these offences, but that you were the subject of psychological stressors to which you reacted in an abnormal manner.

'As Mr Joblin said, to have chosen the behaviour you did itself indicates abnormality. Such a conclusion neither justifies nor excuses your conduct. It throws but little light on the question of why an otherwise law-abiding member of society would do what you did when legal mechanisms, however imperfect, exist to settle matrimonial disharmony without recourse to violence,' Justice Bongiorno said.

'That what you did was egregiously wicked cannot be gainsaid even if it is more difficult to reach the same conclusion as to your subjective moral culpability beyond reasonable doubt. However that may be, your preparations for these crimes and your attempts to hide their perpetration, as well as the method you chose for carrying them out, strongly support a conclusion, for sentencing purposes, that you were at all times fully aware of what you were doing and that what you were doing was objectively wrong.'

Victim impact statements, including those filed by Lilia Gebler and Anna Kemp's two brothers, Gerald and Joe, were presented to the Supreme Court for the judge to take into account when fixing the sentence.

Justice Bongiorno told the Court that the statements described the Kemp family's love for Anna and Gracie, and their shattered expectation of the birth of her second child. He told Sharpe, 'The effect of Anna and Gracie's deaths, the manner of their occurrence and the lengths to which you went to disguise your involvement in them, including the slurs you cast on your wife's character in the course of doing so, have all had a devastating effect on her family and some members, at least, of yours.'

Justice Bongiorno explained to Sharpe and the Court that he also had to consider a number of aggravating factors relating to the commission of the murders.

'With respect to the murder of your wife, Anna Kemp, there are significant matters of aggravation. First, there is the question of premeditation. Whether you formed an intention to kill her when you bought the spear gun or when you tested it in your backyard some time before 23 March as the Crown submitted, you had certainly formed that intention when you went to your garage on the evening of that day, retrieved it, loaded it and returned to your bedroom. Your killing your wife was no impulsive act of desperation.

'Secondly, there was the method of carrying out this crime,' Justice Bongiorno said. 'It was singular in its barbarity. Thirdly, there was the fact that your wife was pregnant. Your act effectively destroyed two lives, not one. Fourthly, there was the desecration of your wife's body in the manner of its disposal as already described. Fifthly, there was the extensive charade in which you engaged to try to conceal your involvement in this crime. Sixthly, there is the effect that Anna's death and the method of its occurrence has had on those closest to her. Finally, there was the enormous cost to the State of the investigation of the circumstances of Anna's disappearance and the ultimate search for her remains.

'With respect to the murder of Gracie,' Justice Bongiorno said, 'all of the aggravating and mitigating factors referred to were equally applicable except, of course, the fact of your wife's pregnancy.

'However, there are further significant aggravating factors in Gracie's case which are not present in the case of your wife. Gracie was a defenceless child for whom you had a legal and, more importantly, a moral responsibility and whatever your motive for killing Anna might have been, in Gracie's case it was simply so that your first crime would not be discovered. Having regard to these additional factors, it would have been logically possible to impose different sentences for each of these offences. However, distinctions at this level of heinousness invite unseemly comparisons which are, in the circumstances, unnecessary.'

The judge explained that against the aggravating factors of his crime, Sharpe was entitled to have taken into account his previous good character, including his lack of prior convictions; his ultimate confession; and his plea of guilty, which obviated the necessity of a lengthy trial that would have increased the anguish of Anna's family.

He said the Defence Counsel had urged the Court that remorse should be found in Sharpe's confession to investigators and his guilty plea.

But, Justice Bongiorno said, 'Remorse is an elusive concept. A confession and a plea of guilty will not always denote its existence. They may be as consistent with the existence of a strong Crown case as with repentance. In your case, although your actions during and after the commission of these crimes would tend to suggest a lack of any concern for what you had done, at least until 22 June … Mr Joblin's assessment that you were well aware of the gravity of your actions indicates the commencement of a contrition process.

'No doubt in the coming years the gravity of your actions will weigh more heavily on you. You may reach a state of genuine remorse; it is to be hoped that you do. A positive finding that you have done so yet, however, cannot be made.'

Justice Bongiorno said that the most significant principles in the sentencing process in John Sharpe's case were punishment and the condemnation of the community of these offences. He added that, fortunately, crimes of this nature are rare so that general deterrence has little role to play in sentencing.

'The aims of sentencing in this case can only be appropriately met by the imposition of sentences of life imprisonment on each of the two counts of murder to which you have pleaded guilty.'

The Crown Prosecutor, Jeremy Rapke SC, had argued that Sharpe should never be released from prison. But, as the judge explained, the state of Victoria required the fixing of a non-parole period.

He told the prisoner that this would not mean he would be released when that period expired; but it did mean he would serve every single day of it without any possibility of remission.

On 5 August 2005, Justice Bernard Bongiorno announced his decision on the fate of John Myles Sharpe.

'It is the sentence of the Court that on the count of having murdered Anna Marie Kemp you be imprisoned for the term of your natural life and on the count of having murdered Gracie Louise Sharpe you be imprisoned for the term of your natural life. It is further ordered that you serve a minimum of 33 years in prison before being eligible for parole. It is declared that a period of 409 days has been served by you as pre-sentence detention in respect of this sentence and it is directed that this declaration and its effect be entered in the records of the Court.'

☠ ☠ ☠

Gerald and Joe Kemp had already made the trip from New Zealand to escort the remains of their sister and niece home to Dunedin. They were accompanied by Constable John Woodhouse, whose persistence from a whole country away launched the investigation, and Father Tony Harrison.

Father Harrison and the Kemp brothers organised a funeral service for Anna and Gracie in Mornington, so that Anna's many friends and the police involved in the investigation and search could pay their respects.

'That was an important part of the healing process before the funeral in New Zealand,' Constable Woodhouse said.

Five months after her mother had last spoken to her, two bishops, five priests, the Kemp family and a large congregation of friends attended the funeral of Anna Marie and her daughter Gracie Louise.

Lilia Gebler named her unborn grandson Francis.

Chapter Seven

BYERS BEWARE

Nobody may ever know what happened to Carel Theodorus Gottgens. Nobody, that is, except his de facto wife, Patricia Margaret Byers. Carel Gottgens has been neither seen nor heard of since July 1990, and yet for more than 25 years the last person to see him alive swore that he still *was* alive.

There's no doubting that Patricia Byers is a shrewd and calculating woman, and one who is willing to kill to get what she wants. She is also an articulate and confident woman, a devious fraudster and an expert at inventing plausible stories to cover her dastardly deeds. A former secretary of a Sunshine Coast branch of the National Party, she has also applied her hand to forgery and has tried her hand at fighting her own legal battles. In what has become a 30-year saga of love, murder, betrayal and most of all greed, Patricia Byers has ruined countless lives.

These days, however, she bides her time in prison.

Now 74 years old, the woman dubbed 'the black widow' is in jail for life, having been found guilty in the Brisbane Supreme Court in 1999 of murdering Gottgens nine years earlier. At the time of her sentencing, she was already serving a 12-year prison term for the attempted murder of a second partner.

Oddly – or not – her first husband, Steven, who she married when she was a teenager, died in a mysterious car accident in 1965, leaving her a widow at age 19, with two sons.

Byers and Gottgens were in the throes of separating when Gottgens, who travelled extensively as a marine engineer on merchant ships, returned from a trip to Thailand, dropped off at the home he shared with Byers on 2 July 1990. He had become involved with a bar girl and was planning to fly back to Bangkok to marry the woman. But he never boarded that plane and his new fiancée, later brought to Australia to testify, was left waiting for him at Bangkok Airport. The last time he was seen by anybody other than Byers was on 2 or 3 July 1990.

The black widow then began spinning her web of intrigue. Within a few days of Gottgens' disappearance, she started a campaign of deception to take control of his assets and to convince his family, and the police, that he was still alive. She even claimed, years later in court, that she had spoken to Gottgens two years after his disappearance.

It is hard to believe, though, that in the past 30 years, Gottgens has never contacted his daughters, Ella Celon and Carla Gottgens. And while never knowing exactly what happened to their father, the two sisters also had to wait 16 years for the courts to facilitate their inheritance of what little remained of their father's estate.

Byers managed to get control of Gottgens' estate in the months after he disappeared by forging his signature on transfer documents for his property at Yatala, estimated in 2007 to be worth $500,000. She also altered his will to make herself a beneficiary, drained his bank accounts, ran up huge credit-card debts and cashed in his insurance policies through the use of forged signatures.

Speaking in August 2007, Paul Rutledge, the Crown Prosecutor whose case ensured Byers was put away for life, recalled that the evidence of her forgeries turned out to be 'the biggest document examination case I can think of in Australia'. Rutledge, who was Queensland's Deputy Director of Public Prosecutions at the time, said that hundreds of documents were studied and admitted as evidence and this alone took up about two weeks of the total trial time.

'We proved that shortly after Carel Gottgens returned home from that trip, every asset in his name was transferred into her name. His credit card was maxed out, the house transferred into her name and his bank accounts virtually drained.

'We found out that she'd made an inquiry about his will before he disappeared, and she realised she would have to share his inheritance with his daughters. She didn't want to do that of course, so it wasn't good enough to just kill him – she had to make him "disappear" but still be presumed to be alive so that she could get her hands on his money by forging his signature,' Rutledge said.

'There were also various letters purporting to be written by Gottgens, including a resignation letter to his boss saying that he wouldn't be coming back to work and, I might say, referring to Byers in glowing terms. We proved she'd written that letter and also connected some other documents to a typewriter at her home.'

Rutledge said the prosecution was able to connect the dates of many of these documents to entries in a diary of Byers', which police found in the house.

'So basically, all these forgeries led to her conviction for murder.

'We had no body, no weapon and really no crime scene, but we had a motive and a lot of evidence.'

Being able to get a conviction without a body in Byers' case was not a first for Paul Rutledge, however. He believed he held the accolade of having achieved 'the most convictions for bodiless murders in the world'.

Although the prosecution's case was largely regarded as circumstantial – because of the lack of a body, a weapon or even an exact time of death – the jury was convinced that not only was Carel Gottgens dead, but that Byers had killed him. Paul Rutledge acknowledged that the prosecution didn't set out to demonstrate exactly *how* Gottgens was killed and even 17 years later, he preferred not to speculate.

His only comment was that with 'the hindsight of Byers' act of shooting John Asquith in the head as he slept and the bloodstains beside Carel's bed ... well it makes you think, doesn't it?'

Hang on – Byers shot *who* in the head?

☠ ☠ ☠

Patricia Byers could have committed the perfect crime because police didn't initially suspect foul play in the disappearance of Carel Gottgens. But Byers got greedy again and tried the same stunt three years later.

In a bizarre episode aboard the luxury boat *Misty Blue* on the night of 12 April 1993, Byers shot her then boyfriend in the head in what she imaginatively described to police as a 'pirate attack'.

It was only when police began investigating the shooting and could find no trace of any so-called 'pirates', or any other boats or suspects, that they became suspicious.

Astonishingly, the victim of this attack, John Victor Asquith, survived being shot in the forehead as he slept aboard the boat. More astonishingly, it didn't initially occur to Asquith that he *had* been shot; and it was he who contacted the coast guard that night to get assistance. He told the operator that he was bleeding from a head wound, but was concerned about Byers, who appeared to be unconscious on the boat's upper deck.

It was evident that Asquith had no idea what had happened, and it would be several months before he accepted the fact that it was the woman with whom he had just shared a romantic candlelight dinner who had pulled the trigger. In fact, it wasn't until Asquith began to suspect that Byers was trying to drug him, by lacing his coffee and an egg-and-bacon sandwich with poison, that he finally acknowledged the police's theory might be right: that 'Trish' had in fact tried to kill him.

Little had he realised, that romantic evening anchored in Moreton Bay aboard the *Misty Blue* was just the beginning of a chain of events that would turn Asquith's life upside down. He found himself subjected to years of trauma at Byers' hands.

He spent five weeks in hospital and several more weeks in a rehabilitation unit recovering from the gunshot wound she had inflicted. His miraculous survival was attributed to the fact that the .22-calibre bullet shattered on his skull and the few fragments that entered his brain had caused no significant injury and were able to be removed.

Rejecting the notion that Byers had deliberately shot him, and accepting her claim that it was an accident, he continued working with her in their joint takeaway food business for about 10 weeks. Then, after acknowledging that the shooting was intentional and breaking off his relationship with Byers, he embarked on a turbulent legal battle with her to dissolve their business partnership so he could close the business and sell it. The rancorous trial between them in the District Court was the first of many times Asquith would have to appear in court over the next six years to face the woman who had tried to kill him.

He had to come to terms with the fact that the woman he evidently loved had betrayed him in the worst possible way; that she had plotted to kill him for his share of the business and for his life insurance.

Police investigations revealed that Byers had forged her name on Asquith's will and had taken out a $275,000 life insurance policy on him. She had also bought the .22-calibre rifle with which she'd shot him. But though she was clever and calculating, she made a grave mistake that would come back to bite her. She had sawn off the barrel of the shotgun prior to the boating trip, and then used the wrong ammunition – a bullet that shattered instead of penetrating Asquith's skull.

In a magazine story in 2019, Asquith recalled the events of that night; recalled waking in a daze. 'I felt warm blood trickle down my head.' Surprised that Byers was not beside him in the bed, he staggered up onto deck and found her groaning. 'As I wobbled towards her, I saw what looked like a discarded sawn-off rifle on the floor. "We've been attacked by pirates," she whispered.'

Asquith grabbed the radio and called the coastguard. He was barely conscious when they reached the *Misty Blue*. However, while in the ambulance being rushed to hospital for emergency surgery, Asquith overheard one of his rescuers say, 'There's no sign of a gun.'

'Even when police matched wood shavings from Trish's work bench to the barrel of a sawn-off shotgun our neighbour had fished out of the nearby river, I didn't want to believe it. It was irrefutable evidence that her crime was premeditated, and that Trish had shortened the rifle before shooting me in the head while I slept.'

Patricia Byers was convicted in 1994 of the attempted murder of John Asquith and sentenced to 12 years' jail.

It took Asquith a further five years to get any compensation for the injuries and trauma he'd suffered at her hands. In an extraordinary turn of events, Patricia Byers was allowed out of prison to represent herself at a Queensland Supreme Court hearing of an application by Asquith for criminal compensation in April 1999.

At Asquith's compensation hearing, Justice Desmond Derrington outlined the various medical and psychological problems Asquith had suffered in the aftermath of the shooting. In summing up, Justice Derrington indicated that while Asquith's physical injuries were 'no doubt painful at the time', he had recovered quickly and well. He acknowledged, however, that much of Asquith's ongoing symptoms such as anxiety, loss of concentration, depression, irritability, a loss of self-esteem and sleeping problems were attributable more to the stresses after the event than to the original injury itself.

'One of the problems of this matter is that Mr Asquith's condition is caused by a mixture of the limited trauma which he suffered, his emotional feelings of betrayal, and his ongoing anxiety in relation to his fairly extensive litigation with Mrs Byers,' Justice Derrington told the hearing.

He had earlier noted, 'There is no doubt but that Mrs Byers' cold-blooded, planned act of horrifying cruelty must have distressed him deeply, the more so because of his loss of the enjoyment of their relationship and the trust he reposed in her which was betrayed.'

Asquith had said his hardest problem was reflecting on being with Trish; the good parts and bad parts came back to haunt him.

Asquith had not worked in the six years between the shooting and his compensation hearing and that fact went against him in respect to the amount of compensation he might have received.

Justice Derrington said, 'While Mrs Byers' conduct was disgraceful and abhorrent and she deserves no sympathy, this is not an occasion of punishment of her but of compensating the victim on the same level as in a civil suit for damages of personal injury.'

He ordered Byers, whose self-representation at the hearing he described as 'not very effective', to pay Asquith $26,500 in compensation, of which $15,000 was for his pain and suffering (including $8000 attributable to his physical injuries and scarring) and $11,500 was for loss of earning capacity.

☠ ☠ ☠

It was surprising that Byers got away with Carel Gottgens' murder for as long as she did. But it was the suspicions of Gottgens' daughters, especially after the publicity surrounding Byers' trial for shooting John Asquith, that compelled police to re-investigate Gottgens' disappearance.

When they searched Gottgens' house, seven years after he disappeared, they found minute traces of blood on the wall near the couple's bed, which, when DNA tested, was found to be consistent with Gottgens' blood. They also found Byers' diary, later admitted as evidence at her trial.

Strangely, police never dug up a concrete patio that was being poured in Byers' backyard a week after Carel Gottgens had – according to Byers – moved to Thailand.

To this day, that concrete slab apparently remains intact.

Paul Rutledge recalls it as a long and very complex investigation and one that involved talking to witnesses who were, by that time, 'spread all over the place'. But although Byers' signature forgeries became key evidence at the murder trial, she was never actually pursued on fraud charges, and it wasn't until late in 2006 that those forgeries received another airing.

That was when the state of Queensland and Gottgens's daughters launched a joint bid to have Byers struck off Gottgens' will and to have his Yatala property transferred back into his name so it could be passed on to them. At this hearing, at which Byers once again represented herself, several witnesses, including a forensic expert, were able to convince the court that a number of documents had been signed by Byers, *not* Carel Gottgens.

The primary issue was the title document for 25 Glen Osmond Road, Yatala, which had been transferred into Byers' name on 25 July 1990 – just 23 days after Gottgens was last seen alive. Bernard Clarke, for the state, accused Byers of fraudulently obtaining the property by forging his signature.

'This transfer was a forgery ... all the signatures were forged. They have been the work of one maker ... and Ms Byers was the maker of them all,' Mr Clarke told the court.

Forensic document examiner Mr Gregory Marheime told the court the signature was a 'simulated forgery'. He said that in studying various versions of the signature, he believed 'an attempt had been made by their author to reproduce a signature bearing a pictorial and structural likeness to the genuine signature of Mr Gottgens'.

Two independent witnesses also gave evidence; one attested to the transparency of Byers' deceit and the other to having been incorrectly named by Byers as a witness to the signing of the title transfer. It was also revealed that even the signature of the purported witness to the signing of the document was probably a forgery. Bronwyn Louise Fossey told the court that not only did she not recall being present during the signing of the document, she also did not believe the signature was hers. Mr Marheime agreed that Ms Fossey's signature was again a simulated forgery and that the printing of her name by hand on the transfer also was probably not written by her. Despite this expert testimony, Byers later accused Ms Fossey of 'blatantly' lying.

But even more damning was the evidence given by a Mr Stewart from a local company, The Pergola Centre, who told the court that in November 1990, Byers had contracted the company to build a pergola in her backyard. Mr Stewart said that Byers had signed 'CT Gottgens' on three documents in front of him: the building contract, a work order and an American Express credit card docket.

Byers, in cross-examining Mr Stewart, tried to discredit his testimony, claiming that she had taken the American Express docket from his house on 26 November 1990 and had returned it signed the following day.

However, Justice James Douglas disagreed that Mr Thomas's evidence had been 'shaken' by Byers' cross examination. He described Mr Thomas as a 'credible witness' who was willing to make concessions where appropriate.

'There was no reason suggested why he would lie about these issues and he appeared to me to be careful and accurate in his evidence,' Justice Douglas said.

Lawyer Rebecca Burness, appearing for Gottgens' daughter Ella (who was also executor of his estate), drew on 'the forfeiture rule' to defend Ella's right to have Byers cut from her father's will. The forfeiture rule establishes that 'where a person who would otherwise obtain a benefit by the death of another has brought about that other's death by violent means, he/she shall not be entitled to take that benefit'.

Byers did not enter the witness box at this hearing but at one point, when Justice Douglas asked her whether she had killed Gottgens, she replied, 'In my view he is not dead.'

She said, 'In 1992 [two years after he disappeared] he rang me – I know he is still alive.' Continuing to profess her innocence, she tearily told the court, 'I've been wrongfully jailed.'

At one point, she even likened herself to Lindy Chamberlain: 'With all due respect, Your Honour, there was evidence against Lindy Chamberlain, but that was later overturned.'

Byers ultimately lost the court battle and apart from being struck off Gottgens' will, she was also ordered to pay $54,000 in legal costs. She was then escorted back to prison.

Paul Rutledge is still certain that is where she belongs. When pressed to describe Byers, his only words were 'tough lady'. But he concluded with an appeal to Byers: 'After all these years, perhaps Patricia Byers might like to show some remorse for what she did and let his daughters finally give him a proper burial.'

☠ ☠ ☠

Patricia Byers spent the first 10 years of her life sentence at the Brisbane Women's Correctional Centre, during which time she completed a law degree. That, it seems, was a means to an end. In 2009, she managed to finagle a transfer to a South Australian prison so she could be closer to one of her two sons.

Then, in 2016, Byers finally confessed to having killed Carel Gottgens. But even this turned out to be a ploy. A year earlier, South Australia had introduced a 'No body, no parole' law. As with most other Australian states, this law prevents convicted murderers who deliberately lie about the whereabouts of a body from being considered for release by a parole board. It is also designed to reunite grieving families with the bodies of their loved ones.

Given that Byers wanted to apply for parole (for the fourth time), she told Queensland detectives – who had flown to South Australia to speak to her – that while with Gottgens at Queensland's Coomera River in July 1990, she had hit him with a blunt object (another report suggested a machete) and that he had fallen into the river.

However, because of the blood found in Gottgens' home, the detectives were sceptical of her confession. Though they searched the area where she claimed to have killed Gottgens, Homicide detective Acting Superintendent Damien Hansen said, 'We did not find any remains and we have reported that back.'

Chapter Eight

THE TO-DO LIST

Early one morning in the autumn of 1996, Steven Bailey was visited by the young guy who lived across the street from him in the Shellharbour suburb of Albion Park Rail. Eighteen-year-old Matthew was crying and obviously in need of help.

Matthew told him, 'There's something wrong with Mum and Sarah.'

Steven Bailey entered his neighbour's house in Shearwater Boulevard and found the body of Matthew's mother Jennifer in her bed in the master bedroom. She had been bashed to death.

Bailey left to call 000, then he returned to the house, where he discovered Sarah, Matthew's 13-year-old sister, also brutally murdered. It was just after 9 am on Wednesday 13 March.

Matthew had spent the previous night at his girlfriend's place and had returned home shortly after 8 am. As the house was quiet, he'd assumed someone had taken his brother and sister to school, so he'd ducked up to the nearby supermarket to get some cigarettes. It was on his return that he discovered his mother.

When the police arrived, they found not only the bodies of Sarah and her mother, in their own beds, but also the body of Jennifer's other child, 15-year-old Adrian. All three had died of massive head wounds. Adrian, who was found in the garage, was also soaked in petrol, which had blistered his skin. He was partly covered with a doona.

By this stage another neighbour, Laurens Hoogvliet, noted that Matthew – whose own home had now become a major crime scene – was so distressed he was lying down and sobbing outside Steven Bailey's house. Two ambulance officers decided he needed hospitalisation and took him to Shellharbour Hospital.

As detectives from the Crime Scene Unit began conducting their investigation of the house, it looked at first like a robbery had gone horribly wrong. A video recorder was obviously missing from the cabinet in the lounge, and several drawers and cupboards in other rooms were open as if they'd been searched.

At around 11 am, unaware that Jennifer and his children lay murdered in the family home, Matthew's father Wayne – who'd spent the previous night with his own parents – was surprised to hear a strange man's voice on the phone when he rang his wife. For a moment Wayne thought he'd dialled the wrong number but after the police officer who'd answered the phone ascertained who was calling, he instructed Wayne to hand the phone to anyone who might be with him. Wayne's secretary then informed him that the police would pick him up from his office and take him to Parramatta police station.

The guilt and pain of the two remaining members of this family must have been unbearable. For Wayne, the convenience of staying overnight with his parents in Moorebank because it was closer to work meant he had not been home to protect his wife and children from a brutal killer.

☠ ☠ ☠

For Matthew, the simple decision to spend the night with his girlfriend had consequences that no young man would expect from such a choice. The bloody nightmare he found on his return was no doubt made worse for him because he *had* stayed home longer than planned the previous night because his mother had been worried about some prank phone calls.

At around 10 pm he'd borrowed her Toyota Corolla and driven over to stay with his girlfriend Alyssa, arriving there sometime between 11 and 11.30 pm.

Now, Matthew may not have been the strongest, beefiest 18-year-old – in truth he was rather weedy, once even described as a 'frail little sparrow' – but if he'd stayed home that night this 'gentle quiet lad' might have been able to do *something*.

He left Alyssa's the following morning at 8 am in order to be home in time for his mother to use her car to drive Adrian and Sarah to school.

The autopsies were carried out by forensic pathologist Dr Allan Cala. Time of death, when there are no eyewitnesses, is always given in terms of a likely time frame based on a number of factors, including when the victims were last known to be alive. Dr Cala believed that Jennifer, Adrian and Sarah all died around the same time, some time between 8 pm Tuesday 12 March and 1 am on 13 March.

In his opinion, the killer most likely used a jack handle, a wheel brace or a sledgehammer to beat all three victims to death.

Detailed forensic examination of the crime scene revealed several small blood smears and a smeared fingerprint in the main bathroom, blood smears on the wall above the bed in the master bedroom, and spots of blood or red smears on the hallway floor and on the kitchen wall near the light switch. The washing machine contained two towels, one with a reddish stain, and a pair of rubber gloves, and there was an open jerry can of petrol near Adrian's body in the garage. There were no signs of damage to any doors or windows of the house to indicate forced entry.

Detective Senior Constable Doherty, of the Crime Scene Unit, noted that a towel had been placed over Jennifer's face. A large square of carpet had also been cut out and was missing from in front of the bedside table in the master bedroom, and two smaller sections had been cut and taken from near the foot of the bed.

Several weeks after the murders, children playing near a dam at the old Boral Brickworks at Woonona, 31 kilometres away, found a red bag containing a sheet and a small sledgehammer wrapped in a towel. When police were called to the scene they recovered a red and white Le Sport bag, a black backpack and a number of loose items, including Sega game cases and control pads, a purse with credit cards and a licence bearing Jennifer's name, a hanky, a bottle of Zambucca, a video recorder, two T-shirts, a pair of track pants, some pieces of carpet, and a ziplock bag containing a highly incriminating piece of paper torn into pieces.

☠ ☠ ☠

On 22 June 1996, 18-year-old Matthew De Gruchy was arrested for the unbelievably vicious murders of his mother, brother and sister. His father offered the $100,000 bail.

Detective Sergeant Daniel Sharkey, the officer in charge of the investigation, said Matthew had become the major suspect in the case after it was revealed that the jack handle and wheel brace were missing from Jennifer De Gruchy's car, the one Matthew had borrowed the night of the murders.

While several aspects of Matthew's initial statements did not gel completely with those given by other witnesses, it was the contents of the note found in the sports bag with the items allegedly stolen from the house that proved the most damning.

This to-do list, in Matthew's handwriting, said:

open gate
throw bottle down the back
throw things down wall in roof
track suit pants 1
knife 1
T shirts 2
Shoes 2
hanky
pole
towel
open blinds to see through
Sarah Mum
Adrian
head butt mirror (mirror crossed out) bench
have shower
throw hi fi down back
hit arm with pole
hit leg pole
cut somewhere with knife

There was also a series of numbers on the other side of the page.

☠ ☠ ☠

Post-mortem examinations of the three deceased revealed the gruesome details.

Jennifer De Gruchy had a severe depressed fracture between the eyes, severe lacerations in conjunction with skull fracturing in the left forehead region, fractures of the cheekbones and extensive underlying brain trauma, along with a number of abrasions and bruises.

Dr Cala believed the injuries were caused by a wheel brace or sledgehammer while she slept.

Sarah De Gruchy suffered 10 injuries to her head and neck, mainly confined to the right side. There was marked skull fracturing of the forehead, and of the right side and base of the skull, as well as extensive lacerations, abrasions and bruising. There were three bruises on the right arm, including one tram track or linear bruise, consistent with it having been struck with a tyre lever.

Dr Cala said she had some defence type injuries to her right arm.

Adrian De Gruchy had approximately 21 injuries to his neck and head. He had a grossly fractured face and base of the skull, along with numerous lacerations to the back of the head, right forehead and mouth, as well as fractures to the cheekbones and jawbone. There were six injuries to the trunk, including some tram track bruises to the chest.

Dr Cala believed the head injuries were similar to those suffered by his mother and sister, and could have been caused by a similar weapon to that used to inflict the chest injuries. He believed that weapon to have been a heavy, straight object approximately one centimetre wide and at least 15 centimetres long, such as a jack handle or a wheel brace. He said a sledgehammer may have caused the head injuries.

Dr Cala said the peeling skin on Adrian's body was consistent with petrol having been poured on him in preparation for setting him alight.

Some of the police officers on the scene likened the victims' injuries to gunshot wounds or the aftermath of a plane crash.

☠ ☠ ☠

In his taped interview conducted by Detective Sergeant Sharkey on 17 March, four days after the murders, Matthew said that when he'd returned home on the morning of 13 March he'd gone into the kitchen/dining area but nowhere else. He did not see anyone around, so he drove the car to a supermarket to purchase some cigarettes. It was upon his return that he discovered the body of his mother. He placed a towel over her and ran outside for help. He did not go into Sarah's room or Adrian's room.

Strange, then, that when Matthew ran crying to Steven Bailey for help, he had said, 'There's something wrong with Mum and Sarah.'

In the same interview, he also said he had not at any stage that morning entered the bathroom, the laundry or the main bedroom ensuite, or opened any cupboards, drawers or doors.

Matthew's fingerprint, however, was found in the smear that appeared to be blood on the cupboard doorknob of the main bathroom's vanity unit, and on the open jerry can of petrol. DNA of the blood on the wall above Jennifer De Gruchy's bed matched that of her son Matthew.

His girlfriend and her mother, Alyssa and Gail Brindley, verified that he had arrived at their place between 11 and 11.30 pm. This was later than he'd been expected but he had explained he was late because 'my mum was having prank calls and she asked me to stay'. Alyssa said she had phoned his place at around 10.30 pm, but had repeatedly received an engaged signal.

Matthew left their place at 8 am on the Wednesday morning.

It wasn't until later that day, after he'd returned from the hospital, that Alyssa talked to him about the prank calls and Matthew had elaborated. He told her the caller had said, 'Three people in your family will be deceased'.

Mathew did not mention this specific threat to the police in either his preliminary statement given that afternoon, or when he was interviewed on 17 March. In the recorded interview he maintained there had been about five prank calls on the Tuesday night up until about 9.40 pm. He said that when the phone had been picked up, all he could hear were the beeps, indicating the caller had hung up.

☠ ☠ ☠

The case went to trial two years later in the Supreme Court of New South Wales, before Justice Michael Grove. It was the Crown Prosecution case that Matthew De Gruchy had murdered his mother, brother and sister some time after 8 pm on the evening of 12 March 1996. He had then driven to the quarry at Woonona, where he had disposed of various items taken from the house in the dam. His purpose in removing the items from the home was to create the pretence of a robbery, and having done that, Matthew went to his girlfriend's house. He returned home the following morning, where he pretended surprise at the discovery of his mother and sister.

Matthew De Gruchy claimed he knew nothing about the murders and that they must have been the work of someone other than himself. He gave evidence that the last time he saw his family alive was when he left his home at around 10 pm on 12 March 1996, before driving to his girlfriend's home in his mother's Toyota Corolla.

Matthew said that when he left home his mother and sister were in their rooms. He did not know where Adrian was and assumed that he had gone out. He said that when he arrived home the next day the house was quiet and he assumed that someone else had taken Adrian and Sarah to school. It was on his return from the supermarket that he found his mother. All he remembered after that was running outside to find help.

The Crown accepted that its case was entirely circumstantial, and that it could not point to any motive on the part of the accused to murder his mother and siblings.

Matthew claimed he could not remember writing the note that was recovered from the dam, but accepted that the handwriting was his. He testified that some of the things on the note were consistent with activities involved in the organisation of his eighteenth birthday party, held at the family home in December of 1995. He had received gifts that matched some of the things listed, and the numbers on the reverse side of the paper may have been CD tracks selected for the party.

The prosecutor, Paul Conlon, argued that Matthew's assertion that there had been prank calls to his mother, and his suggestion that the caller had said that 'three of your family will be deceased', bore the hallmarks of invention to divert attention to a non-existent marauder. Mr Conlon said this was particularly so as the accused had made no mention of such a chilling and accurate prophecy when police interviewed him on 13 and 17 March, and because it was curious that such a threat was confined to only three members of a family of five.

Mr Conlon also asked why, in the face of such a threat and the number of anonymous calls that the accused said were made,

Matthew would have left the house at all. Especially if, as he himself claimed, his mother was concerned about them.

Jennifer De Gruchy was known to be alive at least until 8 pm on 12 March because she had spoken on the phone to her husband Wayne from 6 to 6.30 pm, her mother Dorothy Halliwell between 7 and 7.30 pm, and her uncle Raymond Halliwell at about 7.45 pm. Matthew's girlfriend, Alyssa, had also rung the house, and spoken to Matthew at about 8 pm.

The Crown said these times were relevant to the case in so far as they assisted 'in fixing a possible time frame for the killings, and in so far as they establish a window of opportunity for the accused to have committed the crimes'.

Interestingly, these verified phone calls leave little time for the series of prank phone calls that Matthew alleged his mother had been receiving up until 9.40 pm.

The forensic pathologist Dr Allan Cala said the time of death of each of the deceased was similar and occurred between 8 pm and 1 am, but conceded it could have been as late as 3 am.

Matthew said when he'd left the house just before 10 pm his mother and sister were still alive. Alyssa Brindley told police that when she'd rung the De Gruchy residence at 10.30 pm, to find out why Matthew was so late to her place, the phone was engaged.

The prosecution told the court that the trip from the De Gruchy house to Alyssa Brindley's home took approximately 28 minutes. Matthew arrived at his girlfriend's place sometime between 11 and 11.30 pm, at least an hour after leaving home and already late for his date.

Detective Sergeant Sharkey and Detective Palamera told the court that the dam at the old Boral Brickworks was 31 kilometres from the De Gruchy house in Albion Park Rail, and two kilometres from the Brindley home in Woonona. Travel time, at just under the speed limit, was 26 minutes to the brickworks and then another two minutes to the Brindley residence.

The prosecution submitted that Matthew De Gruchy had ample opportunity in the time available between 8 and 11 pm to carry out the killings, to collect various items from the scene and drive to the dam to dispose of them, and then to drive on to his girlfriend's house.

A witness, Stephen Heyman, gave evidence that a couple of times prior to 1996 he'd seen Matthew riding his bike with friends at the brickyard.

The dam where the sports bag was found was therefore not only known to the accused, but was also on the route he took to his girlfriend's house on the night of the killings.

Defence counsel Malcolm Ramage QC maintained that: many other people were familiar with the dam; there was an adequate explanation for a robber disposing of the items taken from the house, in so far as it would have been sensible for him or her to get rid of any items that might provide a link to the killings; the note found with those items contained a number of events that did not occur; and there was no sensible reason for leaving the list in a torn-up state together with other items connected with the murders (rather than destroying it in a more effective way).

Mr Ramage said Matthew De Gruchy had no motive to kill his mother, to whom he was attached, or his brother and sister, whom he loved.

Alyssa testified that when he arrived at her house there was no blood on his clothes, he had no apparent injuries to his face or body, and he did not seem depressed, anxious or upset. Her mother Gail Brindley said she noticed nothing unusual about his demeanour.

It was suggested in court, however, that there was no reason to inspect Matthew for any kind of injury; nor, in the absence of immediate suspicion of his involvement, was he subjected to medical or other examination for possible minor injuries such as a nosebleed or small cut. Yet there was little doubt, in view of the spots of blood found in the hall and on the wall above his mother's bed, that he did lose some blood in the house that night.

The prosecution raised the obvious point that when Matthew first sought help from his neighbour Steven Bailey, allegedly immediately after discovering his mother, he had said there was 'something wrong with Mum and Sarah'. Mr Conlon pointed out that according to the sequence of events that Matthew recounted to police, he could not have known there was anything wrong with Sarah because he did not enter her room. In fact, according to his own preliminary statement to police, he'd assumed when he first got home that she had already left for school.

Mr Ramage suggested that Matthew's conversation with Steven Bailey was explicable by his distraught state and by the possibility that he may not have been sure whose body he had seen.

Objecting to the Crown Prosecutor's argument that 'a disturbed mind' had inflicted the fatal wounds on the De Gruchy family, Mr Ramage told the Supreme Court jury that Matthew De Gruchy was not a mentally disturbed killer, but a 'weedy little man' who was devoted to the family members he was accused of slaying.

He told the jury that when Matthew gave evidence they would hear from 'this frail, little sparrow of a man' with no history of violence. Mr Ramage asked his client if he got on well with his mother.

Matthew De Gruchy said, 'Yes, I did.'

'Did you love your mother?' Mr Ramage asked him.

'Yes, I did,' was the reply.

Matthew was given positive character references by his father, Wayne, his uncle, Paul, and Gail Brindley.

Under cross-examination by the prosecutor, Matthew De Gruchy denied that he had committed the murders. He also denied Mr Conlon's suggestion that he had made a checklist of things to do to conceal his involvement in the crime.

With a breaking voice, Matthew sobbed as he told the court about finding the battered body of his mother.

'There was a lot of blood ... I really didn't know what to do.'

On 14 October 1998, Matthew Wayne De Gruchy was convicted of the murder of his mother Jennifer Ann De Gruchy, his sister Sarah De Gruchy and his brother Adrian De Gruchy. He was sentenced on each count of murder to concurrent terms of 28 years.

☠ ☠ ☠

When the trial was over, another uncle, Steven De Gruchy, read a statement to the media expressing his family's belief that his nephew was innocent. On behalf of Matthew's father Wayne and the De Gruchy family, he said that the emotional toll of losing three family members, only to see another charged with murder, had been devastating.

'The family has been to hell and back,' he said. 'We continue to believe he is not guilty of the acts.'

Steven De Gruchy criticised the approach taken by the media throughout the investigation and trial. 'Some members of the media think they're doing their job but they have shown no regard for the families involved. Families who just want to be left alone and try to bring some normality back to their lives.

'Our lives will never be the same again after what has happened. We have lost our loved ones Jennifer, Adrian and Sarah. They continue to be with us and in our hearts forever.'

On the other side of the family, Jennifer De Gruchy's brother Ray Halliwell said he could not find a bad word to say about his nephew.

Jennifer and Ray's sister, however, was not so sure. After the trial, Liz Karhof admitted that she believed Matthew was guilty. She said he'd been a loving and untroubled child until he became involved in drugs and his moods became erratic. She said his cannabis use had made him a bit of a Jekyll and Hyde.

Although Matthew's defence told the court that he did not argue with Jennifer about borrowing her car, Liz Karhof said the vehicle had, in fact, been a constant source of tension between mother and son.

Matthew's girlfriend Alyssa had made a similar observation during his committal hearing.

'During the time I have known Matthew,' she said, 'I have found him to be just a normal sort of person who, on the odd occasion, gets into arguments with his family and myself.

'When he argues with his family it is usually about his access to his mother's or father's car.'

In her victim impact statement, which was read to the court by Justice Michael Grove, Liz Karhof revealed the anguish she'd felt on seeing the brutal injuries that had been inflicted on her family.

She said she could never forget the shock of seeing her sister's badly beaten body at the Glebe Morgue and the coldness of holding her hand.

'I wanted to be there with her forever, I did not want to leave her alone,' she said. 'I wanted to pick her up and hold her but couldn't. It would be the last time I would ever see her again. I was heartbroken.'

Her statement described how she'd then held onto Sarah's hand and then moved towards Adrian.

'I actually put my hand over my mouth when I saw him so that I would not scream out because his injuries were so horrific,' she said. 'I could not bring myself to touch Adrian because although I knew he was dead, I felt I didn't want to hurt him and that I might if I touched him.'

Liz Karhof also described the day she'd gone to clean the family home in Albion Park Rail as one of the most painful of her life.

'I went back to the house to clean it up so that my brother-in-law could move back home,' she said. 'It took me six hours to clean the blood from Jenny and Sarah's bedrooms.'

☠ ☠ ☠

In November 1999, Matthew appealed against the convictions. His counsel also included an application for leave to appeal against the sentences.

In the original trial there was much talk about the use of the words 'disturbed mind', including what was meant by them, what the jury could have inferred from them, and ultimately why they should be ignored.

Even so, one of the grounds for the appeal against the convictions related to the directions Justice Grove gave the jury concerning remarks made by the prosecutor.

Mr Conlon had suggested, in his closing address, that the person who committed the murders 'must have had a disturbed mind'. This followed his earlier observation that in cases where there has been extreme and apparently senseless violence visited upon a victim, there is quite often no motive.

Defence counsel jumped on this at the time, stating that by these observations the prosecutor had offered the jury an explanation for the absence of any apparent motive for the crime. Mr Ramage said this explanation was totally lacking in support as there was no evidence presented at trial as to whether Matthew De Gruchy had, or had not, been psychiatrically examined, let alone been shown to have a disturbed mind.

Mr Conlon pointed out that the Crown did not have to prove a motive. He said the justification for the other comment lay in the 'nature of the acts themselves' and that 'as a general proposition anybody responsible for these acts must have had a disturbed mind'.

It was the opinion of the Appeal Court judge, Justice James

Wood, that this approach by the prosecutor had been ill-advised; was curious, as it didn't necessarily advance his case; and involved a degree of circularity.

Basically, in the absence of any evidence that Matthew De Gruchy had a disturbed mind, Mr Conlon's comment could have mistakenly been taken to mean that someone other than the accused was the culprit. To that extent, Justice Wood said, the comments actually favoured the defence case.

The defence, however, believed the prosecutor's comments had offered a possible explanation for Matthew De Gruchy acting in a most disturbing and violent way, which was apparently out of character for him.

At the trial, Justice Grove told the jury that it *was* correct, in law, that the Crown was not required to prove a motive.

'Of course, it is comforting to an ordinary human being where you are seeking to assess somebody's action to know why they did it, but I should tell you the law does not require the Crown to tell you why people commit crimes.'

Justice Grove added that his understanding of what the prosecutor said was that such crimes were known to have happened and the motive was unknown or baffling.

'I did not understand him to say that there was no motive; merely that the motive was unknown.'

In bringing down his judgement on the appeal in March 2000, Justice Wood stated: 'When all of the factors identified by the Crown are taken into consideration, in combination, I am not persuaded that the case is one in which the jury ought to have entertained a reasonable doubt. In particular the combination of the note, the presence of the appellant's fingerprint on the cabinet door knob, the DNA recovered from the carpet tuft, and from the spots of blood in the hallway and bedroom, the comment to Mr Bailey about Sarah, the appellant's unconvincing evidence concerning the note, the absence of any mention to police of the prophecy as to the death of three members of the family, the appearance of a staged robbery, and the finding of the items in a dam with which he was familiar, constituted a powerful circumstantial case. It may also be assumed from the verdict that, having seen and heard the appellant give evidence, the jury were not impressed with his credibility.

'In these circumstances, I am of the view that the appeals against conviction should be dismissed, and the applications for leave to appeal against sentence refused.'

Justice Wood said the sentences imposed were manifestly appropriate for the offences of which Matthew De Gruchy was convicted.

☠ ☠ ☠

Matthew and his defence team did not give up – but to no avail. In 2000, his appeal against conviction was unanimously dismissed in the New South Wales Court of Criminal Appeal by chief judge James Wood and his colleagues Caroline Simpson and Brian Sully. The murders were said to involve 'brutality beyond description'.

In 2002, when Matthew was 24 years old, the High Court rejected his last chance for appeal and his conviction was again upheld. The five judges of the High Court's full bench, again unanimously, agreed that the arguments offered against his guilt were 'too improbable'.

Justice Ian Callinan said the circumstances of the murders that had rocked the Illawarra region in 1996 were horrific.

'The mind recoils from the idea that an apparently quiet, gentle young man of good character and with no known animus against his family should brutally slay his mother and young sister and brother.'

☠ ☠ ☠

The big questions in any murder case are always who, how, and why. The how is invariably the first thing established, and the why – if not immediately obvious – is usually revealed when the who is identified.

But in most domestic homicides, even when the motive is known, it's still almost impossible for those outside the family to comprehend that a son *could* kill his mother, or a mother her child, or a father his daughter.

And when there is no apparent, established or known motive – as in the case of the De Gruchy family homicides – it *is* almost easier to believe that Matthew is innocent.

But only because the alternative is too horrible to think about.

Despite having the opportunity, despite his DNA in the blood on the wall above his mother's bed and his bloodied fingerprints in the house, despite the incriminating note found with the goods 'stolen' from the house and the items being found in a dam en route to his girlfriend's place, and regardless of the fact there was no evidence indicating the involvement of anyone other than Matthew De Gruchy, he continued to proclaim his innocence, even going as far as to say he was framed.

The only thing lacking was – and still is – a motive.

But, as Justice Grove said during the original trial, the prosecution's point was not that Matthew had no motive – simply that his motive was unknown.

There have, of course, been a few theories. The ongoing argument over Matthew's use of his mother's car may have escalated that night into the violence that tore the entire family apart.

Matthew's drug use may have triggered a violent episode that didn't stop until everyone in the house was dead.

Matthew De Gruchy may, in fact, have a mind so disturbed that he has wiped out all memory of his actions; or one so inherently devious and violent that he simply prefers to give no reason for what he chose to do, because there is none that anyone else would understand.

Defence counsel Malcolm Ramage had said his client was 'guileless … not very bright and possibly stupid'.

Crown Prosecutor Paul Conlon, however, described him as 'a lying killer, willing to go to any lengths to get away with murder; a schemer who planned the murder of his loved ones to appear as though he was the last man standing after a bungled burglary'.

☠ ☠ ☠

Until that night, the De Gruchy family had been a normal one. Wayne was the state administration manager for Pioneer Concrete, his wife Jennifer kept their Federation-style brick house scrupulously clean, and they and their children were financially comfortable.

Eighteen-year-old Matthew, then with a ponytail of long dark hair, was good looking, popular with his friends and into surfing. He'd spent his early teenage years riding around the suburbs on his BMX bike, going rollerblading with his brother and sister and surfing with his Uncle Paul. He'd never been good at school and dropped out at the start of Year 11 in 1995. Although he worked some weekends at a mechanic's workshop, he was unemployed and living at home until the night of 12 March 1996.

Most people could agree that under 'normal circumstances' the strongest bonds and the most common fights, rivalries, even jealousies within families are between parents or between siblings.

It seems odd that Matthew claimed he didn't know where his brother Adrian was when he left the house that night to go to his girlfriend's place.

He'd told police and he told the court, 'I didn't know where he was, but I presumed he was out with friends.'

Matthew 'presumed' his little brother was out with friends? He honestly thought his 15-year-old brother was 'out' with friends, at 10 pm, on a school night?

So, here's another theory: perhaps the carnage that was unleashed that night in March 1996 began in the garage.

Perhaps Matthew De Gruchy had an argument – probably a stupid, meaningless, trivial disagreement over nothing much at all – with his little brother.

The damage inflicted on young Adrian De Gruchy was by far the worst of the three victims. He suffered massive head trauma. Such was the ferocity of the attack that his teeth were scattered across the cement floor of the garage. His body had been doused in petrol in a failed or rejected attempt to set him alight. And then, he'd been covered with a doona – in a futile attempt to hide what had been done to him.

What would *you* do next if, in a fit of rage, you had bludgeoned your little brother to death for no good reason?

It's not something you can hide from your family. From your mother.

What on earth are you going to tell your mother?

Think about it: there's only one way that she'll never find out what you've done.

☠ ☠ ☠

The Goulburn Correctional Centre – aka Goulburn Jail or Goulbourn Main Prison and originally opened in 1884 – is a high-security facility 195 kilometres from Sydney, which houses some of Australia's most notorious prisoners. In the early 2000s a supermaximum facility was opened within the confines of the original prison grounds. The infamous Circle inside the supermax – once described by a Corrections Minister as a 'godless place' – is home to the state's worst murderers, gang rapists, violent armed robbers and paedophiles.

Among the inmates, until 2019, were the four notorious 'K' brothers, convicted in 2002 of the gang rapes of eight Sydney girls aged 13 to 18; the Murphy brothers, who abducted, raped and killed Anita Cobby; the now-late backpacker serial killer, Ivan Milat; and family killer Matthew De Gruchy.

In March of 2009, Matthew, then 31-years old, fronted Goulburn Court via videolink, charged over a 2007 jail-yard gang-bashing that almost killed one of the infamous 'K' brother pack rapists. (The identities of the so-called 'K' brothers cannot be revealed for legal reasons.)

Matthew was one of six inmates, including three other convicted killers and two violent sex offenders, charged over the brutal attack on the two eldest brothers. He pleaded not guilty to four assault charges, including two charges of maliciously inflicting grievous bodily harm.

Matthew's full sentence expired in June 2024. His earliest possible release was June 2017, when he was first eligible to apply for parole. By then, he was an inmate of the Junee Correctional Facility, had been approved for day release, and had been working in an abattoir in Junee – in the chill room with no access to knives. Despite the day release, his parole was refused, as the State Parole Authority (SPA) found he presented an 'unacceptable risk to the community'.

Two years later, however, on 15 August 2019, Matthew De Gruchy walked free from Long Bay Jail in Sydney, after his parole was granted – on the strict condition that he never enters the Illawarra or Shoalhaven areas; and he never contacts, stalks, harasses or intimidates any of the family members of his victims.

Matthew De Gruchy served 23 years of his 28-year sentence and was 41 years old when he left prison – the same age his mother was when he killed her.

Danny Deacon appeared on Crime Stoppers Northern Territory on 9 July 2013, to beg his partner Carlie Sinclair to come home.

ABC News

Karen Ristevski's aunt, Patricia Gray, with Borce and Sarah, fields questions at a press gathering two weeks after Karen's disappearance.

Penny Stephens/Fairfax

Police and SES crews search for missing woman Karen Ristevski.
Penny Stephens/Fairfax

In happier times, a family portrait of Zialloh and Zahra Abrahimzadeh with two of their children, Atena and Arman

Arman Abrahimzadeh, coming to terms with the fact that his father cold-bloodedly murdered his mother

Newspix/Chris Higgins

Gemma Gaye Killeen, who left her toddler son, Kayden, to drown at Hillarys Boat Harbour in Perth in 2010

The last family picture of Anna Marie Kemp, her husband, John Sharpe, and their daughter, Gracie Louise, in March 2004. The picture was taken a few days before John Sharpe used a speargun to kill Anna and Gracie

Ian Currie/Newspix

Gunshot victim John Asquith and his de facto wife, Patricia Byers. Asquith survived being shot in the head by Patricia Byers, who was later found guilty of the murder of her second husband

Newspix

Police investigators at the waste management site on Victoria's Mornington Peninsula in July 2004, where they were searching for the bodies of 41-year-old Anna Marie Kemp and her 20-month-old daughter Gracie Louise Sharpe

AAP Images/Julian Smith

Sally Brooks, bludgeoned
and left to die by her former
husband, Robert Meade, in her
Donvale home

Matthew De Gruchy in prison, awaiting
trial for the murder of his mother,
Jennifer, his brother, Adrian, and his
sister, Sarah, at their Albion Park home
in March 1996

Newspix/Dravuj Medak

Darcey Freeman

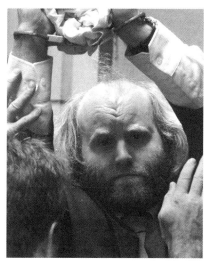

Arthur Freeman following his arrest. He was charged that afternoon with the murder of his daughter Darcey

John Hargest/Newspix

A dishevelled Arthur Freeman during his murder trial

Trevor Pinder/Newspix

The West Gate Bridge, 58 metres at its highest point and from which Arthur Freeman threw his four-year-old daughter Darcey

David Geraghty/Newspix

Kevin Matthews, accused of the contract murder of his wife, Carolyn, outside his former home at West Lakes Shore, Adelaide, South Australia, in August 2003
Michael Milnes/Newspix

Michelle Burgess, who with Kevin Matthews planned the death of Carolyn Matthews and who, with David William Edgar Key, helped carry it out
Lindsay Moller/Newspix

Chapter Nine

I GOT THE SHIT CAR

One otherwise ordinary day in June 2005, Greg King was chatting to his mate Rob outside their local fish and chip shop. Rob was complaining about the raw deal he'd got in the separation from his wife. He not only had to pay this and pay that for his kids, who continued to live with her, but now she was going to marry 'the fucking dickhead' that was her new boyfriend.

What's more, he whinged, 'I got the shit car; she gets to drive around in the good car.'

Given the rate of separation and divorce in Australia – or, indeed, the western world – this gripe probably gets aired somewhere in the country on at least a daily basis. Some blokes, who are really pissed off about the car, might accidentally drive it into a tree so they can get a newer one on the insurance. Some blokes might do a runner so they don't have to pay maintenance.

For some blokes, though, it's not really about the car, or even the money; it's not even about supporting the kids – because they love their kids. For some blokes it's all about the ex-wife.

Greg King had possibly heard that whinge about the car from his mate Rob before, but he'd never heard what came next before. And though he was shocked, he didn't believe what he heard; or rather, he didn't believe his childhood friend was serious.

For the rest of his life, however, Greg King – bus driver and father – will regret that he didn't realise how angry his mate was; that it wasn't just talk; that his mate was serious about getting back at his ex-wife – in the most vindictive, horrible and final way possible.

As King stood there that day listening to the litany of ex-husband woes, who should pull up in 'the better car' and head into the same takeaway shop but Rob's ex-wife.

And that's when the whinge turned nasty. That's when Robert Farquharson revealed the blight on his soul; or what the judge at his trial later called his 'dark contemplation'.

Looking through the window at Cindy Gambino, the mother of his sons, Farquharson said, 'She is not going to do that to me and get away with it.'

Robert Farquharson confided that he wanted to take away the things that were most important to her.

King asked him, 'What would that be, Robbie?' When Farquharson nodded through the window, King said, 'What, the kids?'

When Farquharson said yes, King asked, 'What would you do, would you take them away or something?'

Farquharson stared at his friend. 'Kill them.'

'Bullshit,' King said to him. 'It's her own flesh and blood, Robbie.'

'So I hate them.'

King asked Farquharson how he would do this thing.

Robert Farquharson said, 'It would be close by. There'd be an accident involving a dam where I survive and the kids don't. It would be on a special day.'

'What kind of special day?' King asked him.

'Something like Father's Day,' Farquharson said, 'so she'd remember it when it was Father's Day; and I was the last one to have them for the last time, not her. Then she would suffer every Father's Day for the rest of her life.'

King warned his mate, 'You don't even dream of that stuff, Robbie.'

☠ ☠ ☠

Greg King shouldn't feel bad because he didn't do anything about what he heard that day. And he certainly shouldn't feel guilty, though his experience could now serve as a warning to other men whose mates confide in them.

But really, without hindsight, who the hell *would* have believed that kind of threat?

For a start, what kind of man could even *say* he hated his owns sons – just because they were also hers – let alone mean it?

Secondly, who would be stupid enough to describe exactly what eventually came to pass, and then claim it was an accident?

An accident?

Not even coincidence is that cruel – or specific.

☗ ☗ ☗

Three months later, when the TV and radio news broke one Sunday night that a family car had plunged into a dam west of Geelong and that three young boys, at least, had not survived the crash, the wider community took a collective breath of shock and grief.

It was Father's Day.

What a horrible thing to have happen on Father's Day. What a tragedy. How must the poor parents, if they survived, be feeling?

Then the news carried a bit more detail. The only other person in the car had been the boys' father, who'd been taking his sons home to their mother after an access visit.

Community sympathy twisted in a moment. Although many people – many of us – probably cursed our cynicism, we still thought, 'Oh my god, what a bastard. He obviously drove into that dam on purpose.'

We were even more convinced when we learned that the father, the bastard, had survived.

His sons, aged 10, seven and two years old, had not.

But while we all just put two and two together – unfairly and with no evidence – there was one man who knew that it was in fact so.

Greg King broke down at work on 5 September, the morning after Father's Day, when he learned that Robert Farquharson's three boys had died exactly the way his good mate had said they would.

The young Farquharson brothers, Jai, Tyler and Bailey, had drowned in a dam not too far from home, trapped in their father's shit car.

☗ ☗ ☗

Police, emergency services and even the media gave Farquharson the benefit of the doubt in those first few days after the tragedy.

Initial news stories told how, just after 7 pm, Farquharson's car had run off the road about seven kilometres east of Winchelsea; how he had tried unsuccessfully to save his sons; how he'd then struggled from the dam and made it to the road where he flagged down a car.

His own mobile was wet and useless and the driver of the car that stopped didn't have one. Farquharson begged to be taken into Winchelsea to raise the alarm.

Friends and family members then rushed back to the dam.

When the CFA and SES crews arrived at the chaotic scene at about 8 pm, other people were already desperately searching for the boys. But it was dark, and no-one had been able to determine exactly where the car had entered the water.

CFA volunteers, attached to ropes, dived into the dam to join the search, but it wasn't until close to 11 pm that police divers finally found the car and its little occupants.

Acting Inspector Mick Talbot, of the Major Collision Investigation Unit, announced that the Farquharson bothers had been freed from their seatbelts. 'We don't know for sure, but our belief is that one of the children has released them all from their seatbelts ... but they have been unable to get out of the car,' he said.

Newspapers the next day said the incident was being treated by police as a 'tragic accident'. Inspector Talbot said that 'somehow' the Farquharson family car left its lane on the Princes Highway, crossed the opposite Geelong-bound lane, broke through a post-and-wire farm fence, and skipped 'like a stone' into the dam before vanishing into eight metres of dark water.

The car left no skid marks; there were no signs of speeding; and the breath tests done after the accident showed that no alcohol was involved in the tragedy.

Inspector Talbot said police had 'spoken to the driver of the car very, very briefly'.

'As you can appreciate,' he said, 'we haven't been able to get much sense out of him at the moment because his three kids have been killed.'

☠ ☠ ☠

Gradually, although it didn't take long, the facts of what really happened that Father's Day night began to emerge. One of the strangest things, at first, was that the driver of the car that Farquharson flagged down did, in fact, have a mobile phone.

Shane Atkinson, and his friend and passenger Tony McClelland, were heading home to Winchelsea just before 7.30 pm when they stopped after seeing a bloke on the side of the road waving frantically.

The 24-year-old Atkinson, not realising then that he actually knew the man, ran over to him and said, 'What the fuck are you doing standing on the side of the road – are you trying to trying to kill yourself?'

The man said, 'No, no, no; fuck, fuck, fuck; what have I done? Give me a lift back to Winch. I've got to tell Cindy I've killed the kids.'

Atkinson said the man told him he had 'put his car into a dam' and that he'd 'either had a coughing fit or had done the wheel bearing'.

Even though he was soaking wet it was also dark, so it took Atkinson and McClelland a moment to realise what Farquharson, who kept swearing and repeating himself, actually meant. That his car was in a nearby dam – with his kids in it.

The young men offered to jump into the water and take a look, and Atkinson offered his mobile phone to call an ambulance.

But Farquharson refused both the rescue offers and the chance to call for help.

'No, don't go down there, it's too late. They're already gone,' he said. 'Just take me to Cindy. Come on, come on, get me back. I will just have to go back and tell Cindy.' He then asked for a cigarette.

It was only when the interior car light came on that Shane Atkinson recognised his passenger, from when he was a little fella; it was Mr Farquharson, who had mown the lawns around town.

According to Tony McClelland, Farquharson at first blamed his car. He recalled him saying, 'I couldn't get them out. I must have done a wheel bearing.'

McClelland said that shortly after, on the drive into town, Farquharson told them he 'must have had a coughing fit and blacked out and he just woke up in the water'.

'He said that when he came to, the water was up to his chest,' McClelland said.

As they drove at speed to Ms Gambino's house, Atkinson again offered his mobile to Farquharson so he could call 000, but he pushed it away again and kept saying – 'about 100 times' – that he had to get to Cindy's house to break the news first; to 'tell my missus that I've killed the kids'.

When they pulled up in Cindy Gambino's driveway, she came out of the house expecting to greet her children. Instead Robert Farquharson, soaking wet and babbling, told her he had killed them.

Atkinson said Farquharson was not knowing what to say, except that he kept saying, 'The kids are in the car and they're in the water.'

Atkinson later said that driving Mr Farquharson away from the dam, and not calling emergency services himself, was 'the stupidest thing' he'd ever done.

'As soon as I've pulled into the driveway I've, I've known that I shouldn't have even left the scene,' he said.

After his passenger told Cindy Gambino 'I killed the kids', she started crying and tried to hit Farquharson.

Atkinson and Tony McClelland left them, immediately raised the alarm back in Winchelsea and then returned to the dam with help. By that time, according to Atkinson, Cindy Gambino was there, her partner Stephen Moules was in the water, and Farquharson was pacing up and down the road 'smoking cigarette after cigarette'.

☠ ☠ ☠

Cindy Gambino had been having an ordinary night; waiting with Stephen Moules' nine-year-old son Zach for her own boys to come home. When her ex-husband, muddled and saturated, broke the most awful of news, she phoned Stephen to tell him where she was going. Then she bundled Zach into her car and drove – with Robert Farquharson – seven kilometres back down the Princes Highway to the dam.

She said that when her speedometer hit 145 kilometres an hour, Zach started to get upset and begged her to slow down. He said, 'Cindy, you're frightening me. Can you slow down?'

Cindy remembered saying, 'I've got to get to the kids, got to get to the kids.'

☠ ☠ ☠

Robert Farquharson was seen by many who knew him as a loving father a bit down on his luck. Since separating from Cindy he'd been sharing a small home with his own father. He was working as a cleaner at a resort in nearby Lorne, but the wage wasn't great, so along with the maintenance he forked out for the kids, he was financially pressed.

He had taken the positive step of seeing a counsellor because he was having difficulty coping with the boys when he did have access to them. But Farquharson was clearly not happy or accepting of the reality that Cindy had not only moved on from him, but moved on with someone else.

A lot of men, and some women, find themselves in this unenviable position. It's not nice, it's heartbreaking, and it's bound to wreck their confidence, their idea of control, the way they look at the world.

Most men learn to deal with it. Most men find their own way to move on, get their own new life. Most men hope that new life will be one that continues to include their children.

But not all men; not Robert Farquharson.

But then, maybe he'd always been a bit of a loser.

Cindy Gambino's stated reasons for ending their marriage may have revealed another side to Robert Farquharson – had anyone been looking. She said she was 'having trouble giving my heart to Rob' and that she'd gotten tired of him not finishing things.

In one statement she'd admitted she'd never really loved him, and she told the court that Farquharson was always down and out. She said, 'I just didn't want the marriage anymore. I asked him to leave.'

She wanted to separate quietly and amicably, always putting the boys first.

Farquharson, already depressed about losing his family, later feared he would be replaced altogether in his boys' lives by the new man in his house, even though Cindy assured him that would never happen. They were still friends, after all.

They'd been separated about a year when Farquharson told Greg King of his plan; a vindictive, dreadful, unthinkable and cowardly plan.

'There's no way I'm going to let him, her and the kids live together in my house and I have to fucking pay for it and also pay fucking maintenance for the kids,' Farquharson told King.

'Nobody does that to me and gets away with it.'

☠ ☠ ☠

Three months after his conversation with King – and a couple of days before Father's Day 2005 – Rob Farquharson cuddled two-year-old Bailey as he proudly watched his eldest son Jai accept the flag for his footy team's win in the under-12s grand final.

At about 3 pm on the following Sunday, Cindy Gambino dropped her kids off at her ex-husband's house for an access visit. She said it was okay for them to stay for tea.

The Farquharson boys gave their dad a photo of themselves and some saucepans for Father's Day. Jai was also excited about another present, a wooden back scratcher, that he had waiting at home for his dad.

Farquharson and his three sons piled into his 16-year-old Holden Commodore and headed off to Geelong for the afternoon. They called in to Kmart, where Farquharson bought the footy-mad Jai a cricket ball, because he was soon to play his first season; they had KFC for tea; and then dropped in to Mount Moriac to pick up something the kids had left at Farquharson's sister's place on their last visit.

After that they headed back to Winchelsea, a drive of just over 18 kilometres. Halfway home, about seven minutes out from the town, that old Commodore veered across the road and ended up in the dam.

Robert Farquharson continues to protest his complete innocence, so we'll never know if the actual decision to carry out his dark intentions was made in the split second after he crossed the overpass; or if what he did in that same moment had been his plan all along for that particular Father's Day.

The incident was originally handled by the Major Collision Investigation Unit but was soon referred to the Homicide Squad when doubts were raised about Farquharson's version of events.

Crash experts say the Commodore turned right at a sharp angle, crossed the opposite lane, ran through long grass down an embankment, ploughed through a wire fence, made three steering corrections, swiped a tree and entered the dam. It was found nearly three hours later, nose-down in 7.4 metres of water and about 28 metres from the edge of the dam. There were no marks on the road or in the grass leading to the dam that showed the car was 'ever out of control'.

Police divers said Jai was found halfway out of the open driver's door of the submerged car; and his brothers Tyler and Bailey were also free of their safety belts, but died trapped in the locked back section of the car.

Crash investigator Sergeant Geoffrey Exton said that when the vehicle was pulled from the water, he found the ignition was turned off and in the locked position, the headlights and fan were switched off, and the child locks on the rear doors were on. There was significant damage to the front of the car and the driver's-side mirror was missing.

Debris, including part of the mirror and headlight glass, was found by a tree near the edge of the dam.

☠ ☠ ☠

On the roadside Robert Farquharson told Atkinson he'd put the car in the dam because he'd either done the wheel bearing or had a coughing fit.

In the car on the way into Winchelsea he told McClelland he must have done a wheel bearing. A moment later he said he must have had a coughing fit and blacked out.

Back at the dam afterwards he told a Geelong police officer, Senior Constable Edward Harmon, that he'd 'had a chest pain' and 'just blacked out'. No mention of a coughing fit.

He told Belmont paramedic David Watson, who coaxed him into the ambulance at the scene, that he'd had a dry cough for a few days and had suffered a coughing fit, blacked out and woke as the car floated in the dam.

He told Torquay paramedic Lindsay Robinson, who helped Watson in the ambulance, that he'd had a bad cold. He also told Robinson that he had 'no history of blackouts'.

In a bedside interview, recorded at Geelong Hospital that night, he told police he 'couldn't really say' how his car had run off the road and into the water.

He told Senior Constable Rohan Courtis, from the Major Collision Investigation Unit, 'I had this coughing sort of fit and I don't know.' He said he was always cautious when driving with the children and guessed that his coughing fit had started after he turned the car heater on.

☠ ☠ ☠

The 'I must have done a wheel bearing' excuse was never heard again after that Father's Day night – except in witness statements. Farquharson shelved it himself, and stuck with the blackout excuse, which was sensible because tests on the car revealed there was nothing mechanically wrong with it.

Farquharson was first interviewed by Homicide detectives two days after the event. By then a doctor had helpfully diagnosed him with a condition, one with a name.

Cough syncope explained everything. A rare condition – and one that Farquharson soon claimed had struck him before, at work, just a couple of weeks prior to that tragic Sunday – cough syncope causes a brief period of unconsciousness triggered by a coughing fit.

Farquharson told police that he'd turned the car heater on because of the cough. Odd, then, that when the car was pulled from the dam, the heater was off – just like ignition and headlights.

Robert Farquharson also told Watson, the paramedic, that his eldest son Jai opened the front passenger door, causing water to flood into the car, sinking it.

When questioned by Homicide detectives, Farquharson denied deliberately drowning his sons. 'I'd do anything to have them back, and I've got to live with this for the rest of my life that I couldn't save my kids,' he said.

'I have two arms, two legs. I can't save three. How was I supposed to do it? I tried and tried and tried.'

Farquharson said the car floated for some time until water began rushing in when Jai opened his door to try to get out.

According to Farquharson, 'Jai said, "Dad, we're in the water."

'I said, "Just sit there, mate," and he panicked and opened the door and I went to shut it.

'I said, "No, don't … don't panic, mate. Don't panic."

'I just must have said, "Hold on, hold on. I'll get out and get you out."'

Robert Farquharson shut his son's car door, then opened his own. The cold dam water rushed in. Even if he'd wanted to save his boys, the nosediving car made it impossible.

He told detectives he'd freed himself and tried to rescue the children, but had no hope because the car was sinking too fast. He left them and swam to shore.

During the interview at the St Kilda Road Homicide Squad office on 6 September, Detective-Sergeant Clanchy asked; 'Why did you want to go to Cindy?'

Farquharson replied: 'To get help. I had no phone, nothing to ring anyone or anything. I did – well, not that that was my concern – I – I don't know. I said, I need to see her to tell her, "Look, we've had an accident", or "take me to the police". I – I don't know. She was probably the first thing – the first person I thought of. I don't know. I can't answer that.'

Clanchy told Farquharson that 'the examination that's been done in relation to how the car ... came into the dam, there's no – there's no indication at this stage of any loss of control of the vehicle'.

Farquharson: 'Well, I'm telling the truth. I blacked out. I had a coughing fit and I blacked out. I mean, I wouldn't do that.'

Detective-Sergeant Clanchy: 'When – when you say that, what wouldn't you do?'

Farquharson: 'I mean, I wouldn't do something deliberately like that, what people are trying to say. I had a coughing fit, and I blacked out and I can't remember anything. That's the honest truth.'

🕱 🕱 🕱

During his first interview with detectives on 6 September, Farquharson offered to take a lie detector test. He took that polygraph, conducted by a non-police expert, at Geelong police station on 21 September 2005. Lie detector results are inadmissible in court, which, as it transpired, is just as well.

When a devastated Greg King told police what Farquharson had said to him three months before, he said he'd thought his mate had just been 'bullshitting'. King volunteered to help police by talking to Farquharson while wearing a concealed recording device.

During one exchange, King asked if the accident had anything to do with what he'd said earlier in the year about his threat to pay back Cindy.

Farquharson stated, 'No, no way, I was just angry ... You've misinterpreted me, it's not what you thought you heard. I would never do that.

'I would never hurt her, and I definitely would never hurt my kids.

Never. Why would anyone go from not smacking them to killing them?'

Farquharson urged his friend, 'Wipe that right out of your head ... For god's sake, please don't mention that sort of stuff ... that's going to incriminate me.'

He asked King to tell the police positive things about him and his relationship with his sons.

'I've got to live with this for the rest of my life ... Don't freak out, just tell who I am, what I represent and all that.'

During that first interview with the Homicide Squad in September 2005, Farquharson said that, as he dragged himself out of the dam, he thought, 'If I can wave someone down they might be able to come and help me ... I swam ... and walked back to the road and tried to wave people down to stop and help me ... I went to the road to get people to help me.'

But he didn't do that.

Robert Farquharson did not dive and dive and dive in any desperate attempt to save his boys; he did not go back for them. He refused immediate help to rescue them and rebuffed the mobile phone offer to call 000.

He asked instead to be driven straight to his wife's place so he could tell her what he'd done.

He told the two young men he'd flagged down – and who offered to dive in and search for the boys – 'It's too late, they're gone.'

He left his sons in a car at the bottom of a dam so he could tell his ex-wife that he'd done just that.

It was Stephen Moules, not Robert Farquharson, who later stripped off his shoes and jumper and dived into the freezing water. Cindy Gambino's new man dived for her boys, repeatedly and frantically, until paramedics forced him to stop, fearing hypothermia. Her ex-husband, meanwhile, stood around or paced and asked people for cigarettes.

No-one who attended the scene observed Robert Farquharson make any attempt to rescue his children.

He told his ex-wife that he'd killed the kids. He claimed it was an accident and that he'd tried to rescue them.

Cindy Gambino believed him – then, and apparently she still believes him. As do the rest of his family.

His oldest friend Greg King wanted to believe, but couldn't.

The police believed him at first; but not for long.

Robert Farquharson was formally charged with the murders of his three sons on 14 December 2005.

Crown Prosecutor Jeremy Rapke QC simply had a job to do.

Mr Rapke told the jury during the six-week trial, before Justice Philip Cummins in the Victorian Supreme Court, that Robert Farquharson had committed 'an incredibly cruel act ... which completely turned on its head the notion that a father would do anything to protect his children.

'It was a shockingly wicked and callous act.'

Defence lawyer Peter Morrissey said, 'There are three beautiful kids dead, their father is on trial, and what he has said – and you will hear it – is that he loved those kids and he'd never hurt them.'

He said his client blacked out after suffering a coughing fit as he drove along the Princes Highway, and woke to find himself in the submerged car.

Mr Morrissey told the jury that Mr Farquharson suffered cough syncope, a rare disorder in which sustained and forceful coughing causes people to black out.

Mr Rapke said the accused was conscious and acting voluntarily when he drove his car into the dam. He said crash experts found no indication of any loss of control by the driver; that the car made three separate steering alterations after the time Mr Farquharson claimed he lost consciousness.

'Obviously, cars don't steer themselves,' Mr Rapke said.

During the pre-trial hearings (before the jury was empanelled), and as was his duty to his client, Defence lawyer Peter Morrissey submitted that there was no case for the accused to answer on the three charges of murder. One of the many pieces of prosecution evidence that he argued against was the expert testimony of the Major Collision Investigation Unit.

He suggested that, but for the unit's evidence of the three steering corrections, there was 'an absence of any objective evidence that my client was conscious when the car entered the dam'.

Justice Cummins, however, reminded Mr Morrissey that a trial commences 'with the presumption of innocence ... which is not the same as a presumption of unconsciousness'.

During another pre-trial hearing, Mr Morrissey argued that statements made by his client to various people, and gained from telephone intercept (TI) warrants between 11 and 21 September 2005, should be admitted to evidence.

He said that, although these were out-of-court statements, they could be used by the defence in its rebuttal of the awareness of guilt proposition being put forward by the prosecution.

In other words, they could be used to counter the covertly taped conversations between his client and Gregory King that the prosecution planned to use against Mr Farquharson, because the content of telephone intercepts to other people were likewise made by a man who did not wish to be wrongly charged with an offence that he did not commit.

Justice Cummins ruled that in his view the telephone intercept material was inadmissible. He said they were self-serving hearsay statements made by an accused out of court.

'They are no more admissible,' he said, 'than the accused going around Winchelsea saying to people that he is innocent.'

Justice Cummins also pointed out to Mr Morrissey a related issue that had been raised by the prosecution. 'In my view it is not necessary to go to this, but I simply record it,' he said.

Inherent in the issue of the TIs requested by the defence, he said, was the 'spectre of a lie detector test, which was in fact conducted on 20 September 2005.

'Mr Rapke has put that if the TI self-serving proclamations of innocence, with their emotional panoply, go in, the prosecution, in order to properly present that material, would need to have in the lie detector test aspects of it because ... they are integral to the holistic entity.

'Demonstrably,' Justice Cummins reminded defence counsel, 'it would be undesirable for the accused if any lie detector reference went in, let alone any suggestion that he failed it. That plainly should never go before the jury, and it will not.'

The evidence given at trial in support of Robert Farquharson's rare medical condition was given by Dr Chris Steinfort, who diagnosed Mr Farquharson with cough syncope. His diagnosis and evidence were based on his own study of the 6573 patients in his database, 32 of whom suffered syncope, and 14 of them cough syncope.

Respiratory specialist associate Professor Matthew Naughton and neurologist Dr John King testified on the unlikelihood of the occurrence of cough syncope in a man with a healthy heart and lungs.

Professor Naughton told the jury he had never seen such an episode in 25 years as a doctor. 'We are dealing with an extremely rare condition for which there is no test,' he said, adding that the chance Mr Farquharson suffered from the disorder was extremely unlikely.

'I think a single episode of cough syncope in an environment where it's relatively warm and was not replicated thereafter I think is highly unusual. I mean, I just think the whole circumstance is an unusual environment for cough syncope to occur.'

Paramedic David Watson testified that he had listened to Farquharson's chest in the back of the ambulance by the dam and there were 'no wheezes or crackles; the chest was normal'.

The prosecution also pointed out that Dr Steinfort's research indicated that Farquharson's cough syncope defence was based on a statistical rarity of less than 0.003 per cent of the general population.

The suggestion that this rare and unlikely condition could then manifest itself on the 140-metre stretch of road, on the 39 kilometres between Geelong and Winchelsea, where there just happened to be a dam – and on Father's Day – was too farfetched to take seriously.

☠ ☠ ☠

Cindy Gambino's then new partner, now husband, testified how he tried to find the boys that night but the water was too cold.

Stephen Moules said he went to the accident site after getting a frantic phone call from Ms Gambino saying there had been an accident and that the car her sons were in had gone into a dam.

He told the court that when he arrived there, he asked Rob Farquharson what had happened and was told, 'I blacked out.'

'So I asked him if he had been drinking, and he said no. He said, "I had a coughing fit and I blacked out, and when I woke I was in the water."'

Mr Moules said he took his boots off and went into the water where he thought the car may have gone in. 'The water was ice cold.

It took my breath away … The longest I stayed in at any one time was five or six minutes.'

Mr Moules said he finally gave up looking for the car and the boys when it just became too cold.

'I was swallowing water,' he told the court, 'and I thought, this is ridiculous.'

Cindy Gambino had already told the court how her former husband appeared at her place in a hysterical state to tell her the bad news.

Giving evidence in his defence, Ms Gambino said the night the children died Farquharson turned up at her house distraught. He'd had a Father's Day access visit with their three children. 'He was very hysterical. He didn't know where the car was,' she said. 'He kept saying "some dam or some water".'

Ms Gambino said she drove to the place where Rob told her the car had gone into a dam. 'We couldn't find where the car was, we couldn't see the dam. It was so dark.'

Acting Sergeant Glen Urquhart, an accident reconstruction expert with Victoria Police, told the court he estimated Farquharson's car was travelling between 60 and 80 kilometres per hour before it went into the dam.

He said that in his opinion the car made an initial sharp turn to the right, then straightened and finally made a more subtle turn to the right before it entered the water.

☠ ☠ ☠

In his closing address, Mr Morrissey told the jury that the evidence against Robert Farquharson was speculative, hopeful and infected by tunnel vision.

'The evidence is pitiful. It's distant. It's long shot after long shot,' he said. 'He's not some monster. He's not a brooding, angry, rage-filled person at all, he's just Rob. He's been dealt a hard hit.'

Mr Morrissey said that if Mr Farquharson was lying to police he would never have told them about closing Jai's car door when the boy opened it and water began rushing in.

'It's a tragic and sad and horrible detail … because in theory you couldn't help but reflect on this, that if he didn't shut the door maybe Jai would have got out.

'That detail there, we say, is an indicator that he's telling the truth because it's a painful thing for him to say and it doesn't cast him in a good light.'

In his closing, the Crown Prosecutor said, 'It would be artificial and potentially misleading to look at the case without considering Farquharson's break-up with his wife Cindy Gambino, his professed love for his children, his financial position and his long-term depressive illness.'

Mr Rapke said those factors had a bearing on the likelihood that Farquharson was a murderer, rather than an unlucky and tragic man.

He said Ms Gambino initiated the break-up after realising she did not love Farquharson. She formed an attachment with another man, who Farquharson apparently feared would supplant him as a father figure for his children.

Mr Rapke said the statements made by Farquharson to Greg King showed he had antipathy, if not hatred, for Ms Gambino.

'If this hatred is then overlaid on a chronic depressive illness, then there is a dangerous and volatile mix just waiting to be ignited.'

The lawyers in the fictional TV drama *The Practice*, when facing a likely defeat in the defence of a client charged with murder, often resorted to what they called Plan B. During their closing argument they would try to deflect the jury's attention away from their client by presenting a second or third person as a possible – and just as likely – suspect for the crime.

In the defence of Robert Farquharson his defence team's Plan B was to offer Jai Farquharson.

What if the 10-year-old, who drowned with his brothers when their car plunged into a dam, grabbed the steering wheel after his father blacked out?

Mr Morrissey asked the jury to consider if Jai Farquharson was responsible for the steering changes between the car leaving the Princes Highway and running into the farm dam. He said the police reconstruction of the incident was a disaster, and it was possible Jai had moved the steering wheel at some point.

'You need to consider in this case whether that's a realistic possibility or not, whether Jai Farquharson is a boy who would have been capable of reacting to a crisis by trying to help,' he said.

'I cannot prove to you or point to any evidence that he in fact did do that. But it's a factor. Jai might have had an impact on that steering wheel at some point in the journey down.'

☠ ☠ ☠

After the crash in 2005, Cindy Gambino told police, 'I believe with all my heart that this was just an accident. Rob would not have hurt a hair on their heads.'

She told Farquharson's committal hearing on 14 August 2006, a year before the trial, that she did not believe her ex-husband murdered their sons. She said their separation had been 'reasonably amicable', though they had argued over the boys spending time with her new boyfriend, Stephen Moules.

When Justice Cummins asked for the jury's verdict in October 2007, Cindy Gambino began to sob. As the foreman announced that the jury had found the 38-year-old Robert Farquharson 'Guilty, Guilty, Guilty' of each of the three charges of murder, his ex-wife wailed, 'Why? Why? Why?'

Whether it was still denial or a horrifying revelation, Cindy Gambino's pain that day could never be imagined. When a woman thinks she has an amicable separation from a man she didn't really love, when she believes him to be, at least, a loving doting dad, it would be impossible to imagine, let alone accept, he had become a vile and selfish monster.

Cindy Gambino was taken from court crying uncontrollably. Her mother, Beverley Gambino – grandmother of Jai, Tyler and Bailey – then fainted and was taken out on a stretcher. She was treated by paramedics in the courtyard of the Supreme Court building.

The nuggety, pudgy-faced Robert Farquharson had tried to remain blank-faced as the verdict was read but his expression turned to shock when he heard he'd been found guilty of murdering his eldest son, Jai. By the time he sat down, after the next two verdicts for the murders of Tyler and Bailey were announced, he looked stunned.

Not long after his ex-wife and mother-in-law left the Supreme Court in an ambulance that day, Robert Donald William Farquharson left in handcuffs.

At his pre-sentence hearing on 27 October, Crown Prosecutor Jeremy Rapke said Robert Farquharson had 'wiped out his entire family in the one act' to punish his former wife and had shown no remorse.

'The children were all of tender years ... but not so young that they would have been immune from fear, shock, feelings of abandonment and plain terror in the last few moments of their lives. We shall not dwell on the scene that must have played out in the car as it sank below the surface of the dam and slowly filled with water.'

Mr Rapke asked, 'Where was the father of these children as they fought for their lives?

'He swam for his life, made – according to him – some desultory attempts to save his children and thereafter discouraged rescue attempts from brave strangers and others prepared to dive into the icy water to try to save the children.

'A father does not abandon his children like that.'

☠ ☠ ☠

During the sentencing on 16 November 2007, family members and supporters staged a walk-out less than five minutes into the proceedings. Wearing *In Rob We Trust* badges, and others that said *Fact Before Theory* and *Robbed*, they left the court before the full sentence was announced.

Outside court, brother-in-law Ian Ross, flanked by Farquharson's sisters, read a statement on behalf of the convicted killer.

'The court has found me guilty but I did not murder my children. I received a life sentence on the night my boys died so I don't care much about what other people think of me.

'I do care how people remember or think of Jai, Tyler and Bailey because they are three special boys and their lives were very important to me and all their family.

'I will appeal the verdict because I will not have the public believe that Jai, Tyler and Bailey were anything less than the most important part of both my life and the lives of their families.

'I will fight to clear the names of my three boys. They are what keeps me going because there is nothing much else more important to me.

'I cannot change what people think of me now so, with all my heart, I ask you to respect my children, Cindy and both our families.'

Inside the court, Justice Philip Cummins was explaining that one of the functions of the law was to protect the weak from the strong. He said nowhere was this more so than in criminal law.

'And in criminal law, nowhere is it more so than in the protection of children.

'Children are precious and are vulnerable,' he said. 'They are entitled to love, to care, to health, to education, to security and to safety. Most of all, they are entitled to life.

'Parents of children have correlative duties to the rights of their children. Parents have a duty to nurture with love and care, to provide, as best they are able and with the help of the State, health and education for their children, and hopefully to give their children happiness. Most fundamentally of all, parents have a duty to protect their children.

'The criminal law is not coextensive with parental duty. The criminal law should not overreach itself. Much parental duty is at a higher level than the reach of the criminal law … The criminal law is concerned with the bedrock of society – safety. Where the criminal law and the duty of parents coalesce is at the base – the duty to protect children. If the law fails there, the law fails. If the law is inadequate there, the law is inadequate. The protective mantle of the criminal law applies especially to children.

'The protection of the law arrives too late for these three children. However, punishment of the offender is justified; and hopefully deterrence of others will flow from that punishment.'

Justice Cummins addressed the prisoner. 'Mr Farquharson, you have been found guilty by a jury of the murder of your three sons, Jai, aged 10 years, Tyler, aged seven years and Bailey, aged two years. As the learned Director [Prosecutor Rapke] has stated, you wiped out your entire family in one act. Only the two parents remained: you, because you had always intended to save yourself; and their mother, because you intended her to live a life of suffering.

'You had a burning resentment that you were financing your estranged wife's new life. She had the better house; the better car; the children all financially provided or supported by you; and now she had a new relationship.

'You said to a friend, Mr Gregory King, "Nobody does that to me and gets away with it."

'From that personal and financial genesis, you formed a dark contemplation.

'Three months before you took your children's lives on 4 September 2005, you spoke of your dark contemplation to Mr King outside a fish and chip shop in Winchelsea. You said that there would be an accident involving a dam where you survived and the children did not.'

Justice Cummins said that Mr King, a decent man, did not believe him, because such a dark contemplation is almost inconceivable to a decent person.

'But that year it came to pass. There was an accident involving a dam where you survived and the children did not, and for which your estranged wife will suffer for the rest of her life. On Father's Day.'

Justice Cummins then described the particulars of the incident on Sunday 4 September 2005 — as they were found to have happened 'beyond reasonable doubt' by the jury.

'In your 1989 Holden VN Commodore sedan you were driving your three children back to their mother's house in Winchelsea. Jai was in the front passenger seat, Tyler and Bailey in the rear, Bailey in a child's seat. All were restrained by seatbelts. Seven kilometres north of Winchelsea your vehicle traversed a railway overpass. The dam was on your right. As you approached the dam you steered the vehicle off the road at a steady speed, avoided the trunk of a tree near the water's edge, and drove the vehicle into the dam.'

The judge said the vehicle travelled 28 metres across the dam and sank seven metres to its floor.

'You extricated yourself from the vehicle, rose to the surface, swam to the shore and left your three children to drown. As you intended.

'When, hours later, a brave police diver found the children, Jai was partly out of the vehicle and the two younger children still in the rear. The seat belts which had been restraining the children as your vehicle drove along the Princes Highway all were unbuckled. Each child was dead.

'Although your vehicle had been driven along the Princes Highway with its headlights on, when found, its headlights had been turned off. Although as part of your coughing story you said to the police that you had turned on the heater in the vehicle, when found, its heater was off. The ignition also had been turned off.'

Justice Cummins said Farquharson's conduct beside the dam demonstrated his self-centredness. When two young men came across the scene, they offered to dive into the dark and still water to try and save the children.

'You said it was too late. They offered a mobile telephone for you to ring 000. You refused and asked to be driven to your estranged wife's house so that you could tell her what happened. When the distraught mother returned to the dam with you, you did not join any of the desperate attempts to find the children.

'The partner of your estranged wife, Mr Stephen Moules, a brave and good man, repeatedly dived into the dark waters to seek to find the children.

'You, their father, simply watched him, and when he emerged you asked him for some cigarettes for yourself. When you were being cared for in an ambulance at the scene, a police officer quietly asked a paramedic whether there was any chance of you being breathalysed. You overheard the conversation and stated in a loud voice that you had no problems with being breathalysed and were eager to do so. Although you were affected by the enormity of what you had done and by the extreme cold of the water of the dam, you were alert to your own interests.'

Justice Cummins said Farquharson showed a continuing alertness to his own interests. This was particularly revealed by his question to investigating officers at the Geelong Hospital shortly afterwards. He asked, 'What's the likely scenario for me?' He did not, the judge said, ask one question about the children.

'You said to persons at the scene, and later to investigating police, that while driving along the highway you had a coughing fit, blacked out and woke up in the dam.

'This was a false story; easy to say but demonstrably untrue.

'You did not give evidence at your trial, which is your right.'

Justice Cummins explained that his brief narrative was a necessary consequence of the jury's verdicts and of the evidence at trial proved beyond reasonable doubt.

He said he considered Gregory King was a truthful and accurate witness. He described him as a person himself in suffering because of the terrible knowledge that had been imparted to him by Robert Farquharson and which, very understandably, at the time he did not believe.

Justice Cummins said the sustained manipulation of Mr King by Farquharson, as revealed by the covert tape recordings, revealed the prisoner's self-interest.

'Of the medical witnesses called as to the medical unlikelihood of the occurrence of cough syncope, I was especially impressed with the evidence of Associate Professor Naughton of the Alfred Hospital. He was a witness of great insight and capacity.'

The judge also commended the police who attended the scene; the ambulance and service personnel; the Major Collision Investigation Unit, including Detective Sergeant Glen Urquhart; and the investigating police, including Detective Sergeant Gerard Clanchy, for their work under very difficult conditions.

'I also commend the good persons of Winchelsea and surrounding areas who selflessly sought to help on this terrible night.

'I pay tribute to the application and conscientiousness of the jury. The jury of citizens, randomly brought together to form the tribunal of fact, laboured long and hard. They are a credit to the community from which they come.'

Justice Cummins then got down to the business of the day.

'I take into account in sentencing you, Mr Farquharson, that you are now 38 years of age, that you have no prior convictions, that you have otherwise led a good life, that you had suffered over time from a moderate depressive illness for which you were receiving continuing medication but which illness at the time of the offence was improving, and all the other matters helpfully urged on your behalf by your counsel.

'I take into account the evidence of Mrs C F Ross, your eldest sister, called on the plea. Mrs Ross is a good person, as indeed all your family are.

'You had love for your children, but it was displaced by vindictiveness towards your estranged wife, which led you to these crimes.

'I do not find that you had a fixed intention over months to kill your children. But you contemplated it over months. And on the road back to Winchelsea on Father's Day you finally decided to fulfil your contemplation.

'These were not spontaneous crimes, or crimes occasioned by a temporary or momentary lapse of self-restraint or surge of emotion,' Justice Cummins said.

'It does not avail you that the three children died by one single act. It was your intention to kill them together, and by one act to kill them all.

'You have no remorse for these crimes, although you regret their consequences for you.'

The judge stated that in sentencing Robert Farquharson he took into account, as the primary factors, punishment of him for these crimes and the deterrence of others.

He said, 'You breached in the most profound way the trust which the law, and your children, placed in you as their father. The appropriate sentence on each count is life imprisonment.

'On each count of murder – of Jai, of Tyler, and of Bailey – I sentence you to life imprisonment.

'The question arises whether it is appropriate to set a minimum term of imprisonment whereafter you would be eligible to be granted parole.'

Justice Cummins said it was a most exceptional course not to set a minimum term – for the good reason that wherever possible the law should hold out hope to people. He said it was wrong in itself, and no service to the community, to crush people.

He said, however, that there were seven countervailing factors.

'First, you killed your own children, who put their trust in you and which trust you abused. Second, you killed three children.

'Third, you were in total control of the children. There was no other adult present who could help them. Fourth, they were totally dependent upon you for their safety. They were not in a position to help themselves.

'Fifth, these were crimes you had contemplated over significant time. They were not committed in a momentary lapse of self-restraint or surge of emotion.

'Sixth, your purpose was to inflict punishment upon their mother, your estranged wife.

'Seventh, it was a necessary part of your intention to kill all three children. This is not a case where one or more children were caught up in a fixed intention as to another. Your purpose was to ensure all three were killed, so that their mother was left with no consolation. And that is what you did.

'In all the circumstances, it is not appropriate to set a minimum term of imprisonment after which you would be eligible for parole. I do not set any minimum term.

'Mr Farquharson, for the murder of each of your three children you are sentenced to life imprisonment.'

This was three terms of life imprisonment – without parole. His lawyer stated the defence team's intention to appeal.

☠ ☠ ☠

On 17 December 2009, Farquharson's conviction was unanimously overturned by the three appeal judges. They were critical of the trial judge, the prosecution, and the evidence of key prosecution witness Greg King.

On 21 December, Farquharson was granted bail and released into the care of one of his sisters with a $200,000 surety.

He was back in court five months later; the retrial began on 4 May 2010 before Justice Lex Lasry QC. The jury retired to consider their verdict on 19 July, after hearing 11 weeks of evidence and argument.

On 22 July, after three days of deliberation, Robert Farquharson was again found guilty of murder. He was sentenced, on 15 October 2010, to life imprisonment with a 33-year minimum.

☠ ☠ ☠

Just as Greg King had thought his mate was bullshitting, and Cindy Gambino could not countenance her sons being murdered by their father, we might all ask how a man – a supposedly loving father – could do something so terrible.

The thing is, on that dreadful Father's Day in 2005, Robert Farquharson was taking those boys 'home' to a place that was no longer his; to a woman who was no longer his; to a man who now spent more time in the lives of his sons than he did.

In the moment that Farquharson crossed that overpass that night, those boys were not his; they were hers. They were Cindy's and they were the best way in the world to hurt her – forever.

The plan had been there a long time; the decision to carry it out may have happened in a flash. But once he made the decision, he made the turn, and once he made the turn, there was no turning back.

In that moment, the kids weren't kids anymore; they were the weapon against his wife, against his life, and against the world that had reduced him to that one vengeful and unforgivable act.

This man is serving a life sentence for the three lives he took. Because, at whatever moment he made the decision, Robert Farquharson drove into a dam one Father's Day and then swam away from his three young sons who were trapped inside that shit car as it sank in the freezing water.

Chapter Ten

THE BEST LAID PLANS

Scientists are commonly regarded as intrinsically methodical people. It's the nature of their profession that their working lives are consumed with systematic repetition and disciplined research. For some, this patient attention to detail carries over into their private lives. It certainly did for Robert Arthur Meade, a geologist with more than 30 years' experience in his chosen scientific field. It was, perhaps, a no-brainer that when he decided to murder his ex-wife and the mother of his three children, he would put a lot of thought into his modus operandi. So meticulous was he that he even rehearsed a 'dry run' of a trip from Adelaide to Melbourne three weeks before, so he could time his movements and create an alibi for the time she was attacked.

But unfortunately for him, he maybe over-thought things and the mobile phone technology that he counted on to provide his alibi actually contributed to his undoing. He did the one thing that scientists should never do – he assumed. He assumed that if he turned his mobile phone off for two hours, he couldn't possibly be traced to the address of his former Donvale home at the time his ex-wife was being bludgeoned by an intruder. It seems it didn't occur to him that turning his phone off at the specific time of the attack, when theoretically he shouldn't have known it was happening, was highly suspicious. But then, his behaviour in the few weeks leading up to 1 July 2011, and the few weeks afterwards, was also dubious when taken in context.

The 50-year-old, who had only just remarried, could not come to terms with the fact that his former wife, vivacious 48-year-old Sally Brooks, wanted to take their three children back to her homeland

165

of England to live. Although he had finally consented to signing the release forms for them to be removed from Australia, it was clear he had no intention of letting them go. But his plan to murder his ex-wife so that he would gain custody of the children backfired big time. He now won't get to see them grow up at all.

Despite his methodical planning, Robert Meade made too many mistakes to ever think he could get away with murder and, in trying to cover his tracks, he made himself look all the more guilty. And it evidently didn't occur to him that the fact that he and Sally were not on speaking terms, that he didn't want the children to leave the country and that he was evidently trying to shirk paying child support were red flags in the police investigation into her murder.

☠ ☠ ☠

Robert Meade and Sally Brooks met in Melbourne in 1985 when Sally was working for BP. She was well educated, having achieved tertiary qualifications in business at Bath University in England. Sally was on a backpacking adventure through various countries when she decided to stay a while in Melbourne. Meade, who was born in Melbourne, had graduated from RMIT as a geologist. Although Sally returned to England in 1986, the two stayed in touch and in the mid-1990s she returned to Australia and renewed a relationship with Meade. They lived together for a time in Balmain, New South Wales. They ultimately married, in her home city of Nottingham, in 1999, after which Meade returned to Australia, six months ahead of Sally. Over the next four years the couple had three children: Elizabeth, born in 2000, Archie, born in 2002 and Charlotte, born in 2004.

But all was not well in the Meade household in Limassol Court, Donvale. In May 2003, when Sally was just pregnant with Charlotte, the two separated and Meade moved into a flat in Ringwood, although he maintained contact with his family. In late 2003, he sought a reconciliation and the following year the couple got back together, with Meade returning to the family home around October of that year. But the reunion was to be short-lived as the marriage continued to struggle, especially when Meade tried to start a soft-toy business that put their finances in jeopardy and almost led to bankruptcy. At one stage, Sally returned to the United Kingdom for a while to earn some money. But despite seeking marriage counselling, the couple's relationship continued to deteriorate over the next few years and the arguments increased. Meade did not accompany Sally and the children when they spent Christmas 2008 in the UK. It was about this time that Meade began looking elsewhere for companionship.

He turned to an internet dating site and struck up a friendship with a Russian woman, Irina Arsenova. In January 2009, Meade told Sally that he was leaving her and, a month later, he flew to Russia to meet Irina. Divorce then became inevitable and by June 2009, Meade and Sally had agreed that Sally would retain possession of the Limassol Court home and custody of the children. The divorce was finalised later that year. After the divorce the relationship became even more strained, and it was in late 2010 that Sally first proposed to Meade that she might return to England to live with the children. Meade vehemently opposed this idea, maintaining that the children were Australian, not half-English.

At this stage, Meade was living in Sydney with Irina and her daughter, Valerie, who had immigrated to Australia. But in January 2011, Meade took up a contract as a senior geologist for a minerals exploration company, Uranium Equities Limited, in Adelaide and the three moved there after Meade and Irina were married in February 2011. The only problem was that he didn't tell Sally about his new job, presumably so he could avoid paying child support. Instead, he told her — communicating usually by email or text message - that he was unemployed and trying to initiate various business projects for a company he referred to as Blue Gum International. He did, however, still want access visits with his children and travelled on several occasions, roughly every third weekend, from Adelaide to Melbourne.

His arrangement with Sally was that she would drop the children at school on the Friday morning and leave a bag of clothes for them on the front veranda. He would collect the bag during the day before picking the children up from school and taking them to spend the weekend at his mother Joan's place in Vermont.

At about the time Meade and Irina were getting married, Sally started proceedings in the Family Court to enable her to relocate to the UK with the children. Despite his initial protestations, Meade finally consented to Sally taking the children to the UK in March

2011. But that was most probably when he started plotting. It was probably when he decided that if he couldn't have his children, she couldn't either. And so began an elaborate plot to drive from one state to another – while claiming to his employer that he was ill, but to others, including Sally, that he was on business – so that he could sneakily murder her while creating what he thought was a foolproof alibi.

He wanted to see the children on the weekend of 11 June 2011, but this didn't suit Sally and she expected him the following weekend instead. But for reasons that would only become clear later in court, Meade booked accommodation at the Molesworth Hotel, 117 kilometres north-east of Melbourne, for the nights of Wednesday and Thursday, 8 and 9 June. He didn't attend work in Adelaide on the eighth, but instead started driving to Melbourne. Mobile phone records later showed that he travelled through Kaniva (near the South Australia–Victorian border) at about 9.30 am that morning. His phone records showed that the following morning he was in Yea at 8.33 am, Yarck at 9.12 am and Molesworth by mid-afternoon.

That evening, he texted Sally saying he was in Jamieson (about an hour and a half's drive from Molesworth), trying to sell some interests in a mining tenement and that he would be back home in Adelaide on Saturday 11 June. He wanted more details about her plans to take the children to the UK. But his phone records told a different story. They showed that on 9 June he was, in fact, in Donvale before he headed south to Glen Waverley and Springvale. They also showed that he had returned home to Adelaide on the morning of 10 June. He had gone to work later that day.

It looked very much like this methodical man's unscheduled trip to Melbourne was a dry run for what was to come later. He didn't see Sally, nor his children, nor even his mother that day. Maybe he'd initially planned to carry out the murder that day but, for some reason, hadn't gone ahead with it. But despite his efforts to rehearse the murder – or at least the timing and establishment of an alibi for it – Robert Meade put his foot in it by forecasting the event to a work colleague. On 14 June, just four days after returning from his mystery trip to Melbourne, Meade sent an email to a work colleague, Charles Nesbitt, saying he wanted to talk to him. According to Mr Nesbitt, who later testified in court, Meade had spoken about his wife in acrimonious terms and said she was leaving the country to get away from 'the situation she was in'.

Meade told Mr Nesbitt some extraordinary things about his wife and family, such as that Sally was taking hard drugs and abusing alcohol and that his 11-year-old daughter had been raped earlier that year and that he was a suspect, but that he believed that Sally's boyfriend was the culprit. He also told Mr Nesbitt that his son had been tied to a chair and severely beaten.

None of this was true. Sally's twin sister, Alison, who later travelled from England to testify at Meade's trial, stated categorically that Sally did not even have a boyfriend.

Mr Nesbitt was concerned by Meade's stories and recalled that he had said he'd hired a private investigator to follow Sally. He later told police that Meade had allegedly remarked half-jokingly that 'a couple of .22s and a baseball bat' could solve the problem.

As it transpired, Sally Brooks was killed by blows to the head from a blunt object two weeks later. A coincidence? Not likely.

Meade had what was to have been his second-last access visit with his children on the weekend of 17 to 19 June 2011, again staying with them at his mother's home before returning them home. Sally emailed him on 25 June, telling him that he could have access to the children for the final time between 4 and 6 July, just before their scheduled departure to the UK on 8 July. When he replied to her email, she would have had no reason to expect him to arrive sooner. However, two days later, he went to work as usual at his Adelaide job but claimed during the day to be feeling unwell and so went home, ostensibly to recover. But at 2.17 pm he phoned the Molesworth Hotel and booked a room for 28, 29 and 30 June. So began a long trail of evidence that showed that not only was he not sick, but he was embarking on an unscheduled trip to Victoria that had nothing to do with access visits or employment duties. This was despite his later trying to tell police that he was in the Molesworth area engaged in mining exploration.

He was up bright and early on Tuesday 28 June, and by 8.27 am, when he sent his employer a text message saying he was too sick to go to work, he was, in fact, near the Victorian border on his way to Melbourne. After crossing the border, he stopped in Horsham and bought some items before proceeding to Seymour, where he was seen getting petrol at 2.28 pm. He then drove on to Molesworth and checked in at the hotel at about 3.18 pm, paying for his accommodation with a credit card. He spent the next two days apparently hanging around the Molesworth area and continuing to maintain to his employer that he was too ill to attend work. Evidence later presented in court showed that he bought fuel at Heathcote on the 29th and again in Mansfield on the 30th. Phone records showed that he had been in an area known as Cottons Pinch, near Yea, on both days. At 7.58 am on the 30th, he sent an email to a work colleague claiming that he was in bed at home coughing up blood, but two hours later he was buying petrol at the BP service station in Mansfield. CCTV footage, later collected by police, showed him filling up his vehicle and wearing a light-coloured checked jacket, dark work pants and dark slip-on work boots. At about 11.43 am he bought food at the Bonnie Doon roadhouse. He later exchanged text messages with his wife, Irina, when he was in the vicinity of Cottons Pinch.

Whether Meade was biding his time in the hills north of Melbourne for two days while he plucked up the courage to attack his ex-wife, whether he was there trying to create a plausible reason for being in Victoria at all, or whether he was merely in a confused state of indecision was never absolutely established. But the fact that he lied so elaborately to his employer when he should have known that his movements could be easily traced did not augur well for him in creating a solid alibi.

For some reason, however, and probably because 1 July would be his children's last day at school, he chose that day to set off for Donvale on a mission. He set his phone alarm for 4 am and was thought to have left Molesworth soon after that. He was evidently allowing plenty of time to get to Donvale, avoiding peak-hour traffic and maybe any other possible hold-ups, so that he could carry out his plan. Meade turned off his mobile phone at about 4.30 am and didn't turn it on again until about 11 am, by which time he was in the vicinity of Seymour; this was part of his undoing, as it was entirely uncharacteristic for him to turn it off at that time of day. It had been off when Irina tried to ring him at 8.51 am. The fact that it was off at this time turned out to be as incriminating as if it were on. Obviously, he knew that it would be traced to Donvale if it were on. He later told police, however, that he'd left it in the hotel room in Molesworth.

🐾 🐾 🐾

Not only was 1 July 2011 the last day of the school term in Victoria, but it was also Elizabeth, Archie and Charlotte Meade's last day at school in Australia. It was a big day for them, no doubt occupied with saying their farewells to all their schoolfriends before leaving the country a week later. They could never have anticipated that when their mother bundled them into the car at about 8.30 am to drop them off at the nearby Milgate Primary School for the last time, it would become a momentously dreadful day for them. After leaving the children at school, Sally Brooks drove to Doncaster East Car Repairs to drop off her vehicle for a roadworthy certificate. She told the garage's proprietor that she needed the car back by 2 pm so she could pick the children up from school at 2.30 pm.

She was seen just after 8.50 am walking towards her home. During the half-hour or so that Sally was gone, Meade had parked his car out of sight in a nearby bush reserve, climbed over the back fence and smashed a small window to get into a back lounge room of the house. He then waited in the laundry, correctly presuming that when Sally arrived home she would enter the house through the garage's access door. When she did arrive home, sometime shortly after 9 am, Meade attacked her and struck her on the head at least two, but possibly more, times with a blunt object. He no doubt thought that the mother of his children was dead when he left her, surrounded by blood, on the laundry floor. He also presumably thought that the crime scene would appear as though she had interrupted and been attacked by an unknown intruder.

Sally Brooks lay unconscious on the floor for about seven and a half hours. She didn't respond to the phone calls from the garage at 12.34 and 1.48 pm, letting her know that the car was ready. She didn't arrive to collect the children from school at 2.30 pm, nor did she answer the phone at 2.55 pm and several other times when the school rang to see where she was. The school finally contacted a neighbour, listed as Sally's emergency contact, who went to investigate. The neighbour found Sally lying among bloodied boot prints in the laundry.

Sally was rushed to hospital, unconscious and suffering skull fractures. Police established a crime scene and noted that the intruder who had smashed the window was probably wearing gloves and that muddy boot prints were found leading away from the point of entry towards the kitchen and also on the tiles in the laundry. They noted that there was no sign of sexual interference on Sally and no sign of burglary or ransacking of the house.

By the time Sally was found, Meade was close to crossing the border back into South Australia – no doubt confident that he couldn't possibly be connected to the murder. He arrived home at about 8.30 pm.

Sally remained in a coma for 10 days. Her mother, Audrey, and sister, Alison, arrived from the UK soon after hearing the news of the attack and kept vigil at her bedside at the Royal Melbourne Hospital. Their prayers for recovery, along with those of Sally's children, were fruitless. Sally never regained consciousness and on 11 July 2011 her family made the heart-rending decision to turn off her life support.

Alison told a press conference at the time that the loss of her twin was almost more than she could bear but, she said, 'It was nothing compared to seeing the faces of Sally's children when they were told by police that Sally had been deliberately hurt.' But worse still, she said, was 'when we saw the three children crying hysterically by Mummy's bedside trying to wake her up'.

☠ ☠ ☠

Meade thought he was being clever and careful on the day of the attack when he switched his phone back on at about 11 am. In a bid to deflect suspicion, he rang his mother at 11.33 am – the phone records showed that he was, at that time, at Trawool near Seymour – and then he sent a text message to Sally stating: 'Hi Sally, we'll be staying at Mum's next week, regards, Rob.'

He was back home in Adelaide by 8.45 pm that day, by which time Victorian police had notified South Australian police about the assault on Sally Brooks. Later that evening, the Victorian police contacted Meade by phone, told him about the assault on his former wife and asked him when he had last been in Melbourne. He replied that it had been two to three weeks earlier. He did not mention that he had returned from Victoria to South Australia just a few hours earlier. South Australian detectives then visited him that night. During that discussion, Meade put his foot in it. He told them that the last time he was in Donvale was on 9 June, at which time he had seen a 'for sale' sign at the front of his former home. Of course, police were quickly able to establish that there was no need for him to have been in Donvale that day – his scheduled access visit was supposed to be the following week.

When questioned further, he admitted that he had been in Victoria during the previous three days. He told the police that he had left Adelaide at 5 am on 28 June and had driven to St Arnaud for work. He maintained that he had been working in the Strathbogie Ranges, had stayed at the Molesworth Hotel and had left Victoria at about 10 am that morning. He then literally put his foot in it again. When one of the detectives noticed a well-worn pair of Redback work boots near the front door, Meade commented, 'I didn't take them to Melbourne.'

Victorian police had advised the detectives that bloodied footprints from large-sized workboots had been found in the Donvale house. When detectives executed a search warrant at Meade's home, they collected various receipts from his trip to Victoria, clothing that he said he'd taken with him, his mobile phone, his LandCruiser and the Redback work boots. It was already obvious the police doubted Meade's version of events.

Over the next two months, Meade continued to put his foot in it, with awkward efforts to cover his tracks and deflect suspicion from himself. First, on 6 July, he sent a voicemail message to Mr Nesbitt asking him to delete a potentially incriminating email that Nesbitt had sent him after their discussion on 14 June. What he didn't realise was that the police regarded him as a 'person of interest' in the murder of Sally Brooks, and they had bugged his house and were monitoring his phone calls and movements. Instead of lying low and keeping quiet, Meade instead enlisted his new wife's aid in trying to divert suspicion and embarked on a series of actions that merely implicated him further. Many conversations between the two were recorded during August and September 2011.

On 19 August, Meade was recorded saying to Irina that his children would be 'dead to him' if they were put into the care of Sally's sister and taken back to the UK. He told Irina that he had to prove that he wasn't in Melbourne between 8 and 11 am on the day of the attack. The fact that he was so specific about the time frame – when the police had reported the time of the attack as being between 9 am and 2 pm – was another red flag against him.

On another occasion Meade voiced his concern to Irina that he didn't have any receipts for purchases made on the morning of the attack, but dismissed her suggestions that the shop from which he'd made a purchase might have a record of it. He also mentioned that he would have been seen by a man driving a yellow ute in the Yea area that morning as he had to back up his vehicle to let the other driver cross a one-way bridge. Again he fobbed off Irina's suggestion to search for that 'yellow ute', saying it would be futile. On another occasion, Meade and Irina discussed the possibility of finding somebody who could vouch for him being in the Yea area at the time Sally was attacked. Significantly, he was recorded as saying that it would be good if he could find someone who would place him in the area of Cocker's Sluice at about 9.30 am that day. It was clear he was trying to create an alibi. He also expressed concern about the police's ability to track the location of mobile phones using phone towers and speculated about whether this could be done if the phone was switched off.

The recorded conversations indicated that Meade was even still trying to convince Irina that he wasn't involved with the murder. He told her that he'd left his mobile phone in the bar at the Molesworth Hotel that morning but that when he returned to the hotel it was in his room. On the same day as this was recorded, Meade also discussed a harebrained suggestion by Irina of sending a postcard to Alison Brooks in the UK and pretending it was from her sister's real killer.

Meade was also recorded telling Irina that he hadn't taken the Redback boots seized by the police with him to Victoria, but had worn another pair of shoes not seized by the police. His guilty conscience must have been playing heck with him for two and a half months. Perhaps realising he was the police's main suspect, since no other line of police investigation had turned up any other likely culprit, Meade set off on a bizarre excursion to Victoria on 12 and 13 September 2011, evidently designed to draw attention to himself and make himself appear familiar to locals in the Lake Eildon, Yea and Bonnie Doon area or, at least, as a regular visitor to the area.

During this visit he went to extraordinary lengths to try to create an alibi for the time of the attack on Sally. Without realising he was under covert police surveillance, he went into a takeaway food shop in Yea and struck up a conversation with a staff member, saying that he'd been in the Jamieson area gold prospecting recently and that, one Friday, he'd found three pieces of gold that he gave to his three nephews. He then gave the person a small quantity of gold, saying it was in thanks for the good service and good food. The piece of gold was later handed over to police investigators.

After this peculiar behaviour, the police were pretty sure they had their murderer. Robert Arthur Meade was arrested shortly afterwards and appeared the following day, Tuesday 14 September 2011, at the Melbourne Magistrates' Court charged with the murder of Sally Brooks. He was remanded in custody and was held at the Melbourne Remand Centre. On 24 January 2012, he appeared at the Victorian Supreme Court trying to seek bail. His counsel, barrister Daniel Gurvich, argued that Meade should be released on bail because of exceptional circumstances, which, he said, included Meade's lack of a criminal history, the impact of his imprisonment on his new wife and stepdaughter, his impressive employment record and the length of delay before his trial would begin. Mr Gurvich said that, if granted bail, Meade could live with his mother who had offered to put her house, valued at $575,000, forward as surety for Meade.

Mr Gurvich questioned the strength of the Crown's case against Meade, describing it as 'not overwhelming'. He said that there was no DNA evidence linking him to the crime scene, no blood found in his car and no murder weapon found, and he raised the possibility that somebody else was to blame. 'It looms large in my submission the reasonable possibility that the murder was committed by someone other than the applicant,' he told the court. However, prosecutor Ray Gibson stated there was a strong circumstantial case against Meade. He opposed bail, contending that Meade's counsel had not established that exceptional circumstances existed and that there was an unacceptable risk that he might interfere with witnesses or otherwise obstruct the course of justice if he were granted bail.

The *Bail Act 1997* does not define the expression 'exceptional circumstances' and according to the judge hearing the application, Justice Peter Almond, to be exceptional, the circumstances must be unusual or out of the ordinary. 'Exceptional circumstances may be constituted by a combination of factors which may include factors which relate to the strength of the Crown case or to the personal circumstances of the applicant or both,' Justice Almond told the court.

Mr Gibson told the court that evidence would show that the fact that Meade was upset that his children were about to move overseas was a significant motive for murdering their mother. That, and the fact that Sally was pressing him for child support and that he had lied to her about his financial situation, claiming that he had been unemployed for the previous six months, when he had in fact been working for Uranium Equities, made him more suspect.

The Crown would also raise Meade's behaviour after Sally's death as potential indicators of his guilt. Mr Gibson said the Crown would show that Meade persuaded others to destroy evidence and attempted to bribe witnesses. 'He has revealed his potential and the risk that if he is released on bail for the charge of murder, he is more than capable of carrying out these types of actions that he has been discussing,' Mr Gibson said.

In his decision to refuse bail to Meade, Justice Almond commented that although troubling, evidence of discussions about setting a false trail, bribing someone to provide false evidence and giving away a piece of gold did not provide 'cogent evidence' that Meade would commit any offence if bail were granted. He commented, however, that Meade's behaviour while under police surveillance after the murder formed a major part of the Crown's case against him.

Justice Almond noted that, on the issue of opportunity, the Crown had submitted that Meade had gone to elaborate lengths to orchestrate a trip to Victoria on the week of the murder, including telling his employer that he was unable to go to a work-funded trip to the Nabarlek Mine in the Northern Territory due to a private matter, feigning illness at work on the Monday and continuing to deceive his employer about his health throughout that week, stating on the Thursday that he was still sick in bed and coughing up blood.

'Further,' Justice Almond said, 'the Crown contends that having lived in the deceased's house, the applicant knew the layout of the premises and thus knew how to approach the property unseen using the bush reserve at the rear. The Crown also relies on the fact that 1 July 2011 was the last day of school for the children at the end of the second school term prior to their relocation to the United Kingdom, and that the applicant was aware of the deceased's habit of dropping off the children and picking them up and that she could be expected to be home between 9.00 am and midday.'

He said the Crown also relied on the fact that Meade switched off the GPS function on his mobile phone from 4:22 am on 1 July 2011 until he switched his mobile phone back on at 10.59 am.

Justice Almond told the court that, based on the material before him, he accepted that the Crown case against Meade was 'not overwhelming; however, in my view, it is not a weak Crown case'.

He said the only possible forensic link submitted by the Crown at that stage was the footprints left at the scene, which indicated that the perpetrator was wearing elastic-sided Redback work boots. 'The accused wore Redback work boots and a pair was found at his premises in South Australia. The Crown concedes that the sole pattern of the pair found at the applicant's house does not match the sole pattern in the deceased's house. In the listening device material, the applicant says that he left his work boots at home when he went to Victoria in the week leading up to Friday 1 July 2011. However, on the day before the deceased was attacked the applicant can be seen on CCTV footage taken in Mansfield in Victoria wearing elastic-sided work boots despite statements in the listening device material to the effect that he did not take his boots to Victoria and just had his runners or sneakers,' Justice Almond said.

In summing up his decision to refuse bail, Justice Almond said that having looked at each of the relevant factors, he was not satisfied that 'exceptional circumstances' existed. 'In my opinion, there are a number of unexceptional circumstances which in combination do not amount to exceptional circumstances,' he said.

Meade remained in custody through a committal mention in February 2012 and pre-trial hearings in August 2012, and finally went to trial before Justice Mark Weinberg in the Victorian Supreme Court in September–October 2013. He pleaded not guilty to murder.

Crown prosecutor Ray Elston SC told the court in his opening address that Meade had bashed his former wife in a premeditated attack intended to kill her, and that he had chosen the particular date of the attack because he knew it would be his last opportunity to find her at home alone before she took his children to England. He said Meade had planned his trip to Melbourne in advance with a dry run three weeks earlier.

'This trip from Adelaide to the Donvale area was in fact what we would suggest to you was a dry run, one carried out with the murder of the deceased in mind – a rehearsal,' Mr Elston told the jury.

But Meade's defence counsel, Peter Morrissey SC, raised the possibility that Sally could have been attacked by a burglar who fled the scene empty-handed. 'Whoever did this didn't finish her off, didn't stab her or strangle her,' Mr Morrissey said.

Sally's twin sister Alison was the first witness called to give evidence at the trial. Although they lived on opposite sides of the globe, it was clear the sisters were in regular contact and confided in each other. Alison told the court that she had been aware of strains in her sister's marriage long before her divorce and that Meade tended to be argumentative for no apparent reason and spent more and more time away from home. She said Sally began talking about returning to England with the children in 2010 but was scared of Meade's reaction. She said Meade had initially been upset at Sally's plan but eventually consented to Sally taking the children to Britain.

During the trial it became evident that Meade was an old hand at telling tall stories. Among those who gave evidence was a friend and fellow geologist, Bernard Michaelson, who testified that Meade had once claimed to be an international spy and used geology as a cover for his espionage work. Mr Michaelson told the court that Meade had once told him he'd rescued Chelsea Clinton (daughter of former US President Bill Clinton) from kidnappers.

Mr Morrissey asked Mr Michaelson, 'Did you think Robert had really saved Chelsea Clinton from a fate worse than death?'

'No,' Mr Michaelson replied, 'I didn't. I mean, the information came within a raft of other information, it didn't just come out of the blue like that.'

'As a general proposition he was telling ... what you took to be tall stories?'

'Very tall.'

Mr Morrissey asked Mr Michaelson whether he regarded some of the stories Meade had told him as 'just simply a load of bull, correct?'

'Absolutely. Well, no, it was just so ridiculous. I mean, he made out as if he was an international spy, or rescuer, or espionage person or something, being paid off by governments around the world. He said that geology was an excellent cover. Geology, working in central

Eurasia, Russia and so forth was … an excellent cover for this sort of work,' Mr Michaelson said.

The court heard that although the Redback boots police seized from Meade's home did not match the imprints left at the scene of the crime, since they were different sizes (one size 11 the other 12), and Meade claimed to have been wearing runners during his trip to Victoria during the time in question, Meade was seen wearing similar boots on the CCTV footage at Mansfield.

The court called on evidence from Mr Mark Cloris, who had overseen the manufacture of Redback work boots for many years, who said the boots Meade was seen wearing in the CCTV footage at Mansfield resembled Redbacks. The boots that made the footprints at the scene were never found and no explanation was proffered to the court as to what became of them.

☠ ☠ ☠

After a five-week trial and five days of deliberation, the jury found Robert Arthur Meade guilty of the murder of Sally Brooks on 10 October 2013. Alison Brooks, who was in court for the verdict, said afterwards that she and her family were relieved at the guilty verdict. She said Sally's children had lost the most precious person in the world. 'Our future will forever be tinged with great sadness because Sally is missing from our lives. She brought colour to our world – a world that is now grey without Sally in it.

'We will never understand the actions of this cowardly and pathetic man, nor will we forgive him. While we take some comfort knowing that he will be behind bars, nothing will ever ease the devastation and heartache he has caused.'

Alison now cares for the children in England.

☠ ☠ ☠

In his sentencing report, delivered on 11 December 2013, Justice Weinberg observed that during Meade's plea hearings, the defence had submitted that Meade should not be sentenced on the basis that his attack on Sally was premeditated and also that when he attacked Sally, he intended only to cause her really serious injury, but not to kill her.

Justice Weinberg said, however, that he was satisfied beyond reasonable doubt that the murder of Sally Brooks was a planned killing. He said to Meade: 'There was ample evidence from Mr Nesbitt to the effect that you had become very emotional about the prospect of your children relocating to the United Kingdom, and that you were resentful, bitter, and angry at your former wife's decision to take them out of this country. Your anger was palpable. It reached the point of pure hatred. Your reference to a .22 rifle and a baseball bat may have been half jocular, but it reflected a sinister cast of mind that was developing at the time.'

He said he could see no reasonable explanation for Meade's visit to the Donvale area on 9 June 2011, other than to scope out and plan his attack upon Sally. 'This was not an access visit, and you did not see the children. You did not drive hundreds of miles from Adelaide merely to savour the delights of Donvale. You went there purposefully and with a view to planning what you intended to carry out in the near future,' Justice Weinberg said. He said that various documents, including Google maps and notepaper police found in Meade's car when it was searched after the attack, strongly supported that conclusion. 'The only reasonable inference to be drawn from the notations contained in your handwriting is that you were setting out locations and times, as part of your plan to murder your former wife.'

In further reference to his finding of premeditation, Justice Weinberg referred to evidence that between 1 and 2 July 2011, during the hours of 4.22 am and 11.25 am, a consistent pattern had emerged whereby Meade either made or received multiple calls, or accessed data, on every one of those dates, with one exception. 'Tellingly, that exception was the morning of 1 July 2011. On that day, you neither made nor received any calls (save for the call from Irina at 8.51 am, which was unanswered), and did not access any data, between those hours. The prosecution invited the jury to conclude that you had taken yourself "off air" between those hours because you were well aware of the fact that, if you did not do so, you could be traced to Donvale at the time of the attack. This evidence was relied upon to support the prosecution case that you were the perpetrator of this offence, and also that it was planned,' Justice Weinberg said.

He described the defence's submission that Meade did not necessarily intend to kill Sally when he bashed her as 'entirely fanciful'. 'If she had survived, she would have implicated you, and you would have gone to jail for a very long time. Likewise, if she had survived, she would almost certainly still have relocated with the children to the United Kingdom. Each of those scenarios hardly accords with your strong desire to ensure that they remained in this country. There was only one explanation for your conduct on the day in question. That was that you intended to kill Sally, and thereby prevent the children from being taken from you.'

Justice Weinberg said that although he was satisfied that the attack on Sally was planned, he could not categorically say that the actual decision to go ahead with that plan was made more than a few days before it occurred. He conceded that the 'dry run', on 9 June 2011, may have been undertaken at a preliminary stage, before Meade had finally and irrevocably committed to the murder of his former wife. But he said it was the fact of premeditation, not its actual duration, that was a significant aggravating factor.

'The idea that this was simply a spontaneous explosion of anger on your part, when you confronted Sally out of the blue, in her home, is utterly implausible,' Justice Weinberg told Meade. He said that aside from being premeditated, the offence was further aggravated by the fact that Meade attacked Sally in her own home – 'a place in which she was entitled to feel safe'.

He said Meade's behaviour in the weeks after Sally's death was indicative of his guilty conscience. 'At one point, you discussed the possibility of finding someone to place you in the general Yea area, at the time that Sally was attacked. The plain implication was that you were considering how to create a false alibi for that morning.'

Of the events witnessed by covert surveillance officers just prior to Meade's arrest, when he was seen in Melbourne, Bonnie Doon, Lake Eildon and Yea, Justice Weinberg commented: 'You conducted yourself in an extraordinary manner, plainly designed to draw attention to yourself. You did so, as your counsel conceded, in a foolish attempt to make it seem as though you were a regular in the area, thereby supporting your claim to have been working in the Strathbogie Ranges at the time Sally was attacked. This too was said to be indicative of consciousness of guilt.'

He said that by pleading not guilty, contesting his trial and continuing to maintain his innocence, Meade had done little in terms of trying to mitigate his sentence. 'Accordingly,' Justice Weinberg stated, 'there is not a skerrick of remorse.'

In respect of Meade's mental state at the time of the murder, Justice Weinberg said that '… despite some aspects of your behaviour that seem to have been peculiar, including, in particular, the many lies and fantasies that you wove regarding, for example, having rescued Chelsea Clinton from "the clutches of some kidnappers", it is not suggested that your moral culpability was in any way reduced by reason of your mental state. Nor is it suggested that, by reason of any mental condition that you may have, you will find imprisonment any more burdensome than any other offender'.

Mr Morrissey had contended in court that while Meade may have been delusional at the time of the attack, he had no mental health issues that could have helped reduce the jail term he was about to receive.

The judge noted that Meade's counsel had submitted that any punishment imposed upon him must be viewed in light of the catastrophic effects of the verdict upon his own life. 'He submitted that you have lost everything; family, work, liberty, purpose and meaning. He further submitted that any sentence imposed upon you will have a "crushing quality", which he submitted should be tempered by fixing a lower than normal non-parole period,' Justice Weinberg said.

He also noted that the defence had submitted that Meade's offence did not exhibit some of the aggravating features that were present in other cases of murder. 'For example, there was no "torment" in the lead-up to the attack on Sally, and no attempt to conceal or defile her body. In addition, this case did not have about it any element of a breach of trust.' He said, however, that the absence of these sorts of factors did not of itself mitigate Meade's offence; it merely meant that it didn't fall within an even worse category of offending.

'At the same time,' Justice Weinberg said, 'it is impossible to overstate the gravity of what you did. You deliberately, with premeditation, and without a shadow of justification, took the life of your former wife, the mother of your children, and a woman who, by all accounts, was greatly loved and admired. Your conduct was brutal, callous, and cowardly.'

He said the victim impact statements from Sally's mother, sister and three children tendered to the court on the plea were 'profoundly moving'. 'They tell of ongoing suffering at the loss of their daughter, sister and mother. They speak eloquently of the tragic loss that all who knew Sally have suffered.'

Justice Weinberg said that, in Meade's favour, he considered it unlikely that he would ever offend again after he had served his sentence but he said general deterrence for 'a brutal and premeditated murder' such as this was still of primary importance. 'The fact that you may have been actuated by what you regarded as your love for your children, and your desire to prevent them from being taken from you, provides no excuse whatsoever for your actions.'

He said it was no easy task to sentence someone such as Meade, who he described as 'plainly an intelligent man, with obvious skills and abilities'. He said Meade could have had a happy and rewarding life. 'Instead, by your own selfishness, egotism and controlling nature, you have destroyed the lives of many of those around you.'

Justice Weinberg sentenced Robert Arthur Meade to 23 years' imprisonment with a non-parole period of 19 years and noted that he had already served 820 days of the sentence.

That should give him plenty of time to think about the lives he has destroyed. Aside from Sally herself, who will never get to see her children grow up, hopefully he is thinking about the three children who sat by her bedside and wept, wishing that she would wake up.

☠ ☠ ☠

In April 2017, the Victorian Supreme Court awarded Alison Brooks and Sally's three children a total of $800,000 in compensation. Alison, who works part time as a solicitor in Nottingham, had applied to the court for compensation to cover the costs of caring for the children and for each child's pain and suffering. Alison was awarded $574,208, while each of Sally's children received $75,624.

Meade did not challenge the claim.

Chapter Eleven

AN INCONCEIVABLE ACT

Daniel Valerio, Cody Hutchings, Jaidyn Leskie, Jai Farquharson, Darcey Freeman.

The names of these Australian children are known to many of us for all the wrong reasons.

We know them because a stepfather beat them to death, a mother took their lives, a father murdered them.

In every single case, the question the rest of us ask is: how could they?

What could possess an adult to be so selfish, so angry, so devoid of reason that they would use a child to make them feel tough, feel powerful, feel better about their place in the world?

What kind of mind justifies taking the life of a child, to make their own life easier or to score points against another adult?

What would possess a man – and, with notable exceptions, it is usually a man – to punish the mother of his child by taking that child, not to love and raise, but to kill and have done with it?

As the years pass, those of us not directly affected by such tragedies know that we recognise the names of these children for something big – and probably bad – but need some other clue, or a few words, to remind us why.

Daniel Valerio: the image of his battered body is all we need to recall that he did not survive the next beating by his mother's de facto.

Jaidyn Leskie: the words 'pig's blood', 'Moe' and 'Blue Rock Dam' remind us of the strange saga of a missing boy, an inevitable body, and a controversial and ultimately unresolved outcome.

Cody Hutchings: the words that go with this little boy now are Cody's Law – following the instigation under Victorian law of tougher benchmarks for sentencing people convicted of killing children.

Jai Farquharson: along with his brothers Tyler and Bailey – we need only the words 'Father's Day' to remind us that Robert Farquharson drove his sons into a dam and left them to drown, to keep them from his ex-wife.

While the fates of all of these children, and so many others, are equally unbearable to the families who lost them, the rest of us are simply appalled and saddened by the things that some people do to others.

The degree to which we are affected may even come down to proximity; how close to home the tragedy was. It is in our nature that, if we don't know the victim, their family or the perpetrator, while it is in the news, we take most notice of 'the case' if it's in our own community. We pay attention if it happened somewhere else in our own city; and we're interested, but possibly less so, if it was somewhere else in our own state.

But usually, the further away in time and place, the less we are affected, unless there is something else that marks it beyond being just another terrible tragedy.

For there are cases that transcend communities, cross state borders, even ignore international boundaries. And it's not just the modern 24-hour news cycle and social media that spreads a story like wildfire. With so much news available, an individual crime still needs that 'something else' to forever embed a name in our memories.

When the act itself is inconceivable.

When the murder has witnesses.

When one of those who saw was a sibling.

When some of the observers were otherwise uninvolved.

Then the city suddenly knows a name. The country knows what happened. The world is shocked.

Darcey Freeman is one such name.

We know Darcey's name because what her father did to her, he did in front of his two other children – and in public.

Arthur Freeman took the life of his own daughter in such a way that will haunt the bystanders to his crime for the rest of their lives.

It's this last point that made the tragedy personal to more than just

Darcey's own family. And, in a strange way, even made it 'personal' to many more than those incredulous eyewitnesses, because any one of us — anyone in Melbourne that day — could have been the accidental observer to Arthur Freeman's revenge.

Unable to do anything to stop him. Unable to do anything but watch.

☠ ☠ ☠

On a hot morning in January 2009, Arthur Freeman threw his four-year-old daughter Darcey off the West Gate Bridge.

This father of three discarded his only daughter from Melbourne's highest bridge as if she was a rag doll; a toy to be used in the custody fight with his ex-wife; a thing to be discarded to prove a point.

He did this horrible thing in peak-hour traffic, at 9.15 am on a Thursday, on the day that was to have been Darcey's first day of school.

He committed this act in view of dozens of people in cars that were cresting the bridge at that time.

His did this unimaginable thing while his other children, two young sons, were in the car from which he had just taken Darcey. His eldest child, six-year-old Benjamin, watched him do it.

☠ ☠ ☠

Arthur Freeman's reaction to new custody arrangements for his children was appalling. To say it shocked a city is an understatement. It shocked the nation.

Two years later, Freeman's lawyer and one psychiatrist tried to convince a jury he had been out of his mind at the time; that he was 'mad, not bad'. The Crown and three other psychiatrists tried to convince the jury that Arthur Freeman knew exactly what he was doing.

In both approaches, the facts of the matter were undeniable: Arthur Phillip Freeman killed his only daughter. This meant there were only two verdicts open to the jury in the case against him: that Freeman would be found guilty of murder, or not guilty of murder because of mental impairment. Either way, he would be locked up — in prison or a psychiatric hospital.

☠ ☠ ☠

Arthur Freeman was born in Geelong on 28 June 1973, and grew up there the second of four children. His parents Peter and Nora have since retired to a seaside town on Victoria's Great Ocean Road. His older brother and one sister followed in their father's footsteps and became teachers; his youngest sister is a horticulturalist.

Arthur Freeman's childhood was happy but unremarkable, although he did receive some counselling during primary school because of bullying.

He attended Newcomb High School with no problems, and then went on to study Aquatic Science at Deakin University. After a year, he switched to information technology and graduated with a Bachelor of Computer Science. He lived in various shared accommodation with other students while attending uni.

His first job that made use of his qualifications was in computer programming and data collection; he worked for several employers before eventually landing a job at Colonial First State. It was there Freeman met Peta Barnes. They were married on 31 December 1999.

Early the following year the couple moved to the United Kingdom, where they both got jobs and bought a flat in Maida Vale, in the north of London. Their three children, Benjamin, Darcey and Jack, were all born in England.

In June 2006, the family returned to Australia, because Freeman's wife wanted the children to be educated in one system. They rented a house in Hawthorn, Ms Barnes started work and Freeman remained at home looking after the children.

In March 2007, the marriage of Arthur Freeman and Peta Barnes, despite attempts at counselling, came to an end.

Although Freeman moved out of their rental house, they shared custody and he continued to look after the children during the day. He lived in Geelong for a while and then rented a flat in Hawthorn.

The following year Freeman decided he ultimately wanted to live in Britain so, in August 2008, he returned to the UK in what was an unsuccessful attempt to obtain a British passport. He became romantically involved with an English woman, Elizabeth Lam, and remained in England for several months before returning to Australia.

In the last week of January 2009, Arthur Freeman and Peta Barnes were attending the Family Court in Melbourne conducting a case about new custody arrangements for, and access to, the children following their divorce.

Nerves and tempers all over the city were frayed that month, as an exceptional heatwave was assaulting south-eastern Australia. The state of Victoria had recorded little or no rain for several months, and Melbourne was sweltering through its hottest summer in years. In fact, from 28 to 30 January, Melbourne broke records with three consecutive days above 43 degrees Celsius (109 degrees Fahrenheit).

The state was still just over a week away from what would become known as Black Saturday, when Melbourne reached a high of 46.4 degrees Celsius (115.5 degrees Fahrenheit), and extreme temperatures all over Victoria, along with the tinder-dry landscape and changeable winds of up to 120 kilometres per hour, ignited nearly 400 individual bushfires.

The firestorms on and around Saturday 7 February resulted in the deaths of 173 people – Australia's highest-ever loss of life from bushfire. The fires affected 78 towns, injured 414 people, destroyed more than 2000 homes, 3500 other structures and countless livestock and wildlife, and displaced 7500 people.

In the midst of all that disaster, destruction and loss of life, while the state and country suffered and worried, there was one other name still fresh in people's minds.

☠ ☠ ☠

On Wednesday 28 January, Arthur Freeman and Peta Barnes concluded their case at the Family Court and consent orders were put in place. The previous agreement for custody and access, of equally shared custody, was changed so that Freeman would have less time with his children. The new orders gave him three days' custody every second weekend, and on the afternoon and early evening of the Thursday in the other week.

Freeman had apparently regarded his experience leading up to the hearing as unpleasant. He believed he'd been unfairly treated by Dr Neoh, the court psychologist, who reported that his attitude to the matters to be considered at the Family Court were largely self-centred.

At the conclusion of the case, however, Freeman told friends that he was glad the proceedings were over, and he did not express any particular dissatisfaction with the result. He rang his mother and told her of the result and indicated he would shortly be returning to her home.

Darcey and her brothers, Benjamin and Jack, were technically in Freeman's custody at the time. They had been staying at the beach with his parents while the case was being heard in Melbourne.

With that done and dusted, Freeman was planning to stay that night with his kids and their grandparents, and then return Jack to his mother the following day after dropping Benjamin and Darcey at school. Thursday was to be Darcey's first day at St Joseph's Primary School in Hawthorn.

He drove the 90 minutes from Melbourne via Werribee and Geelong to his parents' home in Aireys Inlet. By the time he got there, around midnight, he was distressed and didn't want to talk about the events of the day.

He had already made several calls to friends to let them know how his day had turned out, telling them that the court was not very supportive of fathers involved in custody disputes.

Between 10 pm and 2 am he also made nine calls to his friend Elizabeth Lam in the UK, but kept getting her answering machine.

Freeman was still upset the following morning, but declined his father's offer to travel to Melbourne with him and the kids. He wouldn't put the journey off either, as Thursday was a big day for Darcey.

Freeman tried calling Ms Lam another seven times after 6 am, before she finally answered just after 8 am while he was en route to Melbourne. It was 10 pm in England.

According to Ms Lam, Freeman was crying and very upset about his reduction in custody access. He claimed that he had 'lost his children', that he felt helpless, and that there were a lot of angry women at the Family Court.

When she later gave evidence at his trial, about their long phone conversation that morning, Ms Lam said: 'He enjoyed being a father of shared care; he loved his children ... he felt they had been taken away from him but he would continue the fight through the court.

'I felt that, you know, he was having a good cry and that the reality of the situation would settle,' she said. 'It didn't even enter my head that he would harm anybody. Artie never said anything that set alarm bells off.'

While this call was going on, the trip from the coast to Hawthorn in peak-hour traffic was taking longer than the usual 90 minutes.

☠ ☠ ☠

No doubt Peta Barnes assumed Freeman's delay was just that – bad traffic on an already hot morning.

She and her mother, not wanting to miss Darcey's first day of school, were waiting at the school gates to see her go in for the first time.

At 8.45 am – having watched all the other children enter school after the morning bell rang – Ms Barnes rang Freeman to find out where they were.

Arthur Freeman said to his ex-wife: 'Say goodbye to your children. Just say goodbye.' Then he hung up.

Ms Barnes tried to ring him back, making several attempts before he answered.

'I managed to get through one more time,' she later told the court, 'and I said to him: "It's me." I think he said, "Who is it?" And I said, "It's me."'

Freeman responded: 'You'll never see your children again.'

Peta Barnes immediately called 000.

☠ ☠ ☠

The West Gate Bridge is a steel box girder cable bridge that spans the Yarra River just north of its mouth into Port Phillip Bay. The bridge is a vital link between the inner city and Melbourne's western suburbs, and with the city of Geelong, 80 kilometres to the south-west.

The main river span is 336 metres in length; the bridge carries five lanes of motor vehicle traffic in each direction of its total 2582.6-metre length; and its maximum height above the water is 58 metres.

Long before Arthur Freeman made his last trip over the West Gate in 2009, the bridge already had a history of deaths attached to it.

Two years into construction of the bridge, at 11.50 am on 15 October 1970, the 112-metre span between piers 10 and 11 collapsed and fell 50 metres to the ground and water below. Thirty-five construction workers were killed. Many of those who perished were on lunch break beneath the structure in workers' huts, which were crushed by the falling span. Others were working on and inside the girder when it fell.

The 2000-tonne mass dropped into the Yarra River mud with an explosion of gas, dust and mangled metal that shook buildings hundreds of metres away, and spattered nearby houses with flying mud. The roar of the impact, the explosion, and the fire that followed, could be clearly heard more than 20 kilometres away.

As is the case with high bridges the world over, another unwanted statistic is the West Gate's suicide record. Until mid-2009, police data showed around one suicide from the structure every three weeks. A 2004 coroner's report recommended anti-suicide barriers be erected on the bridge to deter people from taking their lives. In 2008, the bodies of a mother in her late twenties and her 18-month-old baby were found on the riverbank below the bridge, prompting further calls to erect a barrier.

Those who argued for a suicide barrier claimed that most of those who jumped from the bridge did so on impulse, and that police officers who tried to save those threatening to jump also put their lives at risk. A 2000 Royal Melbourne Hospital study of bridge jumpers found at least 62 cases between 1991 and 1998. Seven people survived the 58-metre fall. Seventy-four per cent of those who jumped from the bridge were male, with an average age of 33. More than 70 per cent were suffering from mental illness. Of those who jumped off the West Gate Bridge, 31 per cent fell on land. Some of those who landed in water drowned afterwards.

☠ ☠ ☠

Whatever possessed Arthur Freeman to do what he did on the West Gate that day has yet to be explained.

He wasn't able to say how he was feeling in those moments, until just over six months later when he talked to Dr Lester Walton. Dr Watson's report (dated 28 September 2009) said:

> *Mr Freeman ... recalls being very worried that he was running late for school for the children, and once he was travelling on the West Gate Freeway, he had a feeling of being trapped. He can recall thinking*

'We're never going to make it' and it seemed like an enormous failure to him that he would not deliver the children on time. He remembers the traffic on the bridge travelling quite slowly and 'It felt like we were not moving at all'. There was a rising sense of anxiety and hopelessness.

But instead of riding out the traffic, or making the most of the time left with his children – who were all in the back seat of the four-wheel drive, two-year-old Jack in a car seat between his brother and sister – Arthur Freeman made an altogether different decision.

He pulled his Toyota LandCruiser over into the left-hand emergency lane, at the highest point of the bridge, parked and put on his hazard lights.

He told Darcey to unbuckle her seat belt and climb over into the front seat.

He reached across from the driver's side, pulled Darcey from the car and led her over to the parapet of the bridge. He then lifted her up and threw her over the edge.

Four-year-old Darcey Freeman fell more than 58 metres, or 17 storeys, to the water below.

Her apparently emotionless father returned to his car and drove away as if nothing had happened.

One eyewitness, Barry Nelson, later told the court the child looked like a rag doll as her father threw her from the bridge. 'I basically saw the child tipped over the side of the bridge,' he said.

Nelson said he called out to Freeman, asking what he was doing, but Freeman had a vacant expression and walked casually to his car and rejoined the traffic.

'He had a completely neutral face as if he was just going about his business every day. He appeared like nothing was wrong. That was the overriding impression.'

☗ ☗ ☗

Melbourne's Water Police, responding immediately to frantic calls from motorists to 000, took 10 minutes to find and pull the little girl from the water. Unbelievably, she was still alive.

Paramedics treated Darcey at the riverside and worked for fifty minutes to keep her alive as she was rushed by police helicopter to the Royal Children's Hospital.

A massive police hunt swung into operation. With so many calls to 000, they already knew the rego of the white Toyota LandCruiser, had a vague description of the man, and also knew there were possibly other children in the car. Their immediate fear was they might encounter a second crime scene if they didn't locate the offender quickly.

Detective Inspector Steve Clark told reporters at the scene, 'A male in that vehicle has taken a young girl, we believe to be four years of age, and dropped her over the side of the bridge and she's landed in the water here at the bottom.

'You think you've seen it all – but obviously you haven't. It's particularly distressing obiously for family members, but for witnesses who saw what occurred, a number of those people are upset, and I've got a number of police here who have young children themselves.'

It took police 90 minutes to find and arrest Arthur Freeman – not that he was hiding, or trying to evade capture.

Freeman had driven straight to the Commonwealth Law Courts Building, on the corner of William and Latrobe streets in the heart of Melbourne. He parked his car lawfully next to the kerb in Latrobe Street, and walked into the court building. It was the same place where his custody case had been heard over the previous two days.

When he entered the building, Freeman was carrying Jack, and leading Ben by the hand. He tried to hand Jack to one of the security officials, saying: 'Take my son,' but the official declined to take the young boy.

CCTV footage of Freeman and his sons from the point shortly after their arrival showed Freeman was distressed and crying, but generally non-responsive both to his children and to court officials.

Ben and Jack were holding their father's hands and clinging on to his legs, but Freeman refused to acknowledge them and just stood staring out a window.

A child psychologist, Ilana Katz, described Freeman as catatonic. 'There were tears rolling down his cheeks, there was liquid running from his nose and mouth. He made no attempt to alter that situation.' She added he was unresponsive to everyone who approached.

As no-one at the court had any idea why he was in such a state – although being the Family Court, they routinely experienced all manner of extreme behaviour – Ms Katz arranged for a crisis assessment team to attend.

Ms Christine Bendall, a court counsellor, also took some effort to comfort and console Freeman. When she eventually got his attention, she said, 'It will be all right.'

Freeman replied, 'No,' and sobbed loudly.

When police officers arrived to deal with him, Freeman apparently said: 'Take me away.'

It was about then – with the discovery of the white LandCruiser in the street, with Peta Barnes' call to 000, with a distressed man in the Family Court foyer – that all the pieces fell into place.

The orders came through to arrest Arthur Freeman for the murder of his daughter. He was taken to the Homicide Squad headquarters.

☠ ☠ ☠

Defence lawyer David Brustman later used that CCT footage as evidence of Arthur Freeman's unbalanced state that day. The only psychiatrist who appeared on his behalf contended that Freeman was mentally impaired at the time of the offence. Professor Graham Burrows testified that in his opinion, Freeman was suffering from severe depression and, as a result of that, he fell into a state of dissociation so that his acts were not conscious, voluntary, deliberate or intentional. That is, he was acting somewhat like an automaton.

Burrows expressed that opinion based on the history given by Freeman on examination, on his father's description of events on the night of 28 January and the morning of 29 January, and the description of how he appeared to some of the witnesses on the West Gate Bridge.

Psychiatrists who testified for the Crown held markedly different opinions. Doctors Skinner and Bell were of the opinion that Freeman was suffering only mild to moderate depression, and if there was any dissociation, it was not such as to have removed his capacity to act consciously, voluntarily and deliberately or intentionally.

Even the doctor who declared Freeman unfit to be interviewed on the afternoon of his arrest – saying he was 'extremely concerned' about the man's mental state as he appeared to be in 'acute, psychic distress' and was 'falling apart' – admitted that Freeman's symptoms could simply have been caused by the shock of having thrown his child off the bridge.

☠ ☠ ☠

Peta Barnes rushed with her mother to the hospital when they learned of the horrifying thing that had been done to her daughter. Paramedics and doctors had tried their best to save Darcey but the massive internal injuries she had sustained were just too severe.

Peta stayed with her daughter after giving her permission to turn off the life support. Darcey Iris Freeman, four years old, died on the afternoon of 29 January.

☠ ☠ ☠

The trial of Arthur Freeman conducted in the Supreme Court of Victoria before Justice Paul Coghlan lasted 19 days. It began on 2 March 2011 – just over two years after Darcey's murder.

At the sentencing on 11 April, Justice Coghlan stated that the trial had been conducted on the basis that, although Freeman did not remember what he had done, he accepted that he was the person responsible for Darcey's death.

But was Mr Freeman mad, or was he bad? That was the question that defence lawyer David Brustman asked the jury to consider in his opening address to the court.

Brustman contended that Freeman had unintentionally, unconsciously and involuntarily thrown his daughter off the bridge, arguing the accused was mentally impaired at the time, rendering him incapable of reasoning in a rational manner.

Freeman's actions, he said, were the result of a 'highly disordered mind, a mind suffering mental illness, a mind which, because of these phenomena, had a number of consequences'.

Chief Crown Prosecutor Gavin Silbert SC disagreed. He told the jury that Arthur Freeman's motive was simple: spousal revenge.

Silbert described a man so angry at his ex-wife after the acrimonious break-up of their seven-year marriage that he resorted to murdering a little girl who loved and trusted him unconditionally.

Evidence was given by psychiatrists, paramedics, police, witnesses from the West Gate Bridge, Freeman's English friend Elizabeth Lam, forensic pathologist Dr Matthew Lynch, Darcey's mother Peta, and – by way of a video-recorded police interview – Darcey's older brother, six-year-old Benjamin.

Professor Graham Burrows, a psychiatrist of 40 years' experience and the sole defence witness, testified that Freeman was suffering from a 'major depressive disorder' at the time of the crime; that he was psychotic, out of touch with reality and in a 'dissociative state'.

Burrows explained that a person in such a state could still do things but have no memory of what they had done – as if they were sleepwalking or had been hypnotised.

Burrows was the only psychiatrist of the six who had assessed Freeman to diagnose severe depression, and to conclude that he did not know that what he was doing was wrong.

The psychiatrists appearing for the prosecution agreed that Freeman was likely suffering from a depressive illness, but not that he was mentally impaired. None were of the opinion that Freeman was suffering from a psychotic illness when he killed his daughter.

Dr Douglas Bell said Freeman's level of depression was of a moderate severity.

'There is minimal evidence of more pervasive and severe depressive cognitions such as thoughts of hopelessness, futility, self-recrimination and despair or other neurovegetative symptoms of severe depression such as loss of libido, anorexia and diurnal mood variation,' he said.

'The observations of Mr Freeman's friends and family of him in the hours following the handing down of the Family Court judgement on 28 January suggest that he was in a heightened state of distress and agitation, expressing an inconsolable feeling that he had lost his children.'

Dr Bell testified, 'All of the observations of witnesses regarding his behaviour on the morning of Darcey Freeman's death suggest that he knew the nature and quality of his conduct.

'Mr Freeman continued to demonstrate that he was able to think purposefully about his situation and to continue to make reasoned judgements about both his own behaviour and the behaviour of others.

'Unfortunately, we do not know what Mr Freeman was thinking at the time he threw his daughter over the rail of the West Gate Bridge. Nevertheless, there is minimal evidence to support a conclusion that at the time of engaging in conduct constituting the offence, Mr Freeman was suffering from a mental illness that had the effect that he did not know that his conduct was wrong, that is that he could not reason with a moderate degree of sense and composure about whether the conduct as perceived by reasonable people was wrong.'

Dr Bell maintained that everything Arthur Freeman did that day, including organising his children into the car, and speaking to several people on the phone while driving 120 kilometres, suggested he was aware of what was going on around him.

The observations of his behaviour by other motorists on the bridge support that. 'Mr Freeman parks his car in the far left emergency lane and puts his hazard lights on,' Dr Bell said.

'He opens the door of his car, reaches in and pulls Darcey from the seat. He holds her firmly and walks her to the side of the bridge, then lifts her above the high side rail and throws her over.

'He then returns to his car, starts it and drives off into the traffic,' he said.

'This is a complex and protracted sequence of goal-directed behaviours that are not compatible with a state of mind in which the behaviour is not conscious or voluntary.'

Dr Yvonne Skinner, also appearing for the prosecution, said: 'I think he was suffering from – well, he was quite distressed and I think suffering from some anxiety and mild to moderate depression.'

She disagreed with Professor Burrows' diagnosis of severe depression and told the court Freeman's actions that day were 'well organised and purposeful' and consistent with 'spousal revenge'.

In the time between arrest and trial, Freeman's appearance had deteriorated from tidy and clean-shaven to unkempt with scraggly long hair and a thick beard. While the defence referenced Freeman's dishevelled appearance as a symptom of his ongoing poor mental state, the prosecution noted his 'presentation' as 'Rasputin-like'.

Throughout the trial Freeman remained emotionless, giving little away by way of reaction – at least in front of the jury. On occasion he wiped away tears after they had left the court.

He did react tearfully during the testimony of Dr Matthew Lynch, the forensic pathologist, who gave details of the damage Darcey had sustained. Dr Lynch described the chest, lung and brain injuries – the 'result of a fall from a great height'.

Freeman was stony-faced again during the testimony of Peta, who had to correct the defence counsel about her marital status.

She indicated the man in the dock and said, 'He is not my husband.'

☠ ☠ ☠

While Peta's stoic but grief-ridden testimony, the evidence of the rescuers' desperate attempts to save Darcey, and the forensic pathologist's clinical description of her fatal injuries were hard for all to hear, there was, perhaps, no account of that day more chilling than that given by Benjamin Freeman.

The video of the police interview recorded with Darcey's six-year-old brother was played to the jury.

Ben explained to a policewoman how he and Darcey were sitting in the back of their father's car, with their little brother in the car seat between them drinking milk from his 'bot-bot'.

Ben described how he was tapping his knees like a drummer while Darcey was pulling faces and making shapes with her hands.

'We were driving along the road and when we got on to the bridge we stopped. And then my dad went out with Darce and then he threw her over the bridge.'

Benjamin explained how his father had told Darcey to climb into the front seat, how he got out, lifted her up and then 'boing – over the bridge.' Then he got back in the car, put on his seatbelt and 'zoomed off'.

'I said, Go back and get her. And Dad keeps driving along. Then I said, Darcey can't swim … and then Dad would just keep on driving, didn't go back to get her. I kept saying it over and over again and he never did.'

Arthur Freeman did pull over again, however, when Benjamin asked if he could sit in the front seat.

☠ ☠ ☠

It took the jury of seven women and five men five days to find Arthur Phillip Freeman guilty of murdering his four-year-old daughter Darcey.

Earlier on their last day of deliberation, Justice Coghlan had given the jury final directions, after allowing seven jurors to asks questions. He told them that, to find Freeman not guilty, they needed to accept that on the balance of probabilities he did not know the 'nature and quality' of his conduct, or know it was wrong when he threw his daughter to her death.

Justice Coghlan also told them they should not 'reason backwards' that Freeman must have been mentally impaired, because no sane person would do what he did.

It was 8 pm on 28 March 2011 when Freeman stood impassively as the verdict was delivered. Peta Barnes also showed no emotion. Both left the court afterwards without a word.

After the verdict, Justice Coghlan excused the jurors from having to serve on another jury for 10 years, at which point four women jurors burst into tears.

☠ ☠ ☠

On 11 April 2011 Arthur Freeman again faced Justice Coghlan in the Supreme Court for sentencing.

The judge began by saying: 'Arthur Phillip Freeman, after a trial lasting 19 days, you were convicted of the murder of your daughter, Darcey, on Thursday 29 January 2009.'

After detailing the basics of the case, Justice Coghlan told Freeman, 'The jury rejected your defence of mental impairment, and once that defence was rejected, it was inevitable that you be convicted of murder. This case was conducted on the basis that the only two verdicts open were guilty of murder or not guilty of murder because of mental impairment. You receive some credit for limiting the way in which the case was conducted.'

The judge explained that there were two major considerations to be addressed in the sentencing exercise. 'The first is whether the appropriate head sentence is life imprisonment. The second is whether, if I impose a sentence of life imprisonment, I should fix a non-parole period and, if so, what non-parole period.

'In deciding whether or not a sentence of life imprisonment should be imposed, I am obliged to have regard to a number of matters. It has long been accepted in this state that a wide range of cases might lead to a sentence of life imprisonment. In some cases, there will be factors personal to a particular accused which might make the imposition of a life sentence inappropriate.

'It was urged on me by Mr D Brustman SC, who appeared with Mr G Georgiou on your behalf, that I should not impose a sentence of life imprisonment. It is fair to say, however, that he pressed his argument as to the fixing of a non-parole period somewhat more forcefully,' he said.

'I now come to look at the matters of aggravation in this case.

'This was the killing of an innocent child.

'The circumstances of the killing were horrible. The throwing of your four-year-old daughter from a bridge more than 50 metres above the ground could not be more horrible. What Darcey's last thoughts might have been does not bear thinking about, and her death must have been a painful and protracted one.

'Your conduct is a most fundamental breach of trust and it is an attack on the institution of the family which is so dear to the community.

'The killing was in the presence of your son, Benjamin, who was then six, and your son, Jack, who was two. The community hopes Jack will be too young to remember.

'Any motive which existed for the killing had nothing to do with the innocent victim. It can only be concluded that you used your daughter in an attempt to hurt your former wife as profoundly as possible.

'You chose a place for the commission of your crime which was remarkably public, and which would have the most dramatic impact.

'It follows that you brought the broader community into this case in a way that has been rarely, if ever, seen before. It offends our collective conscience.

'The threats to your wife on the telephone were in the presence of your children, who were in a position to have heard them.'

Justice Coghlan told Freeman that he had received a number of victim impact statements from family members and witnesses, many of which were read out in court.

'All of the material,' he said, 'in particular that from Darcey's mother, Peta Barnes, and the members of her family, was particularly moving. The fact that in this case the devastation caused to them is an obvious result of your conduct, it is not in any sense diminished by the stating of it. They will live forever with the consequences of what you have done and their lives can never be the same.

'I regard it as important to repeat some of what was said by Peta Barnes. She told us that she has been diagnosed as suffering from post-traumatic stress and that came as no surprise to me or would be any surprise to those who have to deal with matters of this kind.'

Justice Coghlan then read two portions of Peta's victim impact statement.

> Where to start is a challenge as this statement brings to the surface all of the raw emotions I live with daily. Since the loss of Darcey I grieve on a daily basis and realistically do not see how that can ever change. The saying 'time heals all wounds' is not true for myself and I don't ever expect it to be. Not a day goes by where I do not constantly think of Darcey, where I don't miss her and wish with all my heart that she was with me.
>
> I can feel her little hand holding mine when I walk down the street or drive in the car. I lie in bed at night and hold her in my arms. I talk to her and think of her daily wishing she was participating in the activities that were happening at that time. No words could ever truly describe the loss of a child to a parent. The emptiness that sits within you, the piece of you that no longer exists, the fact you no longer go on in life as a complete person.
>
> Seeing little girls who have similar traits or looks to Darcey heightens my already active emotions. Holding myself back from giving the child a hug is always a struggle of self-control.
>
> Not a day goes by where I don't flashback to the emotions I felt when I was told by my ex-husband that I would never see my children again. The panic and fear these words set off inside me resonates within me even today. I feel them now in incidents of my daily life that would not have impacted me prior to Darcey's passing. I notice that I have heightened anxiety in everyday situations and have to manage myself carefully to control this.

The judge read on:

> The events of the day of Darcey's passing are all horrific in their nature. To articulate the impact of this day and the ensuing future it has brought can not truly be expressed in a Victim Impact Statement. No-one can erase the thoughts and associated feelings I have of sitting in the hospital and having to tell the hospital staff that they were allowed to turn the life support machine off. Of holding Darcey in my arms as she

passed away and knowing that this decision would take her from me
again and knowing that there was no other option available to me.

Describing the impact on others involved, Justice Coghlan said emergency services, witnesses and the community as a whole had been affected by Darcey's death, by having the events 'forced upon them'.

He told Freeman, 'In this case, the victim impact material from eyewitnesses demonstrates the way in which those who have had these events forced upon them are affected by your conduct, and in a sense both those witnesses and the emergency services personnel who made statements represent not just themselves, but the community as a whole in expressing their reaction to these events.'

Justice Coghlan told Freeman, 'Mr Brustman [his lawyer] accepted on your behalf that I should give "full and appropriate consideration" to the victim impact statements.

'As I have already indicated, it was submitted that I should not impose a sentence of life imprisonment.

'Mr Brustman concentrated his submission on the imposition of a non-parole period. A large part of his submission was based on how I should apply the principles set out in R v Verdins. Those principles are:

"Impaired mental functioning, whether temporary or permanent ('the condition'), is relevant to sentencing in at least the following six ways:

1. The condition may reduce the moral culpability of the offending conduct, as distinct from the offender's legal responsibility. Where that is so, the condition affects the punishment that is just in all the circumstances; and denunciation is less likely to be a relevant sentencing objective.
2. The condition may have a bearing on the kind of sentence that is imposed and the conditions in which it should be served.
3. Whether general deterrence should be moderated or eliminated as a sentencing consideration depends upon the nature and severity of the symptoms exhibited by the offender, and the effect of the condition on the mental capacity of the offender, whether at the time of the offending or at the date of sentence or both.

4. Whether specific deterrence should be moderated or eliminated as a sentencing consideration likewise depends upon the nature and severity of the symptoms of the condition as exhibited by the offender, and the effect of the condition on the mental capacity of the offender, whether at the time of the offending or at the date of the sentence or both.

5. The existence of the condition at the date of sentencing (or its foreseeable occurrence) may mean that a given sentence will weigh more heavily on the offender than it would on a person in normal health.

6. Where there is a serious risk of imprisonment having a significant adverse effect on the offender's mental health, this will be a factor tending to mitigate punishment.'

Justice Coghlan elaborated:

'Impaired mental functioning at the time of the offending may reduce the offender's moral culpability if it had the effect of:

(a) impairing the offender's ability to exercise appropriate judgement

(b) impairing the offender's ability to make calm and rational choices, or to think clearly

(c) making the offender disinhibited

(d) impairing the offender's ability to appreciate the wrongfulness of the conduct

(e) obscuring the intent to commit the offence, or

(f) contributing (causally) to the commission of the offence.

'As we have said, this is not to be taken as an exhaustive list.'

Justice Coghlan then referenced the reports and testimony given by the psychiatrists during the trial.

'Dr Walton and Professor Mullen ... described you as suffering from a depressive illness, but neither concluded that you were mentally impaired. None of the psychiatrists were of the opinion that you were suffering from a psychotic illness at the time you killed your daughter Darcey.

'Given the relative lack of seriousness of your condition and the grave seriousness of the offending, I have given weight to your condition, but not significant weight as it relates to moral culpability, denunciation and general deterrence,' he said.

'It was urged on me that there was little place for specific deterrence in this case because the circumstances seen here will be incapable of replication in the future. I do not agree with that submission. Given the length of any sentence to be served in this case, specific deterrence is not a matter to which much attention need be paid.'

The judge noted that much emphasis had been placed upon Freeman's relatively young age.

'Your condition appears to have deteriorated, and I have given weight to the extent, as expressed by Dr Walton, that your sentence will weigh more heavily upon you than it would on a person in normal health. That proposition runs in parallel with the proposition that in any event your sentence will be more difficult for you because of the nature of your offending.

'It was accepted that the very public nature of the offending was a consideration to which I should have regard.'

Justice Coghlan stated, 'I accept that your offending was not premeditated, but related to your increasing anger towards your former wife over the Family Court proceedings, exacerbated by your being late for Darcey's first day at school. It should be noted that Professor Burrows did not doubt that you were angry at the time you killed your daughter. I have no doubt that the resentment you bore your wife had been building up for some time.

'It was submitted to me that I should regard your conduct at the court, when seen by Dr DuPlessis and your father, as demonstrating remorse. I accept that it does demonstrate that by that time, you appreciated the enormity of what you had done and there was some aspect of regret.

'I am not satisfied that it does show remorse. Your behaviour through the whole of this period of your life was self-centred, with a strong tendency to blame others. You are yet to say sorry to anyone for what you have done.'

Justice Coghlan said there was an illuminating passage in Dr Walton's most recent report:

> *Mr Freeman indicated that he had a strong desire to be able to meet with his surviving children and explain to them all the circumstances surrounding the death of their sister. However, when I asked him to*

provide me with such an explanation nothing emerged other than peripheral issues.

Justice Coghlan told Freeman, 'I have come to the conclusion that the passage shows that your attitude to this matter is still self-centred. I am satisfied that you continue to lack any insight into your offending and I regard your prospects of rehabilitation as bleak.'

He explained, 'Mr G Silbert SC, Chief Crown Prosecutor, who with Ms D Piekusis, Crown Prosecutor, appeared for the Crown, submitted that I should impose a life sentence on you and that I should decline to fix a non-parole period.

'In his brief but pointed submissions [Silbert] said that this case could be characterised as one of intentionally killing a child without psychiatric illness and such conduct would ordinarily lead to a sentence of life imprisonment.

'He submitted that this case was motivated solely by spousal revenge, was in the worst category of murder and that it was the seriousness of the offending which would also justify not fixing a non-parole period. I have taken those submissions into account.

Justice Coghlan then imposed a life sentence on Arthur Freeman.

'I am obliged to have regard to just punishment, denunciation, general and specific deterrence. I am satisfied there are no particular circumstances in mitigation, to which I refer later on, which would lead me to conclude, having regard to the matters set out above, that I should do anything other than impose a head sentence of life imprisonment and I will impose that sentence upon you.

'That leads me to consider whether or not I should impose a non-parole period. I understand that many will say that your crime is so serious in so many respects that I should not impose a non-parole period; i.e., you deserve to be locked away forever.

'I see the attractiveness of that argument, but the sentencing process is not as simple as that.'

Justice Coghlan explained that he questioned whether or not a non-parole period should be fixed is governed by Section 11 of the *Sentencing Act 1991*.

'A court is obliged to fix a non-parole period "unless it considers that the nature of the offence or past history of the offender makes the fixing of such a period inappropriate".

'I have dealt with the seriousness of the offending. There is nothing in your past history which would make the fixing of a non-parole period inappropriate. It has been decided in this state that however the words of the section are to be interpreted, your age is a relevant consideration in deciding whether to impose life imprisonment and whether or not to fix a non-parole period.

'I am obliged to have regard to the fact that you are 37 years of age. Whatever happens, you will spend what may be regarded by many as the best years of your life in prison.

'I have come to the conclusion that it is appropriate to fix a non-parole period. I do not regard you as being beyond redemption. You are only 37 years of age … I have taken into account your previous good behaviour … and the references tended on your behalf and the support which you have from your direct family.'

The judge said that while Freeman's mental illness was not significant to the seriousness of his crime – which is why he fixed a sentence of life imprisonment – he did take the illness into account in deciding both whether he should fix a non-parole period and in deciding what that non-parole period would be.

'One of the very unfortunate features of this case is that others seem to blame themselves for what you have done. They should not.

'You did what you did, you are responsible for it and nobody else is,' he said.

Justice Coghlan continued, 'You will be sentenced to be imprisoned for life. I fix a period of 32 years before you will be eligible for parole. I declare that you have served 802 days pursuant to this sentence. I direct that this declaration and its details be entered in the records of the Court.

'It means that the earliest date you will qualify to be released will be 29 January 2041, when you will be 67 years of age.'

After the sentence was delivered, Arthur Freeman, who had remained silent through most of his trial and during the sentencing, announced he wished to make a statement.

He backed into a corner of the dock to avoid guards and launched into a bizarre rant in which he accused an in-law of being implicated in the theft of diamonds from a Western Australian mine, talked of Federal Police phone taps, and he claimed he had death threats. He had to be pulled from the courtroom by three guards.

🕱 🕱 🕱

On 27 July 2011, Arthur Freeman sought leave to appeal against the severity of his sentence.

The first ground of appeal was that the minimum term of 32 years was manifestly excessive. In support of this contention, there were three further grounds contending that inadequate weight was given to various matters, including his psychological illness.

Justice Maxwell – who refused the application – said, 'It is a basic principle of sentencing law that there is no single correct sentence in a particular case. On the contrary, there is a "sentencing range" within which views can reasonably differ as to the appropriate sentence.

'A sentence will only be "manifestly excessive" if it falls outside that range; that is, if it was not reasonably open to the sentencing judge to impose that sentence.'

The judge explained that the 'leave to appeal is only granted where one or more of the proposed grounds of appeal is shown to be capable of reasonable argument. In the present case, I do not regard it as reasonably arguable that the non-parole period of 32 years was outside the sentencing range open to the sentencing judge in the circumstances of this case'.

Justice Maxwell said the sentencing judge's findings about the seriousness of this offence were very clear, and were not challenged on Freeman's application. He said Justice Coghlan had identified matters of aggravation that made the offending more, rather than less, serious.

Justice Maxwell also noted that Justice Coghlan also found that Freeman's anger was the operative emotion.

Justice Maxwell said the applicant's submission referred to two then-recent cases that were said to indicate 'appropriate sentences'. Both cases were cited by defence counsel on the plea and the judge referred to them in his reasons.

'The first is R v Fitchett. In that case, a mother killed her two children. She was sentenced to 17 years on each of two counts of murder. With cumulation of 10 years, the total effective sentence was 27 years. A non-parole period of 18 years was fixed.'

Justice Maxwell said Fitchett was a very different case from Freeman's.

'First, the judge in Fitchett accepted that there was a causal link between Mrs Fitchett's depression and the offending. In the present case, as I have said, no such submission was made and the evidence did not support any such finding. Secondly, Mrs Fitchett was found to be "profoundly" remorseful. No such finding was made in the present case.

'Thirdly, and most significantly, the judge was sentencing Mrs Fitchett following a retrial. Her Honour recognised that she was constrained by the sentence which had been imposed at the time of Mrs Fitchett's original conviction. As Her Honour pointed out, it is well established that the sentence imposed following the first trial should ordinarily be regarded as the upper limit of the sentence to be imposed following the second trial.

'The sentence first imposed on Mrs Fitchett in July 2008 was substantially reduced because of the serious mental illness from which she was suffering at the time of sentence,' Justice Maxwell said. 'Although the judge on that occasion did not regard her moral culpability as significantly reduced by her mental condition at the time of the killings, by the time of the sentencing she was severely depressed and at a high risk of suicide.

'Such was the state of Mrs Fitchett's mental illness that the judge was satisfied that he should make a hospital security order.'

Justice Maxwell said the second case relied on in Freeman's application was R v Farquharson.

'In that case, a father drowned his three children by driving the family car into a dam. He was sentenced to life imprisonment on each of the three counts of murder, and a minimum term of 33 years was imposed.

'It is unnecessary to explore the similarities and differences between that case and this. As this Court has made clear, the relevance of comparable cases lies in the ascertainment of the available sentencing range in a particular case. It is sufficient to say that there is nothing about the sentence imposed in Farquharson which suggests that the sentence here in issue was outside the range open to the judge.'

Justice Maxwell added that the conclusion that Freeman's present sentence was within range was reinforced by a recent sentence imposed on a father who murdered his infant daughter. On 1 July

2011, a judge of the Supreme Court sentenced Ramazan Acar to life imprisonment with a non-parole period of 33 years.

'In that case as in this, the offender was found to have been motivated by animosity towards the mother of the child.'

☠ ☠ ☠

On 9 November 2011, Arthur Freeman again tried to appeal his sentence on pretty much the same grounds. On that occasion, judges CJ Warren, JA Nettle and AJA Beach considered and denied the request.

Again Freeman's complaint was that the non-parole period of 32 years was excessive when compared to the non-parole period of 18 years set in R v Fitchett and the non-parole period of 33 years set in R v Farquharson.

The judges said, 'In our view, there is no substance in the argument. Fitchett was sentenced to 27 years' imprisonment with a non-parole period of 18 years after being tried and convicted a second time for the murder of her two infant sons. After she was tried and convicted the first time, she was sentenced to a hospital security order of 27 years' duration with a non-parole period of 17 years (on the basis of uncontested expert evidence that, at the time of sentencing, she was suffering from severe mental illness which made it appropriate that she be sentenced in that fashion).

'Later, the first conviction was quashed on appeal when it was held by three judges of this court that the trial judge had not sufficiently directed the jury as to what would be the consequences of them finding Fitchett to be not guilty by reason of mental impairment. By the time Fitchett was tried and convicted the second time, her mental condition had significantly improved and, other things being equal, would have warranted a greater sentence than had first been imposed.

'But the sentencing judge was in effect bound by the principle of double jeopardy to treat the sentence first imposed as setting the outer limit. It follows that Fitchett is in no way a relevant comparator for present purposes.'

The three judges agreed that Farquharson was a more relevant comparator.

'He was sentenced to life imprisonment with a non-parole period of 33 years for the murder of his three infant sons, by driving them into a dam. He too was found to have been motivated by the wish to harm his former wife by killing their children.

'Granted, Farquharson killed three children and the applicant murdered but one. But the setting of a non-parole period is not a linear function of the number of deaths inflicted. It is a process which requires a sentencing judge to make an order that is of a severity appropriate in all the circumstance of the offence,' they said.

'Given that the crimes committed by Farquharson and the applicant were both of the worst possible kind and the similarities between the circumstances of each offender, it is to be expected that the non-parole periods set in each case would be similar.'

☠ ☠ ☠

One positive and practical thing came about because of what happened to Darcey Freeman.

In the month after her death, in February 2009, the first stage of a temporary suicide barrier was erected on the West Gate Bridge. It was constructed of concrete crash barriers topped with a welded mesh fence.

By June that year it was claimed the fence had prevented two suicides. The permanent barriers, which cost $20 million, now run the full span of the bridge and have reduced the suicide rate by 85 per cent.

The barriers naturally also prevent any repetition of what Arthur Freeman did to his daughter that hot morning in 2009. Not to mention what he put his son through.

Ben Freeman's last impression of his little sister was: 'She didn't even scream on her fall. I didn't hear her scream on the way … no, nothing, nothing.'

Chapter Twelve

THE LOVE PENTANGLE

With a frying pan as her only line of defence, Carolyn Matthews tried desperately to fend off the two strangers threatening her with a knife in the kitchen of her Adelaide home.

Why do this man and woman want to kill me? she must have been thinking.

Carolyn heard the fury in the woman's voice as she goaded the man, who appeared to be having second thoughts. 'Be a man, kill her – show me that you love me,' the woman screamed at him.

And where on earth are my husband and sons when I really need them?

Where? Conveniently out hiring videos. Her husband, Kevin, was gone only 20 minutes; creating a prearranged window of opportunity, and a credible alibi, for his lover and her hired accomplice to get into the Matthews' West Lakes home and stab Carolyn to death.

What appeared to police, at first glance, to be a burglary gone wrong turned out to be something more like a plotline from *The Sopranos*. It was, in fact, a truly bizarre love triangle – no, correction, a love quadrangle – no, try again; a love pentangle.

☙ ☙ ☙

Just after 5 pm on 12 July 2001, Kevin Matthews was about ready to leave Port Adelaide's Beaurepaires tyre service, where he worked as sales manager. Before taking off, he rang home and told his sons that he'd pick them up shortly to take them to the local shopping centre to hire some videos for the evening.

When he pulled up outside his modest brick-veneer house in

Nambucca Avenue, his three sons, aged 16, 13 and 12, were already waiting out the front. When they returned 20 minutes later, the boys entered the house first and found their mother lying unconscious in a pool of blood on the kitchen floor. Blood was spattered down the cream-coloured cupboard doors and tread marks could be seen in the blood on the floor. A frying pan was on the floor near her body.

Matthews called an ambulance and tried to revive her, but she was dead by the time the ambulance arrived.

A local police patrol arrived quickly and cordoned off the crime scene. Shortly afterwards, detectives from Port Adelaide CIB arrived. Their first assumption was that Carolyn Matthews was the victim of a home invasion or burglary gone wrong. But it didn't take long for them to ponder a different and more sinister scenario; that Carolyn had been murdered by someone within – or known to – the family.

By 10 pm, three detectives from South Australia's Major Crime Investigation Branch had also arrived to survey the scene. They found that Carolyn had been stabbed seven times in the chest and once in the back and that it appeared she had tried to fend off the attack with a frying pan.

While detectives remained to process the scene, during which time they discovered a kitchen knife under a bush outside, Kevin Matthews and his sons were taken to Port Adelaide Local Service Area (LSA) headquarters for questioning. Kevin apparently demonstrated an appropriate amount of shock and horror about what had happened and claimed to know nothing about it.

Doorknocks of the neighbourhood by detectives failed to glean any useful information, but four days after the murder, detectives received information through Bank SA Crime Stoppers that steered them towards a possible motive – *the other woman*. Crime Stoppers had been tipped off that Kevin Matthews was having an affair with a woman named Michelle Burgess. This information set the detectives to focus on what had happened earlier on the day of Carolyn's brutal murder.

They visited Kevin's Beaurepaires outlet and spoke to several of his colleagues. But a crucial clue came when they then spoke to the manager of a car service business across the road, who told them he had seen Kevin speaking to a woman fitting the description of Michelle Burgess, and another man, on the afternoon of the murder.

The man was later identified as David Key, who, as it happened, was also having an affair with Michelle.

Police began monitoring all three and were able to verify the affair between Kevin and Michelle. Kevin Matthews therefore became regarded as a 'person of interest' but he continued to deny involvement in the murder or with Michelle. But they were having trouble locating David Key. That was, until he literally put his foot in it. While driving to visit Michelle to discuss the attention being focused on them, David got picked up by an LSA patrol from Elizabeth for outstanding traffic offences. While at the local police station, he rang Michelle, and in so doing alerted the investigating detectives to his whereabouts.

Now, with access to David Key, the detectives found a pair of his boots. Not only did the tread pattern match the ones on the Matthews' kitchen floor, but a DNA test matched blood on the boots to Carolyn's blood. And, although they didn't realise its significance at the time, they also found a handwritten note with a photo of Michelle's husband Darren, also a Beaurepaires manager, and details of his work address, in David's wallet.

Three weeks after Carolyn's death, on 2 August 2001, David Key was charged with her murder. But the detectives already knew he was only the first on their list. They knew he was the hitman hired by Michelle Burgess to kill Carolyn Matthews.

What they didn't know at first was that she and David had agreed on a $50,000 contract to kill not only Carolyn Matthews, but her own husband, Darren, as well. The upshot of this was that she and Kevin Matthews could continue their affair *and* get their hands on Carolyn's $100,000 life insurance policy.

Michelle and David became acquainted only a month or so before the murder, but in that short time they had begun a physical relationship right under Kevin's nose.

Fortunately for Darren, who was the fifth element of this greedy, self-serving pact between Michelle and Kevin, David never got to fulfill the second part of his contract.

With David's arrest, the detectives moved quickly to implicate Kevin, but again he denied involvement. They did, however, have enough evidence to charge Michelle Burgess with murder and their case against her and David was strengthened by his sister's admission that she had passed a 'contract' from Michelle to David. Her description of this 'note' matched the one found earlier in Key's wallet.

But if Kevin ever thought he'd got away with it, he mustn't have counted on Michelle and David blabbing. While in custody, the pair told other prisoners about Kevin's involvement in his wife's murder and pretty soon the word got back to police.

It was obvious that while Michelle and Kevin appeared to have been carrying on ordinary family life with their respective spouses and children, it was all a facade. The evidence of his affair with Burgess (and therefore a motive) was piling up against Kevin Matthews, and on 7 September 2001, he became the third person charged with his wife's murder. He still protested his innocence.

But the prosecution's case became easier when David decided to fess up and directly implicate both Michelle and Kevin.

David Edgar Key, 28, appeared before the South Australian Supreme Court in 2003 and pleaded guilty to the murder. He told the court that Michelle Burgess had, indeed, contracted him to kill her estranged husband, Darren, and Carolyn Matthews. He said he was to be paid $50,000 – $25,000 for each murder – and that his payment would come from the proceeds of the $100,000 life insurance policy Kevin Matthews had taken out in his wife's name.

He told the court that on the afternoon of the murder, he and Michelle had visited Kevin's workplace and Michelle had insisted the job had 'to be done tonight'. He said he and Michelle then drove to the Matthews' house at the prearranged time, knowing Carolyn would be there alone. When Carolyn answered the door, David showed her the contract note to confirm her identity and then Michelle punched her in the face before the two then dragged her into the kitchen. He said he then began stabbing Carolyn at Michelle's insistence. Carolyn had struck him with a frying pan in a vain attempt to fend him off, the court heard. He said Michelle had laughed as they hurriedly left the scene. He said he and Michelle then drove to the beach at Grange, where Michelle rang Kevin from a public phone box and left a five-second voicemail message saying 'the job' had been done.

Because of his guilty plea and the evidence he provided, David Key received a reduced sentence of 20 years. The sentence was handed down on 11 August 2003.

🕱 🕱 🕱

Thirty-year-old mother of two, Michelle Burgess, and her 43-year-old lover, Kevin Matthews, were tried together before Justice Margaret Nyland in the South Australian Supreme Court shortly after Key's sentencing.

Justice Nyland described the murder as 'premeditated, heartless and brutal' and said the plot was born out of lust and greed.

Both pleaded not guilty to the murder of Carolyn Wendy Matthews and continued to deny their affair. But the court heard they were carrying on trysts at several city hotels and had made more than 3000 mobile phone calls and text messages to each other between October 2000 and 12 July 2001.

The court heard that at the time of the murder, Burgess was also having a relationship with a third man, other than Matthews and Key. Matthews' defence lawyer described Burgess in court as a 'black widow'.

Compelling forensic evidence, David Key's testimony and further witness statements were enough to convince the 11-member jury of their guilt. Both were sentenced to life imprisonment in October 2003, and at a further hearing on 2 April 2004, both were given non-parole periods of 30 years.

Prior to that, in February 2004 when Justice Nyland conducted a hearing to consider victim impact statements, Kevin's then 16-year-old son Kenneth said he could never forgive his father for having his mother killed.

In a statement read to the court, Kenneth told his father he had thrown his life away for a 'stupid woman'.

'You had a great life ... and a family that loved you. You threw all that away for one stupid woman.

'You will never be forgiven for this. How could anyone forgive you?'

🕱 🕱 🕱

Burgess and Matthews appealed their sentences on several grounds, including that they should have been tried separately. But their appeal before three justices in South Australia's Court of Criminal Appeal failed on 29 July 2005.

☠ ☠ ☠

Michelle Burgess was evidently a master at using sex to manipulate men. Even in jail, she continued to use her sexual guiles in return for favours. A news report on ABC South Australia in December 2003 revealed that male guards at Adelaide Women's Prison were said to be reluctant to be left alone with Burgess. During the then short time of her incarceration, one guard had already left his job after forming a relationship with her.

Chapter Thirteen

THAT SHOULD MAKE HIM DIE

This case had all the hallmarks of fantastic fiction. We even charged five people with murder, without a body.

Detective Inspector Peter Wheeler, Victoria Police, 2009

Karen Randall had man troubles. An on-again off-again relationship with one of the local guys was currently off. She and Paul had lived together for a while until he started getting rough with her; well, roughed her up, actually. He'd given her a couple of black eyes and a few other bruises. She'd had him charged with assault back in April. He'd copped to it, though, and pleaded guilty in the Moe Magistrates Court. She broke up with him after the assault, and then again a month or so later.

Well, you know, small country town – nearly everybody knows everybody or knows someone who does, and there are not that many guys to go around, so you go with what you know until someone better comes along.

Moe's total population was only around 15,000, which meant way fewer than 5000 who were anywhere near her own age; less than half were men and most of them were already taken. Karen and Paul had known each other for about six years but had only been together for a couple. By most accounts Paul was a nice guy, except that some of the drugs he did made him aggressive – mostly with Karen.

But again – small town, mutual friends, same parties. You can't keep out of each other's way for long, so you learn to ignore or put up with what you can't change. And this is also bogan territory; outsiders joke that Moe is an acronym for Moccasins on Everyone.

Still and all, Paul was getting more than annoying lately. Before Karen and her young son moved to the even smaller nearby town of Mirboo North, Paul kept turning up at her place in Moe banging on the door and windows, begging her to get back with him.

Stupid dope freak. What did she have to do?

No, seriously. What *do* you do with an ex-boyfriend who won't take the hint and leave you the hell alone?

You could get your sister and girlfriends to provide backup while you embarrass him in public and tell him once and for all to take a hike. You could enlist some guys you know to rough him up a bit to make him back off. Or you could take the advice of a friend, one you haven't known all that long, and then just go along with her outrageous and despicable scheme.

Simple as that.

One Sunday in 1989, a group of friends got together in Mirboo North to commit murder. Their crime was premeditated, brutal and callous. And much like the murder itself, the motive – such as it was – was an absurd overreaction.

☠ ☠ ☠

The 134-kilometre Grand Ridge Road, unusually true to its name, traverses the ridge of the beautiful Strzelecki Ranges. It winds its way between the Latrobe Valley and South Gippsland, through beautiful scenery that changes from the rolling pastures of rich farmland to fern forests, towering mountain ash and forestry plantations. It's part two-lane rural highway and part unmade rutted road, travelled mostly by farmers, tourists and a lot of logging trucks.

Mirboo North, the only major town on the route, lies halfway along the Grand Ridge Road. It's around 40 kilometres from Moe, the next big town.

The main industries in the region, in fact for much of Gippsland, are farming – mostly dairy, but also cattle, sheep, vegetables and forestry. Back then, the other main employers were open-cut brown coal mining; the huge paper mill at Maryvale; and the massive Hazelwood, Yallourn and Loy Yang power stations, which use the local brown coal to provide 90 per cent of the electricity for the state of Victoria.

Mirboo North is a hardworking farming community proud of its history and charm, and it was totally unprepared to play host to one of the most bizarre murder cases in Victoria.

☠ ☠ ☠

In late 1989, 26-year-old Karen Randall and her younger sister Donna were both in the midst of moving or settling into new homes. Donna was about to have a housewarming for her new place in Moe, while Karen and her six-year-old son had been sharing a farmhouse with a friend Rhona in Mirboo North, while she waited to move into her new housing commission home.

Karen and Rhona Heaney had only known each other since August, when they'd started the same office skills course at the TAFE college in Traralgon, 50 kilometres away. Both single mothers, they had a few other things in common and quickly became friends, even though Karen dropped out of the course after a month. As this was also during the latest break-up with her boyfriend Paul, Karen was grateful for the opportunity to move in with Rhona and her two kids, and get out of Moe.

Rhona had a sometime live-in boyfriend called Steve and through them Karen met their mutual friends the Maslins, Irene and Jano, who also lived in Mirboo North. The burgeoning friendship between the three women – which by default sometimes included Steve, Jano Maslin and Karen's 22-year-old sister Donna – centred around mutual child-minding, parties, barbecues, motorbikes, drinking and smoking dope.

The Maslins did a bit of dealing; they apparently had a marijuana crop growing in one of the state forests – out Shady Creek way, north of Moe – and sometimes went to stay in another house they had in Geelong, about three hours away, to score or sell.

By the end of October 1989 Karen was waiting on word of her new commission home, partying with her new friends, and still trying to avoid the ex-boyfriend.

The ex, Paul Snabel, was sharing a house with his mate Paul Friend in Moe. Apart from his obsession with Karen Randall, the 28-year-old also had a fondness for the booze and was a bit of a speed freak. That's speed as in the amphetamine, although he did drive a Holden and ride a Yamaha RZ250.

According to Paul Snabel's housemate, the Karen–Paul relationship was stormy. He said Karen would tell Paul to piss off, and then she'd want him back again.

As far as the housemate was concerned, Paul should dump Karen because she wasn't worth the effort.

As far as Karen was concerned, Paul was getting really irritating.

As far as Karen's friends were concerned, Paul Snabel was dangerous.

Rhona and Irene had seen at least one of Karen's black eyes, courtesy of Paul after Karen had accused him of cheating on her, and Rhona had witnessed arguments between the ex-couple on her veranda at Mirboo North after Karen had moved in with her. Irene and Rhona were angry about Paul's behaviour towards Karen, and worried that he might really hurt her.

But it was the beginning of his end when, at the start of November, Paul did two things that were beyond the pale for Karen's friends. He allegedly followed Karen's son home from school; and he visited her new house – the one she hadn't moved into yet, of which she didn't think he knew the address – and slipped a postcard under the door. It said: 'You make me see red'.

That was too much for Irene Maslin. She was already convinced Paul was crazy, dangerous and quite likely to kill Karen, and now reckoned he might hurt her son too. Being worried on behalf of a young single mum was understandable given Irene had kids of her own, and it probably made Karen feel supported knowing her new friend was pissed off on her behalf – but this was where the overreaction to the 'Paul situation' began to get out of control.

Apparently, being on Irene Maslin's bad side was a pretty scary prospect. She was a big woman; loud, threatening and aggressive. She was a 'with her or against her' kind of personality. In fact, more than one Mirboo North resident described her as scary.

'People were frightened of her,' one of the locals said after the fact. 'She could chill you to the bone just by looking at you. Irene Maslin was a real Charles Manson.'

There were other rumours about Irene Maslin: that she 'knew people', you know, who fix things; that she knew hitmen who could deal with shit that needed dealing with. They were probably just that – rumours; but she *was* a drug dealer, so you don't mess with rumours like that.

Not even if you believe she's your friend.

So Karen, who thought she was at her wits' end, consulted that friend. Sometime around 2 November she got together with her sister Donna, Rhona and Irene. One version of the ever-changing story that came out afterwards also placed Irene's husband Jano at this 'planning meeting'.

Irene took the lead; took control. She said something had to be done about Paul Snabel. They all joked about breaking his legs so he'd get the message. Irene then got more serious and talked about 'disposing of Paul'. She and Rhona came up with the idea of injecting Paul with speed laced with something like battery acid. All they had to do was lure Paul to the isolated farmhouse that Rhona and Karen shared on Nicholls Road.

They decided to put the plan into action the following weekend. Donna's housewarming party in Moe was scheduled for the Saturday night and Paul was expected to attend. It would be Karen's job to ring and invite him out to her place, and Donna would encourage him to go out there later, with her. Rhona would get the syringes, and she and Irene would take care of the lethal shot.

They figured it wouldn't take much to talk Paul into going anywhere that Karen was. Stupid bastard – he wouldn't have any idea what he was really in for.

No-one, at any time, said, 'Hang on a sec, this is wrong; we can't do this.' They all agreed it was really the only way to deal with the problem. And everyone would have a part to play.

☠ ☠ ☠

On Saturday 4 November, Donna Randall's party in Moe went off as planned. Karen had decided not to go; or rather, the conspirators deemed it sensible, because Paul would be there. It wouldn't do for her to be seen anywhere he was – especially that night.

Donna laid the groundwork early in the evening by suggesting to Paul that he go with her out to Karen's at Mirboo North after her party wound up. To seal the deal, Karen rang her sister's house during the evening and invited Paul to come along later with Donna. She implied he might have another chance with her.

Meanwhile, out at the Nicholls Road farmhouse in Mirboo North, Rhona, Karen, Irene and Jano – and all their kids – had their own party that night. The adults smoked bongs, and Rhona injected Karen and Irene with speed.

Some time so late on Saturday night that it was really Sunday morning, Paul and Donna left Moe and headed for Rhona's place in Paul's car. Despite being quite drunk, Paul was at the wheel. When they got to the Nicholls Road residence, they found Rhona, Karen and Irene sitting around the kitchen table having a cuppa. Jano had already left the house, taking Karen's son and his own kids home to his place.

Paul had been partying hard all night and maybe didn't even realise how mixed the messages were around that table. There he was, invited into Karen's house, although she wasn't exactly coming on to him; but everyone was talking to him and being nice, and he was even playing with Rhona's kids. He got bored after a while, though, and said he wanted to go get his motorbike.

Paul drove his Holden home to Moe. Rhona went with him, to ensure he came back. They returned about 11 am and then some of the group went for a ride to Leongatha – Rhona and Paul on his red Yamaha, and Karen on the back of one of Irene's bikes with her.

After the ride, Karen took herself off to bed, Donna lay down on the couch for a sleep, Paul started drinking whisky, and Irene and Rhona started talking speed.

Irene and Rhona offered Paul a hit. Apparently, Paul had only ever drunk or snorted the amphetamine before, but it didn't take much to talk him into injecting it. They went into the bathroom.

Irene had laced the speed in the syringe with battery acid, figuring it would give the guy a heart attack and the whole thing would look like an accident.

When they emerged from the bathroom, Irene whispered to Donna, who was still on the couch, that if she didn't want to see what was going to happen, she'd better leave.

'He's going to fall any minute and it won't be nice,' Irene told her.

Rhona let herself into Karen's bedroom, and woke her up to tell her, 'We've just given him a dirty shot but he's still standing.'

Working on the theory that if you've been bitten by a poisonous snake you should remain immobile to slow the rate of poison, Irene and Rhona took Paul for a walk, figuring that the activity would push the battery acid around his system quicker.

Nothing happened. The acid seemed to have no effect on Paul whatsoever.

After an hour of wandering, they headed back to the house, where Paul grabbed one of the motorbikes and started riding around the paddock. When Irene and Rhona began talking about other ways of dealing with Paul, like using a baseball bat or tying him to a tree, the Randall sisters couldn't take the stress and decided to leave.

Donna and Karen headed for the Maslins' place, where all the kids were, including Rhona's, who'd been dropped off sometime after lunch. Also there were Jano Maslin, Rhona's boyfriend Steve, and another guy.

☠ ☠ ☠

If there was ever a guy in the wrong place at the wrong time it was that other guy. Ian Gillin wasn't even a local – not born and bred anyway. The 22-year-old had moved to the area from Shepparton for work and had got an apprenticeship at the SEC in Morwell. It was there he'd met Jano Maslin and over the next couple of years he and Jano had become good mates, despite a 10-year age difference.

Young Ian had almost become part of the Maslin family and they all shared a love of motorbikes – Jano and Irene had five of them. Ian was tall and strong and useful. He was often at their house for dinner, or to help Jano with building and renovations. The latest project was a swimming pool.

Ian had also known Steve, who was there that day, for a while; even before Steve had started dating another of the Irene's friends, Rhona Heaney. Through all of them, Ian had met Karen Randall a few times, enough to know she had a sometime boyfriend who used to beat her up. He'd never met the guy himself though; and until that Sunday in November he'd never even met Karen's sister Donna.

While the three men – Jano, Steve and Ian – continued their digging of the pool foundations, the sisters sat around watching, and the kids were playing.

Then Irene Maslin rang home. She spoke to Karen and then to Jano, whereon Jano asked Ian if he wanted to take a drive with him.

Where they went and what they did in the next hour or so changed Ian Gillin's life forever.

☠ ☠ ☠

Ian and Jano called in to a shop in the main street to pick up some smokes and soft drink and then headed to Rhona's place on Nicholls Road. When the guys got there, they noticed that Irene was in the shed next the house, so they wandered in there first.

'She had something in her hand,' Ian Gillin told police much later. 'It looked like a syringe and she was filling it up with some stuff. I asked what the stuff was and she said, "It's battery acid. There's a guy in there who has to go. If someone doesn't do something about him, he's gonna end up killing Karen."'

When Ian and the Maslins went inside, Paul Snabel was sitting on the couch chatting drunkenly to Rhona. She introduced Ian and Paul, and then the two women retreated to the kitchen to make cuppas for everyone. Ever the helpful young man, Ian left Paul and Jano watching TV and went to see if the women needed any help.

They did, but not the kind Ian was expecting.

Irene pointed to a baseball bat leaning on the kitchen wall and told him, 'I want you to knock this guy over the head.'

Ian figured Irene, who was a bit drunk, wasn't actually serious; at least he hoped not. He took his cup and left the kitchen. Rhona and Irene followed with the other drinks. A little later, when Ian took his cup back to the kitchen, Irene tagged along.

She said, 'Hurry up and do it 'cause he just has to go,' and then she left the room.

Poor Ian. He never was the brightest spark, but the truth was that for all the 'being part of the Maslin family', the young man was intimidated by his mate's wife.

In fact, Ian Gillin was shit scared of Irene Maslin. Always had been. The way she talked; the way she treated people; the way she ordered Jano around and how he had to do everything at the house, and everything she said when she said it. Even though they argued all the time it was Irene who was the boss in that family.

Ian was so scared he was shaking, although part of his fear was not about what Irene wanted him to do, but what she might do to him if he didn't.

He didn't even know this Paul guy. Sure, he knew *who* he was. He knew that he was Karen's skanky ex-boyfriend; that he'd hurt Karen; that no one liked him – well, Karen didn't, and his friends the Maslins didn't ...

Ian picked up the baseball bat with his left hand, and returned to the lounge room. He didn't really think he could do it ...

And then he just did.

Ian walked up behind Paul, a virtual stranger sitting in an armchair watching TV, and swung the bat into the left side of his head.

Paul, instantly out cold, slumped sideways and started bleeding onto the carpet.

Jano and Ian then just stood there, and watched Rhona unsuccessfully try to inject the battery acid into Paul's arm. She and Irene then tried to inject his ankle instead, until they realised the needle was buggered.

The women and Jano retreated to the kitchen for a moment but when Paul started groaning Irene yelled out to Ian, 'Just hit him again.'

So he did.

When Ian realised Jano was standing next to him, he handed the baseball bat to his mate and went outside because he wanted to throw up. He didn't really like the sight of blood, and Paul was bleeding all over the floor.

Rhona joined him outside, briefly, to see how he felt, and then after a little while Ian re-entered the house – just in time to see Jano Maslin belt the victim twice more on the same side of the head with the same bat.

A couple of minutes later the women emerged from the kitchen, where they'd obviously been discussing what the hell they had to do to finish this guy off.

Irene Maslin bent over Paul, put a plastic bag over the unconscious man's head and secured it in place with a rubber band around his neck.

'That should make him die,' Irene said. 'He should suffocate.'

While Rhona Heaney busied herself cleaning up the pool of blood with a towel, the rest of them watched and listened as the plastic bag was sucked in and out with Paul's dying breaths.

Once Irene was satisfied that the problem of Paul Snabel had been solved – that Karen Randall's irritating boyfriend was finally dead – she ordered Jano to fetch a tarpaulin and some rope. Jano spread the green tarp out on the floor, then he and Irene lifted Paul from the chair to the tarp, folded it around the body and tied it up.

Jano and Ian carried the bundle outside and put it into the back of the Maslins' family station wagon, while Rhona scrubbed the carpet with a bucket of water, then washed off the murder weapon and put it back among her son's toys.

Then, with Irene at the wheel of the Subaru, the three conspirators and their terrified accomplice took the back streets to the Maslin house. Irene and Rhona dropped the guys off and headed north to dispose of the body.

☠ ☠ ☠

It may seem like there was a lot of aimless riding and driving around going on that day and night, but country people have to travel for most things; they're accustomed to the distances. For the locals of Mirboo North, for instance, it's a half-hour drive to Moe or Morwell, or 45 minutes to Warragul, to go to the movies or go bowling or to shop in a big shopping centre. Rhona Heaney's trip to the TAFE college in Traralgon took around 50 minutes, and it took an hour or so for the Maslins to get to the necessarily secluded area of bushland where their marijuana crop was hidden.

So, it wasn't a random spot in the middle of nowhere an hour from home that the women chose to dump Paul's body that evening. Irene knew exactly where she was going: beyond Shady Creek – 30 minutes north-west of Moe and north-east of Warragul – up a dirt track in the dense-bush of the 1400-hectare Sweetwater Creek Nature Conservation Reserve. Irene and Jano had been growing dope there for years and the crops had never been found. There was no better place to dump a body.

Irene was so sure Paul's body would never be stumbled on that the women didn't even bother burying him. After bumping the Subaru over a few logs, when the track virtually ran out, Irene just stopped the car and she and Rhona dragged the body from the back. They made a half-hearted attempt at covering it with a few logs and branches and then simply drove home.

Meanwhile, Jano and Ian had a nice cup of tea in the Maslin kitchen and then offered to take the Randall sisters home. After a small detour to Karen's new house in Mirboo North to grab some clothes, they drove the sisters and Karen's son to Donna's place in Moe.

On the drive home afterwards, Ian finally said to his mate, 'What have we done?'

Jano told his mate that they'd all be fine, as long as he didn't talk about it to anyone.

When the men got back to the Maslin house in Mirboo North, Rhona and Irene were already there. There was one loose end that still needed fixing, so Jano and Ian took the Subaru and a trailer and headed over to the house on Nicholls Road to fetch Paul's red and white Yamaha RZ250.

They drove it straight into Jano's garage, where Irene announced they had to strip the bike and dispose of it. The men again did as they were told and, over the next couple of hours, with Irene and Rhona's help, proceeded to take the thing apart.

Jano filed the engine number off and tied up all the wiring in neat left-handed knots. The wiring and smaller bike parts were put into a bunch of plastic bags that he'd brought home from his work at the State Electricity Commission. When they were done, and the Yamaha couldn't be reduced any further, the plastic bags and the larger parts were loaded into the back of the Subaru.

Irene and Rhona wandered inside while Jano and Ian set off on yet another drive to scatter the bike parts as far and wide as they could. The men drove around in the very early hours of Monday 6 November, dropping the larger pieces of the motorcycle – like the engine and the frame – into a couple of dams, and the rest of it at two different local tips. They were done and home again by about 4.30 am.

And that was it. No logical reason. No bike. No evidence. No body. No murder.

☠ ☠ ☠

Seven days later, on Monday 13 November, Paul Friend of Moe reported his housemate missing.

Paul Friend had been away himself for a few days – from Sunday 5 November until the following Tuesday – but then he'd made a few phone calls looking for his mate. Paul Friend didn't really start to worry for another three days though; not until Paul Snabel's mother rang their place looking for her son.

All that the Moe police had to go on, to start with, was what Paul Friend knew: the last time he'd seen his mate was Saturday 4 November. They'd watched *Hey Hey It's Saturday* together, then Paul Snabel had gone out. Friend saw him again a few hours later at the housewarming party of a mutual acquaintance. Since then, he hadn't turned up for work, and his friends and family had not heard from him.

By the time Detective Senior Constable Michael Grunwald of the Morwell Criminal Investigation Branch picked up the case the following weekend, 28-year-old Paul Snabel had been missing for two weeks.

Detective Grunwald began his investigation knowing that Snabel had been in a rocky relationship with one Karen Randall; and that his last known whereabouts was a party in Moe at the home of Donna Randall, the ex-girlfriend's sister.

Grunwald paid a visit to Karen, made a phone call to Donna and on Sunday 19 November met with both sisters in Mirboo North, at the Nicholls Road residence of their friend Rhona Heaney.

Donna Randall verified that Paul had been at her housewarming party in Moe, and the sisters added that Paul had also dropped by Rhona's place the next day. Karen had been busy packing, getting ready for the move into her new house, and Rhona and Donna were helping. The last time either of them had seen Paul, they said, was around 5 pm when he'd left the farmhouse on his Yamaha.

With that new and in-no-way-incriminating piece of information, Detective Grunwald knew that any search for the missing Paul Snabel should begin in Mirboo North, rather than 40 kilometres away in Moe. No-one who knew him believed that Paul would leave town – not to mention his job, friends and family – without telling anyone, so the natural assumption was that he'd had an accident. A ground and police chopper search of the area over the next couple of days found no sign of Paul or his motorbike on or off the roads between Mirboo North and Moe.

Then a stroke of luck not only aroused the investigators' suspicions that the Randall sisters possibly knew more than they were saying, but also suggested that Paul was more than likely a victim of foul play.

Even before the police launched a local media campaign requesting public assistance, the bush telegraph had been working overtime. News of the missing man had spread throughout the district and locals were already on the lookout for him and his red motorcycle.

On 22 November, Detective Grunwald ordered a search of the Boolarra tip (about 13 kilometres from Mirboo North) after a local boy had informed police he'd made some interesting discoveries while foraging there for useful stuff. The teenager had found more than a dozen motorcycle parts, from what was probably a red Yamaha 250, including a front headlight and rear indicator lights, a mudguard, a rear wheel and tyre, foot rests and a windshield. The subsequent police search of the tip uncovered plastic SEC bags containing motorbike wiring and cables, wound and secured in distinctive bundles.

Over the next couple of days, other tip foragers came forward with bits and pieces from a red and white Yamaha – including a fuel tank and a seat. And on Saturday 2 December a local man found a motorcycle engine in a dam. The Search and Rescue Unit dragged that dam, and another nearby, and in no time recovered a red motorbike frame and front fork.

After the discovery of the first bits of the dismantled Yamaha in November, the Morwell CIB realised it was time to call in the big guns. Detective Senior Constable Peter Wheeler and two other detectives from the Victorian Homicide Squad arrived in the district on Friday 24 November.

☠ ☠ ☠

Two decades later, Peter Wheeler – now Detective Superintendent – still marvels at how the physical evidence in this case came together.

'This would've gone down as just another unsolved missing person case, if the bike parts hadn't started turning up,' he said.

'It seems that sometimes, as investigators, we make our own luck. In the end it didn't matter that someone had gone to so much trouble to disassemble that motorcycle and scatter the pieces. Kids just happened to be rummaging around in a couple of local tips, at the right time; their parents happened to notice what their kids had found *and* were paying attention to local gossip and the news; and then put two and two together to arrive at a possibility.

'In the end we were able to almost fully reconstruct the motorcycle.'

While the sheer luck of those discoveries still astounds Wheeler, the gradual unravelling of the conspiracy doesn't – nor did it at the time. Although the number of people involved was highly unusual, it was that very thing that doomed the plan to failure. Once the police had an idea of what might have happened, all they had to do was press on with the investigation and bide their time.

'We were soon able to conclude, with certainty, the circumstances surrounding the death of Paul Snabel,' Detective Wheeler said.

In fact, it was the very care that the conspirators had taken in stripping the bike that proved their undoing. At least one piece of the dismantled Yamaha was found in the Boolarra tip on Monday 6 November, only one day after Paul disappeared. That gave police a new starting point – or rather a likely end point – on their already short timeline.

'It was really quite bizarre,' Wheeler said. 'We were able to identify the people responsible who had a substantial role in the scenario leading to that death, which was very much a planned murder in which people had specific roles to play.'

'What's more, we got to a point in our investigation, in January 1990, where we had enough corroborating evidence to make several arrests for the murder of Paul Snabel – even though we did not have a body. We still had no idea where he was.'

☠ ☠ ☠

Earlier, in November 1989, however, all that the investigating officers had were a few bike parts that *might* belong to the missing man's Yamaha, and a 'trail' that kept returning to the Nicholls Road farmhouse and the three women who'd last seen Paul Snabel on Sunday 5 November.

When Rhona Heaney was first interviewed by Michael Grunwald and his colleague Detective Sergeant Shane Downie, on Thursday

23 November, she gave the same account as the Randall sisters, but added that Paul had been drinking all that Sunday – before riding off on his bike at 5 pm. The officers executed a search warrant on Rhona's house that day, but found nothing.

Police are always suspicious when statements from more than one person are too similar. In reality, no matter what the situation, no two people see or remember things the same way, so for three women to be telling the same basic story in the same way could only mean it was just that: a story. And it wasn't long before that story – of the last time they'd each seen Paul Snabel – began to change in other subtle ways.

On 24 November, when detectives Grunwald and Wheeler talked to Karen Randall again, she told them that she'd noticed, on that Sunday morning, that Paul had obviously taken some speed. She also revealed – probably accidentally – that it was Donna who had brought Paul out to the house at Mirboo North. They'd both arrived in his car, but later in the morning he'd driven back to Moe to switch it for his motorbike.

At that stage, none of the women had even so much as mentioned Irene Maslin's name, let alone placed her at the Nicholls Road house.

But again, that's the problem with a conspiracy: the more people in on it, the more people there are to let something slip. And if the players don't see themselves as equally responsible, or if even one person believes they're going to take the fall, the beans will eventually be spilled, and the truth, or a version of it, will come out.

With each interview, Rhona Heaney and the Randall sisters added something to their account. Each time it was something apparently insignificant but telling: Paul was in a good mood; Paul had taken some speed at the party the night before; Paul had spent the Sunday afternoon drinking; Paul had left at about 5 pm; Paul had left at about 4.15 pm; Paul and Donna got to the Nicholls Road house at 5 am; they got there at 6 am.

On 25 November, when Detective Grunwald talked to Rhona Heaney again, she mentioned Irene Maslin's name for the first time, but only in passing. Rhona told him she'd gone out after lunch on the Sunday, bought a bottle of whisky from the pub, taken all the kids to her friend Irene's house, then gone home again.

When the detectives discovered that Karen and Donna were

also acquainted with the Maslins – and that it seemed these mutual friends had a very large garage – they paid a visit, with a search warrant. It was Monday 4 December.

Irene claimed she'd never heard of Paul Snabel before his disappearance had made the news, and that she'd spent all of that Sunday a month before at home with her husband Jano, two other blokes, her own kids and, from lunchtime until about 7 pm, Rhona's kids as well.

Jano's story matched Irene's perfectly, except he admitted having met Paul a couple of times over at Rhona's place.

The search warrant enabled investigators to collect several items, which would later prove incriminating: some red paint flecks from the otherwise spotless floor of the garage; a file with red paint flecks; and a Yamaha bike tag. They also noticed, with interest, just how neatly Jano Maslin kept his gear, especially the nicely wound wires and ropes, tied with same kind of left-handed knots as the bike cables found in the SEC bags at the tip.

On 18 December, Irene and Jano took their kids out of school and left town. It was a day after the cops had paid another call on them to ask Jano to answer further questions about Paul Snabel. After consulting his wife, Jano had refused to go with the detectives without talking to a solicitor. A day or so later, Rhona told officers that as far as she knew the Maslins had just gone on holidays, but she didn't know where.

Around the same time, a very stressed Karen Randall checked in to a private hospital in Frankston, two hours away, to get treatment for drug and alcohol abuse.

🐾 🐾 🐾

Detective Wheeler said the investigating officers kept returning to Karen, Donna and Rhona because with each new statement the women added something new, or neglected to elaborate on something they should have known – according to one of the others.

'As the pressure from the police intensified, the wheels started to fall off because the women not only knew that we were relentlessly pursuing this, but that we weren't fully accepting the versions we were being given. We were constantly seeking clarification.'

The detectives got their first real break in the case when the Randall sisters decided to come clean – again with their own versions of the truth. And these new stories of what happened on 5 November clearly put Rhona and Irene in the frame for having 'done something to Paul Snabel'.

When Detective Downie spoke to Karen in hospital on 21 December, she finally admitted that she felt something may have happened to Paul. She claimed that Irene had told her, on the day after he was now known to have disappeared, that Paul would never bother or hurt her again. Irene also warned Karen that she'd have to watch herself and do whatever they told her to do.

It was in that interview that Karen became the first person to put Irene Maslin at the Nicholls Road house on the day that Paul was last seen. She added, however, that she had no idea when Irene had arrived at her place.

Karen also changed another part of her earlier account; the bit about watching Paul leave her house on his Yamaha at about 5 pm. In her new version, she said that Paul was still at the Nicholls Road house when she and Donna left to go to the Maslins'. She also stated that the only people at her friends' place when they got there were Jano, Steve and all the kids, and that Jano had later driven her, and her son and sister, to Moe.

On the same day of Karen's revised statement, Donna Randall was invited to the Morwell CIB office to talk to Detective Downie again. This time she too placed Irene Maslin at her sister's house on 5 November. Donna told the detective that when she and Paul arrived at the house in Mirboo North early on that Sunday morning, Irene, Karen and Rhona were all awake and in the kitchen.

Donna verified that when she and Karen left Rhona's house, Paul was still there, as were Rhona and Irene. She added that she'd overheard Irene and Rhona talking about doing something to Paul, like breaking his legs, but that he was on a bike in the house paddock when she had left to go to the Maslins' place.

When Downie asked why she had previously lied, Donna said that Irene and Rhona had told her to, and that she was scared of Irene. Donna explained that it was between the first phone call from Detective Grunwald on 19 November, and the first face-to-face talk she and Karen had with him later that same day, that the original story had been made up.

Irene and Rhona had told the sisters exactly what they should tell police: that they had watched Paul leave Rhona's place on his bike at around 5 in the afternoon. Irene also made it clear that they were *not* to mention that she had ever been at the house that day.

When asked why she thought this meant that something had happened to Paul, Donna claimed Irene had also said things like, 'I'm polishing my barrels; if one of us is gonna go down, we're all gonna go. If this gets out of hand the big boys are gonna have to deal with it.'

One other new and vital piece of information that Detective Downie acquired from Donna Randall that day was a name – mentioned for the first time and only in passing. Donna said that she, Karen and her nephew had been driven home to Moe from the Maslin house that evening by Jano – and his friend Ian Gillin.

At this stage during their constantly evolving stories – which denied any real knowledge of whatever it was that might have happened to Paul – the Randall sisters slowly painted (either deliberately or accidentally) some not very nice pictures of their friends Irene and Rhona.

Detective Wheeler said, 'It soon became obvious that the statements, right from the word go, were concocted and part of the concerted effort on the part of all the females who were giving statements – including Rhona Heaney – to give versions that were false and geared towards minimising their involvement or knowledge as to what had occurred.'

☠ ☠ ☠

In a series of almost-rolling police interviews with Rhona Heaney and the Randalls over the next couple of weeks, the story continued to change and a big ugly picture began to emerge.

On 24 December, Detective Downie spoke to Donna Randall again. She told him that around 3 am the previous morning she'd been collected by a friend of Irene's and driven to the Maslin house at Corio, near Geelong. When Rhona arrived later, she had told her friends that the police seemed to know that Irene had been at her place on that Sunday.

Although Irene was suspicious that 'someone had been talking', she was doubtful the police had that particular piece of information.

'They're just guessing,' Irene had said. 'Because if they knew these things we'd all be behind bars.'

Rhona added that she thought Karen was their weak link.

Donna also told Detective Downie about another one-on-one conversation she'd had that day. Rhona had told her, she said, that Paul's body had been left in the bush near a drug crop that they'd been growing for about five years.

Rhona had said, 'He'd be rotten there, rotting away … if the animals and things hadn't dragged him off.'

On 28 December, Detective Peter Wheeler interviewed the other sister again. Karen Randall was still in the private hospital in Frankston. This time Karen admitted that she, Rhona, the Maslins and everybody's kids had all been at her place on the night of Donna's housewarming. She said the adults had all smoked dope and the Maslin family had stayed the night.

While Karen still maintained that when she and her sister had left the house Paul was fine, she now admitted that from the very next day she knew that something had happened to him. Karen told the detective that Irene had said Paul wouldn't bother her anymore. She claimed Irene had then threatened her.

'When she said that he would no longer bother me, the way that she said it, with evil eyes and an aggressive look on her face, it really scared me and I could tell that Paul was no longer with us. By that I mean that I believed he was dead.'

Karen claimed Irene's threats included the idea that she, Karen, was an accessory and that if she said anything to the police, her head would be blown off.

Karen said Rhona Heaney had later backed up Irene's threats by implying her death would be made to look like a suicide, and that any attempt to leave a note would endanger the rest of her family.

When Detective Wheeler asked if there was anything more she knew about what had happened to Paul Snabel, Karen said that Irene had said things had gone terribly wrong, that there'd been a baseball bat and a lot of blood involved.

☠ ☠ ☠

Once the Maslins were well and truly in the investigation mix, the police began hearing other rumours, such as Irene being into drugs and that Paul Snabel had threatened to dob on her.

Given his predilection for dope and speed, Paul was more likely to have been a disgruntled customer or unreliable with his debts, rather than a snitch. And that possibility, of course, could also have meant there'd been a 'falling out' between dealer and buyer.

Detective Wheeler said, 'Because Irene Maslin never gave us anything – no statement, no information, no admitted association – we could never be entirely sure that Karen Randall's "situation" with her ex-boyfriend was the only reason for Irene to believe Paul Snabel should die.'

An interesting – and ultimately never-explained – thing that came out of the follow-up interview with the missing man's housemate Paul Friend, on 24 November, was the mention of a brief appearance of a gun in their house some months earlier. Paul Friend told the detective that when he'd asked his mate why the gun was there, Paul Snabel had said there were some guys after him.

And of course, according to the Maslins' closest friends, Irene knew people ...

'There were so many parties involved,' Detective Wheeler said. 'It wasn't a matter of mum shot dad, and was standing in the kitchen with the smoking gun when the police arrived; or one known offender had stabbed another known offender and the police just had to file the paperwork.

'Part of the process during the Snabel investigation was trying to get an understanding of the relationships, trying to develop some kind of motive in our minds, and then trying to come up with scenarios as to what potentially may have occurred.'

Wheeler said he still doesn't believe that the full nature and degree of all the relationships of all the parties was ever fully established; but no amount of theorising prepared the investigators for what they were about to find out.

For despite what Rhona and Irene thought, Karen Randall was not the weakest link in their very cheap chain.

On 29 December, the detectives went to take a statement from someone whose place in the story so far had barely raised a blip on their investigation radar. However, from then, and over the following

11 days, the bizarre and complicated plot to murder Paul Snabel was revealed by the one person who hadn't been in on the plan from the start.

Ian Gillin was the first to tell the cops everything he knew – including his part in it – and the only one, ultimately, not to minimise his role.

But even Ian, during his first interview, stuck to the Maslin–Heaney lie. After all, Detective Senior Constable Andrew McLoughlin really only wanted to know what he was doing at the Maslin house on 5 November, and who else he'd seen there on the day.

No-one had placed Ian at the Nicholls Road house and in fact, so far, only Donna had mentioned his name at all. She said he and Jano had driven them home that night.

Ian told McLoughlin about his friendship with Jano and, subsequently, his wife Irene; how he often ate at the Maslin home and helped around the place; and how they were digging a pool that day. Yes, he'd met Karen Randall; no, he'd never met Paul Snabel but knew who he was; and he'd only met Donna Randall that Sunday for the first time.

In this first interview, he said that Irene was home when he arrived there but had later gone somewhere; that he, Jano and Steve worked on the pool all day; and that when he and Steve left the Maslin house around 8 pm, the Randalls were still there.

This already conflicted with Donna's story that Jano and Ian had driven her home, and other statements that put Irene at Rhona's house from the Saturday night to the Sunday night.

On 5 January 1990, Donna Randall declared that she wanted to add to her previous statements, and emphasised that she had previously not told the truth because she was scared of Irene Maslin.

Donna told Detective Wheeler how Rhona had gone with Paul to Moe in his car and ridden back with him on the Yamaha; that Irene and Rhona had talked Paul into injecting some speed on that Sunday afternoon; and that afterwards Irene had told her that if she didn't want to see what was about to happen to him, she should leave because 'he's going to fall any minute and it wouldn't be nice'. Donna revealed she knew her friends had added battery acid to the speed in that syringe.

She also added that when she and Karen were at the Maslins' place later that afternoon, Irene had rung there and then Jano and

Ian had left for an hour or so, after which both men had driven her, and her sister and nephew, home to Moe.

Detective Wheeler said, 'It was obvious by then that there had been a hell of a lot going on behind the scenes influencing the versions that were being given to us.

'The suspects, as so many of them were by then, were feeling pressure not only from the police making the inquiries and questioning the information that was being given to them, but also from the knowledge that if they didn't fulfil their role in accordance with the instructions they'd been given by Irene Maslin, then the threats made by her would be carried out.'

In that same statement of Donna's, she also mentioned having helped Rhona deliver her lounge suite to a friend on 18 November, because she was getting a new one. Apparently, she couldn't get some stains out of the one she was giving away.

Detective Wheeler said that as the others started to buckle under the pressure, the ringleader did not.

'Irene Maslin was different, in that she never provided a statement to police at all. She was obviously pulling the strings behind the scenes, in terms of influencing what people were saying to police, and was accompanying that with the threats.'

Two days after Donna's revised statement, her sister offered new information. On 7 January, Karen Randall told Homicide detective John Robertson that immediately after Irene and Rhona had given Paul the speed, Rhona had told her it was a 'dirty shot'.

Karen also admitted that Irene had, days later, told her about the battery acid in the syringe, the baseball bat, and the plastic bag that she had finally used to suffocate Paul. Irene had also said they'd had to kill Paul because 'he knew too much'. Karen claimed she assumed that necessity referred to Irene's drug dealing.

In the meantime, the physical evidence was mounting up. Forensic tests matched the paint on the almost completely reassembled Yamaha RZ250 to the flakes of paint found on the Maslins' garage floor and captured in the grooves of one of Jano's metal files.

Forensic investigators examined the couch that Rhona had given away because it was stained, and found that an armchair in her house was tinged with blood. They also removed a section of 'cleaned' carpet that had a large bloodstain on it.

The plastic SEC bags in which the cables from the dismantled Yamaha had been found at the tips provided a circumstantial link to Jano and Ian, as they both worked for the electricity commission. More directly incriminating, however, was the way that wiring was coiled and tied in exactly the same kind of left-handed knots that Jano used for his own gear in his garage.

☠ ☠ ☠

On 7 January Ian Gillin gave a second, videotaped interview, conducted outside the home of Irene and Jano Maslin in Mirboo North.

In his new version of the events on that Sunday two months before, he said that Irene was not home that morning; that, according to Jano, she was 'out riding with Paul'; that Jano had left his house that afternoon for a few hours. He first said that he alone had driven the sisters home that evening, then later said Jano was also with them.

He told the detectives Wheeler, Robertson and Downie that when he got back to his mate's place from Moe, Irene and Rhona were there. Shortly after, Jano had driven off in the family's Subaru, with a motorbike trailer, and returned with a red Yamaha RZ250.

Ian said it was after midnight when he helped Jano unload the bike into the shed. 'We were told that we had to strip it down.'

He said it was Irene who gave that instruction, and that it was he, Jano, Irene and Rhona who had taken the bike apart.

Ian denied knowing who owned the bike or why they were dismantling it in the middle of the night, but said dumping the parts in the dams had been his idea. Jano had suggested the tips. Ian then took the detectives on a video tour of the four dump sites.

The next day, Monday 8 January, Ian Gillin was taken to Victoria Police HQ in Melbourne to be formally interviewed by the Homicide Squad about the murder of Paul Snabel.

He told them everything.

While Ian had been unaware of the larger plot to kill Paul, he recounted all that he did know. How he had gone with Jano to the Nicholls Road house on the afternoon of 5 November. How he had seen Irene in the garage loading a syringe up with battery acid. How she'd told him there was a guy inside who had to go or he might kill

Karen Randall. How Rhona Heaney had introduced him to a drunk Paul Snabel. How Irene had told him to hit Paul with a baseball bat. How scared he felt when he realised she was serious, because he knew that if he didn't do what Irene said, it might happen to him.

Ian told the detectives, 'I picked up the baseball bat … I sort of started shaking a bit … Then I didn't know what to do, so I just walked in and knocked him over the head and he fell.'

Ian described how he and a shocked-looking Jano had stood by and watched as the women tried to inject the battery acid into Paul's arm and ankle. He admitted that he'd just obeyed Irene when she told him to hit Paul with the bat again; how he later watched Jano Maslin whack Paul twice on the head. He described the blood on the floor; how Irene Maslin had put a plastic bag over Paul's head and they watched and listened as he slowly suffocated; how Rhona cleaned the floor and the baseball bat; how Irene and Jano wrapped the body in a tarp; and how he and Jano carried it out to the car.

Detective McLoughlin asked Ian why he didn't try and take the bag off Paul's head.

Ian said, 'Because I was that scared, I didn't want to really get involved with it.'

'What did you think was going to happen to Paul with the bag over his head?' McLoughlin asked.

'He was gonna die,' Ian stated. 'I reckon if I stepped in and done something about it … I might've been the next one.'

In trying to explain why he was so scared of Irene Maslin, he recounted an incident from a few months earlier when Irene had left her house in the company of two big guys, who Jano had said were hitmen.

In this formal interview, Ian also admitted that after he and Jano had taken the Randall sisters home to Moe, he had gone with Jano to collect Paul's Yamaha.

Ian Gillin was charged on 8 January 1990 with causing the death of Paul Snabel.

☠ ☠ ☠

Detective Wheeler later said, 'Getting an insight into Irene Maslin was difficult right up until the end of the investigation, when the

Randall girls and Ian Gillin cracked and were interviewed formally as suspects. That's when they finally came out with the true version of what had occurred, and the roles that each of them had played.

'Rhona Heaney was also difficult to get a handle on,' he said, 'but Irene Maslin never provided a version, even when she was formally interviewed.'

The day after Ian Gillin was charged, three of the other conspirators were formally interviewed.

Jano Maslin claimed he had been home all day on Sunday 5 November, digging a pool with Ian and Steve; that Rhona Heaney had popped in during the afternoon to pick up Karen's son, and returned later to watch videos; that he did not see Karen or Donna Randall that day at all.

Jano denied having spent Saturday night and Sunday morning anywhere else; he denied any knowledge of dismantling and disposing of a motorcycle; he denied helping with the removal of a body from Rhona's house on the Sunday. He said he didn't 'know' Paul Snabel but admitted to having met him once at Rhona Heaney's house a couple of months before.

Jano Maslin said he had 'no reason to lie'. Detective Sergeant Shane Downie charged him with the murder of Paul Snabel.

Homicide detective Peter Wheeler interviewed Rhona Heaney. She had been advised by her solicitor to say she had no comments to make. She began by saying she'd got her weekends mixed up and that the visitors she mentioned having dropped by her place on Saturday 4 November had actually called in the previous weekend. She said that only she, Steve, Karen and the kids were home that night. She admitted knowing Paul Snabel; that she had met him a few times through Karen Randall.

Rhona refused to comment on who had been at her place in Nicholls Road on the Sunday; whether she'd gone with Paul to Moe to collect his motorcycle; whether she had later helped dismantle that motorcycle; whether she had played an active role in the murder of Paul Snabel; or whether she had helped to dispose of his body.

Detective Wheeler charged 37-year-old Rhona Heaney with murder.

☠ ☠ ☠

Irene Maslin's formal interview, the same day, was short and virtually silent. She merely stated her name, said she was 32 years old, gave her occupation as 'homebody, home duties care-giver' and asked for a phone book to find a solicitor.

'Irene Maslin was totally uncooperative from the word go,' Detective Wheeler said. 'By saying so very little – and given what we were learning about her from the other parties involved – she came across as a hard, strong woman. She was quite arrogant in her refusal to give anything away.

'We had learned from other sources too that she was active in the drug trade in the Latrobe Valley and had a reputation that caused people to be fearful of the ramifications of not doing whatever she wanted.'

During her interview with Detective Andrew McLoughlin, on 9 January, Irene Maslin sat in seething stony silence. She smoked several cigarettes, and even physically turned away from the interviewing officers.

McLoughlin eventually informed the care-giving homebody that she would be charged with the murder of Paul Snabel.

Peter Wheeler said that two days later the Homicide detectives collected Rhona Heaney from remand, where she was in custody, and directed them to the Shady Creek area 'in a concerted effort to try and locate where the body had been dumped by her and Irene Maslin.

'We didn't find the body that day, but Rhona Heaney did elaborate on what had happened at her house on November 5 – although her statement was still geared towards minimising her role in things.'

Basically, Rhona overlooked everything that happened before Ian hit Paul with the baseball bat. She acknowledged there had been a plan to do something about the way Paul had been badly treating Karen, but she maintained that her solution would have been to have Jano or Ian punch him and send him home.

She told the detectives that she'd been in another room when Ian hit Paul, but returned to the lounge room afterwards because it was 'her job' to inject Paul with battery acid. She said she couldn't do it and instead went outside to find Ian, to whom, she claims, she said, 'This is really fucked, I want to get out of here.'

Omitting all other aspects of how the murder transpired, Rhona said that the next thing she knew they were all in the Subaru, and then she and Irene headed to Shady Creek. Rhona said she knew Paul's body was in the back but when they stopped in the dark in the bush, all she did was drag some branches over to the car because she felt too sick to help Irene with any other part of the body disposal.

It was a week before the Randall sisters were formally interviewed and charged.

Donna was interviewed first, on 19 January, and finally revealed how the plot to murder Paul Snabel had come about; how, at the gathering a few days before her housewarming party, Irene had said something had to be done about Karen's ex-boyfriend before any harm came to her or her son.

Donna detailed how it was her job to get Paul out to the Nicholls Road place on the Saturday night, where Irene and Rhona would inject him with a shot of speed and battery acid.

Donna told Detective Wheeler how the dirty shot had had no apparent effect on Paul and that when it seemed that Irene was instead planning to bash him, she and Karen left the house.

Donna insisted she did not know what happened to Paul until much later. Irene's threats and other 'overheard' conversations between Irene and Rhona soon made her realise they had in fact probably killed Paul Snabel.

When asked why she didn't tell the police the truth any earlier, Donna told Wheeler that she was scared; that she had never come across anything like that before.

'I thought if I'd said something to anyone that they probably would've killed me and if I'd gone to the police, they'd probably arrest me,' she said.

Detectives Wheeler and Robertson then interviewed Karen Randall. She explained how Irene was angry, on her behalf, about her ex-boyfriend's behaviour and had talked about disposing of Paul. Karen said it was Irene's idea to lure Paul out to the house at Mirboo North and inject him with battery acid.

Karen said 'her job' was to ring Paul during her sister's party and entice him out to her place. She admitted that on that Saturday night Rhona had injected both her and Irene with speed.

Most of the rest of her story on this occasion matched her previous statement, except that she now acknowledged that, as far as she

knew, Paul's death had come about because of her bad relationship
with him.

She said that when Ian and Jano returned to the Maslin residence
before taking her and her sister and son home to Moe, Jano had
said: 'Well, he's not going to bother you again.'

Donna and Karen Randall were both charged with causing the
death of Paul Snabel.

☠ ☠ ☠

Detective Inspector Peter Wheeler is still not convinced the whole
truth ever came out.

'We'll never know, with 100 per cent certainty, the full extent of the
relationships of the parties involved; and that includes the deceased.
Because not everyone talked to us, we'll never know whether there
were any other influencing factors as to why these people embarked
on their deadly course of action,' he said.

Detective Wheeler believes it's entirely possible that Irene Maslin
had that secret extra ingredient – that the police never uncovered –
that caused her to be so intent on getting rid of Paul Snabel.

'It's possible that ingredient was even outside the knowledge of
those who were interviewed and they actually gave what we, and
they, believed to be truth as they knew it.

'The fact the people were given an allocated and dedicated
role to play in the overall scheme to lure Paul Snabel out to Rhona
Heaney's farmhouse in order to inject him with a mix of battery acid
and amphetamines, with the idea that that would kill him, says a
great deal about Irene Maslin.

'But then – when things went wrong, when he didn't die from
that – the extraordinary behaviour to ensure that it did happen was
clearly indicative of the fact that Irene Maslin was very, very keen to
ensure that Paul Snabel died that day,' Wheeler said.

'Despite getting nothing from Irene herself, the fact remains that
the investigation got to a point in time that there was substantial
evidence there to justify the arrest of all the parties for murder –
even though we didn't know the whereabouts of the victim. To be
able to arrest people and charge them with murder when you don't
have a body is fairly significant.

'And then of course the icing on the cake – from a prosecution point of view – was that we were able to locate Paul Snabel's remains, which then provided a whole range of corroboration in terms of the versions we'd been given about how he'd met his death.'

🐛 🐛 🐛

On the day that the Homicide Squad detectives got Rhona Heaney out of jail so she could show them where she and Irene had dumped Paul's body, they had been unable to locate it. Detective Wheeler said the investigators accepted, however, that Rhona's effort to help them was genuine and that where she took them that day was within a reasonable proximity of where his remains might be.

Two weeks later, on 25 January, Detective Sergeant Shane Downie of the Morwell CIB coordinated a combined Victoria Police and State Emergency Services (SES) search of an expansive area of bushland around Shady Creek.

Detective Wheeler said this was another example of how luck can play a big role in any investigation.

'That day an SES worker was walking down a bush track and the wind just happened to blow in the right direction at the right time. This fellow got a whiff of something that was a bit off and just walked off the track a short distance into the bush and located Paul Snabel's remains.

'The wild dogs had been into him and scattered him all around the place. He was skeletal at that stage obviously; but there were also some remnants of his clothing,' Wheeler said.

'Most importantly, we found his skull, with the caved-in left-hand side of his head, which was consistent with the information we'd been provided with regarding the use of the baseball bat.

'So it was just an incredible set of circumstances, where on the particular day that we went back and revisited the scene with all those people searching the bushland area, the wind happened to blow at the right time as a fellow was walking by the right spot.'

Detective Wheeler said it wasn't until Paul's remains were found that he and fellow Homicide detective John Robertson – along with two state pathologists, doctors David Ranson and Alison Cluroe – returned to the region to investigate and recover the remains.

While the forensic search grids of active crime scenes are fastidiously thorough, this location was not only *not* the primary scene, but it was also nearly three months old and open to the unforgiving elements of a hot Australian summer. Due to the scavenging of wild animals, the dump site was also compromised and uncontained; it had no real borders. The pathologists, for instance, found human bones in eight scattered spots. Two parts of the skull were found in two different areas.

Therefore, another discovery, by the crime scene examiner Tony Kealy, could also be put in the category of 'lucky find'. Sixteen metres from the designated centre point of the crime scene he found a 'slightly damaged' log with paint on it. This was later matched to a small dint and some missing paint on the Maslins' Subaru.

Detective Wheeler still says that even though they had enough evidence to charge all those involved, and that they would've been held responsible for their horrendous activities, there was an incredible sense of relief and high degree of satisfaction in also finding the body.

'We were able to put that part of the case to rest as well, which was especially important for the sake of the family,' he said.

But it was Detective Shane Downie who took on the terrible task that day in 1990 of informing Paul's Snabel's parents that they had more than likely found their son, but would need his dental records to identify him properly.

☠ ☠ ☠

Despite the evidence, both physical and in the statements of their co-accused, Irene and Jano Maslin were at first not committed to stand trial.

'Ian Gillin was only ever going to go down for manslaughter,' Detective Wheeler said.

But even though he offered to plead guilty to that charge – and to testify against the Maslins – he was tried for murder, along with Rhona Heaney and the Randall sisters, in 1991.

Ian Gillin was indeed found guilty of manslaughter and sentenced to six years with a minimum of four. He served three.

Rhona Heaney was sentenced to 15 years in jail, with a minimum of 10 years.

Karen and Donna Randall each received 14 years, with a minimum of nine.

All four appealed their sentences but only the Randalls were granted new trials.

Detective Wheeler explained the grounds for the retrial. 'Even though they were part of the plot to kill Paul Snabel, the sisters did not take part in the actual murder, and in fact were not present at the time. And because the original plan, of which they *were* a party, did not work and the co-conspirators killed him in a manner unknown to the Randalls, it was ultimately decided they should be not be charged with murder.'

Karen and Donna Randall were found guilty instead of attempted murder and both sentenced to four years, with two-year minimums.

At his later trial, Jano Maslin was found not guilty.

In the end – nearly four years after the fact – Irene Maslin pleaded guilty to the murder of Paul Snabel.

'That decision was a consequence of the combination of the convictions of the others involved, and the overwhelming evidence the prosecution would bring against her,' Detective Wheeler said.

'There is usually a lesser sentence involved by pleading guilty, and Irene and her legal team would've taken that on board as they weighed pros and cons of contesting the matter or throwing her on the mercy of the court.'

Irene Maslin decided not to take her chances with a jury.

On sentencing Irene, on 21 June 1993, Justice Vincent said, 'The circumstances surrounding the death of Mr Snabel have been canvassed at length in two trials over which I have presided. In the first of these, two persons, Karen and Donna Randall, who played important roles in the activities which led to the death of your victim, were presented for their involvement. In the second trial, your husband Jan Maslin was found not guilty by the jury which had been impanelled to hear the matter.

'I have now heard a version given in evidence by each of the other five people who were involved in one way or another in the various events,' he said. 'Naturally, when considering your case, I have approached it on the basis that great care must be taken to avoid the possibility that injustice may be occasioned to you by virtue of that circumstance ...'

Justice Vincent continued, 'I have been conscious from a relatively early stage of my acquaintanceship with this matter that the participants were only too prepared to place total responsibility for the killing of Mr Snabel on your shoulders and all attempted to present themselves as either pawns or victims.

'It is not in my view possible to weave the disparate, and on occasions self-justifying, threads provided by these various versions into a tapestry which faithfully represents the history and detail of this terrible crime. However, sufficient findings can be made on the evidence properly admissible against you for its essential features to be discerned and the level of your responsibility to be determined.'

Justice Vincent went further. 'The extent to which this idea [to kill Snabel] crystallised into a plan of action is not completely clear. What is apparent is that you embraced it and became an enthusiastic participant in all that occurred from that time onward.'

He said, 'As I have remarked on two occasions, I find it difficult to identify with any confidence the point at which agreement was reached among those present to kill the deceased. However, I am satisfied that the idea took root in your mind, at least, at a quite early stage and that you became committed to its fulfilment from then onwards. I accept that each of the others involved in the plan, which was eventually agreed upon, made separate decisions with respect to it; but I have no doubt that it would not have been carried out without the active participation and strength of will that you provided. Certainly, it would appear that by the time at which the telephone call was made by Karen Randall on the night of Saturday 4 November, the die was cast.

'Nevertheless, as I have indicated, on any basis, you played a very important role in bringing about his death. It seems likely that it was you who first determined that he was to die and it was, to a significant extent, the force of your personality which ensured that the others involved agreed to participate and performed the roles assigned to them. Your final decision to commit the crime of murder, whenever it was made, was not reached in haste or without careful consideration, even allowing for the possibility that you may have been affected by the consumption of methylamphetamine. You acted resolutely and over a relatively long period. The failure of a first attempt did not result in the abandonment or reconsideration of the scheme, and did little more than reveal the extent of your determination ...'

Justice Vincent pointed out, 'The motivation underlying your actions is also unclear. You have provided no explanation. More than one possibility has been suggested in the course of various proceedings but, at the end of the day, no finding can be made.

'It is hardly necessary to say that the crime which you committed is and must be viewed with the utmost seriousness by the Court. Through the sentences they impose, the Courts must demonstrate the abhorrence with which the unlawful taking of a human life is properly regarded by all decent members of our community.

'From the personal perspective which I have formed of your crime, perhaps the most surprising feature of the whole matter is the apparent ease with which the decision was made to kill another human being and the pitifully small value which you appear to have placed upon the life of that person.'

He continued, 'Naturally, I have taken into account your plea of guilty – noting, however, that it was entered at a very late stage. I accept the statement of [your counsel] Mr Slade that you have found yourself unable to cope with the enormity of the situation in which you have been placed since the end of 1989 and that you have become both depressed and remorseful for your actions. I accept that you are concerned about the welfare of your child and will suffer a deep sense of loss with respect to your relationship with him during the period of imprisonment which I must impose on you.

'I have taken into account the absence of any prior convictions and your general background. I note that you are now 36 years of age and that as far as your background is concerned, although it would appear you have encountered a number of personal or relationship problems, there is nothing remarkable in your history which could have been seen to provide any convincing explanation of your actions.

'Finally, I have given consideration of parity with the sentence which was imposed on your co-offender, Rhona Heaney ... I do not consider that any differentiation ought to be made between the sentences imposed upon each of you.'

Justice Vincent sentenced Irene Maslin to 15 years' jail; with a minimum of 10 years.

All those involved in the murder of Paul Snabel served their minimum sentences. Irene Maslin died of cancer a few years after her release.

☠ ☠ ☠

So how does someone like Irene Maslin coerce a group of people – allegedly her friends – to do such a despicable thing?

Detective Wheeler says there was no question the woman was intimidating and that she did have a bad reputation, but it was more than that.

'She was a manipulator, who relied on the fear factor of her notorious reputation. She relished that power and control,' he said.

'Our impressions of Irene were all as a consequence of the interviews with the others involved in the crime, particularly Ian Gillin and the Randall girls. They gave us our only insight into Irene Maslin and the fact that she was the one who had driven the discussion about how something had to be done to get Paul Snabel out of the picture.

'She was the driving force in all the various scenarios considered and, ultimately, was the one who decided on the means by which his fate would be applied. She then allocated tasks and roles to the other participants to ensure that everything would occur in accordance with the plot. It was also she who called the shots when the original plan went wrong,' Detective Wheeler said.

'There was also the strong demeanour that she displayed in terms of the pressure being applied to the other women; so much so that if they said anything that was not in accordance with her script, and which caused the police to focus their attention on her, she was going to take everyone down with her.'

'Even during her formal interview with Andrew McLoughlin, when it was obvious their murder plot had come apart at the seams, Irene Maslin remained stone-faced. There was a complete lack of emotion – except for an underlying anger – and absolutely no expression of regret.

'And that's the way she conducted herself to the end.'